LEADING
AMERICA

★ ★ ★ ★ ★ ★ ★ ★ ★ ★ ★ ★ ★ ★

LEADING AMERICA

★ ★ ★ ★ ★ ★ ★ ★ ★ ★ ★ ★ ★ ★ ★

PRESIDENT TRUMP'S
COMMITMENT TO PEOPLE, PATRIOTISM, AND CAPITALISM

SEAN SPICER

CENTER
STREET®

NEW YORK   NASHVILLE

Center Street
Hachette Book Group
1290 Avenue of the Americas, New York, NY 10104
centerstreet.com
twitter.com/centerstreet

First Edition: October 2020

Center Street is a division of Hachette Book Group, Inc. The Center Street name and logo are trademarks of Hachette Book Group, Inc.

The publisher is not responsible for websites (or their content) that are not owned by the publisher.

Print book interior design by Timothy Shaner, NightandDayDesign.biz

Library of Congress Control Number: 2020943618

ISBN: 978-1-5460-5944-8 (hardcover), 978-1-5460-5945-5 (ebook)

Printed in the United States of America

LSC-C

10 9 8 7 6 5 4 3 2 1

To my family

CONTENTS

LEADING
AMERICA

★ ★ ★ ★ ★ ★ ★ ★ ★ ★ ★ ★ ★ ★

CHAPTER ONE

2020: THE BATTLE FOR THE SOUL OF AMERICA

Every four years voters are told the upcoming election is the most important election of their lifetime. The 2020 presidential election is the election that will not only define the next four years but I believe the direction of our nation for years to come. There is no doubt in my mind that the principles that our nation was founded on are at stake.

Only by looking past President Trump's tweets and the media's never-ending critique of him can you stop and appreciate all that he has accomplished in just four years. Whether it's strengthening our economy through a pro-growth agenda of deregulation, tax cuts, and revising trade agreements, rebuilding our military, enacting criminal justice reform, defending religious liberty, protecting the unborn, or appointing two hundred federal judges—which will undoubtedly leave a multigenerational impact on the landscape of our judicial branch—or ensuring our veterans get the services they have earned, President Trump is leading America and has a tremendous record of accomplishments.

For as much as the left likes to talk about justice and compassion, you would think they would be overjoyed to hear that under Trump, Hispanic-Americans, Asian-Americans, and African-Americans have achieved the lowest unemployment rate ever recorded, while veterans' unemployment reached a twenty-year low, women's unemployment reached a sixty-five-year low, 4 million Americans have been lifted off food stamps, nearly 9,000 Opportunity Zones have been built to invest in minority communities, and the FIRST STEP ACT was passed in what was a historic achievement that ended decades of establishment complacency on criminal justice reform. The act addressed the problems of over-incarceration, racially biased sentencing laws, and recidivism that undermined public trust in the justice system—things that the left claims to champion but were largely silent about when Trump got it done. This should tell you a thing or two about the left's obsession with identity politics when politically advantageous.

President Trump continues to lead the country forward through action and legislation. The progress of the past four years can all be undone in one election.

Four years ago, Senator Bernie Sanders's socialist policies were still on the fringe of the Democratic Party. Capitalism was still largely embraced as the backbone of our country. Today Sanders's ideas are mainstream as the Democratic Party is increasingly embracing the tenets of socialism. Democrats who were once considered moderate now face primaries from the far left. They either adapt and embrace the far left or face defeat. Presumptive Democratic nominee for president Joe Biden is no exception.

These are not vague statements about the left. They are quite literally pledges from the party leaders. This past summer, Biden released a 110-page manifesto of platform proposals penned by none other than himself and Bernie Sanders. Ironically dubbed the "Unity Task Force," the list is riddled with radical policies that will undoubtedly fuel disunity and division. The two not only vow to erase the monumental progress that President Trump has made on tax reform, immigration, criminal justice reform, and the military, but they also promise to replace it with an agenda that embraces job-killing tax increases, costly and burdensome environmental regulations, government-run health care, open borders, and even an effort to "reimagine policing" by adhering to the radical demands of the "defund the police" movement. At its core, the plan seeks to redefine our great nation as a mere tool of oppression—one that rightfully succumbs to "abolish" culture and, in the words of Biden, needs "revolutionary institutional changes."

It's not only capitalism that's at stake, it is also our constitution. For as long as I can remember, I was taught that the guiding principle of the First Amendment to the U.S. Constitution was based on the concept of allowing for the free expression—and exchange—of ideas. While I might not like or agree with what someone said, I would fight for their right to express it no matter how much I may disagree with it. Unfortunately, this understanding is fading quickly. More and more, our society has delved into a mob mentality that believes that if you don't share the prevailing leftist view, then you need to be canceled and pushed out to the margins of society.

In July 2020, 153 prominent writers, artists, and thought leaders signed their names to an opinion piece in *Harper's Magazine* titled "A Letter on Justice and Open Debate." They wrote that "the free exchange of information and ideas, the lifeblood of a liberal society, is daily becoming more constricted." They further noted that "an intolerance of opposing views, a vogue for public shaming and ostracism and the tendency to dissolve complex policy issues in a blinding moral certainty" was becoming an increasing problem in society. The piece ran in the wake of racial unrest stemming from the killing of George Floyd by a Minneapolis police officer and noted: "we refuse any false choice between justice and freedom, which cannot exist without each other . . . as writers we need a culture that leaves us room for experimentation, risk taking, and even mistakes."

It wasn't long before backlash and even retractions from some of the signers ensued. Something that appeared to be uncontroversial and unifying resulted in liberals having to apologize for briefly making so much sense. Welcome to the current state of American society—one in which all politics is personal and all persons are forced to be political.

As White House press secretary, I said, "Democrats are using every tool at their disposal to get in the way of President Trump's attempt at making America great again." At the time, I was talking about the obstruction and boycotts of hearings for President Trump's cabinet members and judicial appointments, but since then, I have seen it not only in the obstruction to the entire Trump agenda, but also within every aspect of life and in every sector of society. I've started to realize just how pervasive and cynical their efforts are. If you're not actively looking for them, much of it can be easily missed. In fact, there are so many things that we see in our day-to-day lives that we don't realize.

When you send your kids off to school, you're probably not wondering whether the teachers are instilling in them values that run contrary to your own. I can guarantee you're not wondering if the lesson plans include the act of stomping on the American flag or if the teachers are instructed to "explicitly reject and resist" your role as a parent. Those ideas certainly never crossed my mind.

Likewise, your college student could probably graduate with honors and go on to earn a PhD without realizing how indoctrinated they are. It happens all the time—and quite frankly, it explains why we're seeing so many of today's thought leaders and academic elites lead the liberal agenda at the local level and on the national stage.

You could binge-watch an entire Netflix series without noticing the underlying political agenda that it's planting into your subconscious. For many folks, tuning into a late-night show or going to see a movie is a way to unwind. But if you pay close attention, you'll see that Hollywood is one of the left's most effective tools when it comes to seeding a political narrative or influencing culture.

You could spend hours browsing social media without knowing that your newsfeed is carefully crafted to present you with the information that Silicon Valley leftists want you to see.

You could spend thousands of dollars at your favorite retail chain, never knowing that your money might be funding a political cause that diametrically opposes your values.

We didn't get here overnight. Each of these institutions in society has been subtly pushing an agenda for decades.

For the left, it's all politics, all the time. Our country has become so divided that everything now devolves into politics and pits regular Americans against one another. Too often, politics is brought up and people are forced to choose a side.

Are you going to kneel or not?

Will they go to the White House or not?

Will they apologize?

Will they boycott this company?

I'm no stranger to politically charged questions. My job as White House press secretary was to answer them. But these are questions that reflect the partisan political lens that we're conditioned to look at everything through, politically related or not.

Working in the Trump White House has given me great insight into the inner workings of one of the most out-of-the-box presidential communications operations in modern history. From the outside looking in, the media would have you believe that President Trump is some out-of-control madman because he doesn't conform to their definition of what a "normal" president should be. They hate that he refuses to stay inside the lines they have drawn for him and instead prefers to circumvent their outdated legacy structures altogether to talk to the people directly.

Left-wing media figures seem to be in a constant state of manufactured outrage because President Trump doesn't communicate the same way President Obama did. They would have you believe that their frustrations with President Trump stem from his "unpresidential" style of communication. Like most gripes from the mainstream media, this is far from the truth.

Does President Trump tell it like it is? Yes. Does he let the American people know his thoughts through Twitter? Of course. Has he been one of the most consequential presidents in modern American history? Yes.

The fact is the blue checkmark mafia is really just operating from a place of desperation. They have no option but to cling to their poor attempts at moral indignation to promote a clearly partisan agenda. They despise that President Trump understands that speeches don't change lives—policies do. Where President Obama talked about relief for the poor and middle class, Trump actually cut taxes. Where Obama gave wonderful speeches about creating jobs, President Trump actually cut regulations and ignited an economic boom.

President Obama might have said the right things, but at the end of the day, President Trump is the one implementing the right policies. The left-dominated media can't report that, though. If they did they would be betraying their true motivating force, the domination of a liberal agenda. The White House press corps is obsessed with tweets, not results. I have come to discover that the questions they don't ask, the headlines they won't write, and the stories they chose not to cover are more telling than what they do ask, write, and cover.

I've always known that the media and Hollywood tilted left, but over the last couple of years, I've experienced firsthand the tactics of the left to control the narrative and drown out voices on the right within every major American institution. From preschools to college campuses, from corporations to Hollywood, from Big Tech to the media, the left has long dominated the most powerful institutions in America. The mainstream media, while popular to blame, is not the cause; rather, it is a symptom of a much broader and multifaceted effort to dominate culture and derail the Trump agenda.

Working with the Republican National Committee (RNC) and the Trump campaign, transition team, and administration, serving as a Hollywood character cast member, being a target of Big Tech censorship, speaking on college campuses, and raising children in American schools, I have seen the left from many different angles over the past several years. I've been on both sides of the newsroom. I've been both the strategist and the interviewer. I've shaped the national media narrative and have been shaped by it. I've been boycotted, protested, banned, and smeared by the very people I had worked *with* for years. The boycotts didn't end when I left the White House, though. As you'll explore in the forthcoming chapters, I've been boycotted and protested everywhere from college campuses to bookstores, and maybe the most absurd, a reality dancing competition.

My experience with *Dancing with the Stars* is indicative of just that. When simply having a diverse group of people with different opinions on the same stage can no longer be tolerated by the left, you know there's something much larger at stake. It was not the first time I sparked national outrage, and I'll be lucky if it is the last. Like millions of Americans, I was guilty of the ultimate crime: being a conservative and supporting the Trump agenda.

Just as they've done with everything else, the left turned a dancing reality show into a political battleground. For the left, it wasn't a dancing competition—it was a competition for everyone, that is, except for anyone who they might disagree with politically. They will stop at nothing in their attempt to turn capitalism into socialism, patriotism into globalism, and American values into progressive values. They're willing to run small businesses into economic ruin, turn academic institutions into harmful social experiment centers, use children as political pawns, and ruin America's favorite pastimes with political polarization—and they're leaving a nearly unrecognizable country in their wake.

Democrats realized that attacking President Trump directly doesn't get results and are instead directing their disdain at his supporters, so we can only expect my experience to become a reality for millions of more freedom-loving Americans who haven't already experienced it. The subtle tactics are becoming less subtle by the day, and no American can afford to sit back and watch.

As we go through this book, I'll be pointing out all of the major attacks on our country, from our history to our Constitution to our deeply held values and beliefs, but my hope is that if we stay the course, we can overcome these things. After reading this book, you will have a clear picture of what's exactly at stake in the 2020 election and beyond. More important, you will become more intuitively aware of the multifaceted forces, both covert and overt, that are being used to sow division in our country and transform these core values established in the U.S. Constitution. The next time you turn on a TV show, send your kid to school, read your favorite newspaper, or browse the web, you will be equipped with the knowledge to understand the past, present, and future of the leftist movement and the wherewithal to uphold your own ideas and defend your own beliefs—which is exactly what our country's founders meant when they drafted the First Amendment.

CHAPTER TWO

AN OUTSIDER:
DANCING WITH THE STARS

Working for President Trump left a lasting impression on my outlook on the intersection of pop culture and politics. He always encouraged people to push the envelope. Without that mentality, he never would have gone from a real estate mogul to reality TV star, and he certainly never would have gone from reality TV star to president of the United States.

He felt that leadership, whether political or not, is about meeting people where they're at, engaging with them over the things they care about, and then fighting for what you believe in. It's what allowed him to go against the grain in every industry he was a part of. It's also his driving force for his current life in public service. He was never one to stick with the status quo or follow the crowd. He recognized that sharing conservative beliefs, or simply being an outspoken conservative in leftist-dominated industries, is harder, but no less important, than sharing beliefs with like-minded people.

As I walk through my entire experience on *Dancing with the Stars* in this chapter, from my initial conversations with producers to my final goodbye onstage, I highlight the memorable moments, the obstacles, and the lessons I learned along the way. Though each week was different and came with its own unique challenges, I always carried these lessons from working in the White House—the same lessons that encouraged me to dive headfirst into something I never in a million years imagined I would do.

On August 31, 2017, I departed the White House for the last time as an employee. As I walked through the towering black gates, I paused as the metal slammed shut. They seemed unusually loud to me at that moment, and I hesitated just a beat to absorb the magnitude of what remained inside those gates and to reflect on the honor it was to serve. I also knew that this would be the first time in my adult life that I would not be working for a political campaign, the government, or the military. (As with most people who have spent significant time in the political arena, I did have a couple of exceptions to that rule—you could call them small stints "between jobs.") I was beginning a new chapter of my life, looking forward to exploring new possibilities. The only certainty that I knew was that I had no idea what was to come.

I carved out a nice niche doing some consulting work, doing the rounds on the speaking circuit, making a surprise cameo appearance at the opening of the Emmys in September 2017, and even publishing my first book—*The Briefing*—in July 2018; it became a *New York Times* bestseller. I was spending more time with my family and meeting a lot of interesting people along the way, and I was having a lot of fun.

Just prior to leaving the White House, I received a phone call from Deena Katz, one of the co-executive producers of ABC's *Dancing with the Stars*. She had tracked down my contact information through a mutual friend, Jason Recher, who had worked for high-profile Republicans including Sarah Palin. Governor Palin's daughter Bristol had appeared on the show, and Jason had gotten to know Deena. Deena flew from Los Angeles to Washington, D.C., to meet with me and had scheduled lunch for us at the Hay-Adams, a dignified historic hotel situated on 16th Street, on the north side of Lafayette Square, overlooking the White House. It's a landmark in the nation's capital, known for having doormen in perfectly pressed suits, polished brass doorknobs, and the scent of fresh lilies filling the air in the lobby. Lunchtime is marked by DC "A-listers" having quiet, confidential conversations. I walked through Lafayette Square and headed to meet Deena to discuss the upcoming season of the show.

As we sat at a table covered with crisp white linens, Deena ran through all of the particulars of the show—how the show worked, how dance partners were chosen, how the practices and preparation were handled. After careful consideration, I had decided the timing was not right, nor did I think it was the appropriate thing to do after immediately leaving the White House. I had already lined up several speeches and appearances and had some leads on consulting opportunities. I was in no position to jump headfirst into something like this, especially considering I was very aware that I lacked any sense of rhythm and would have very little time to prepare prior to launch which would be just a few weeks later.

After leaving the White House, I received quite a few opportunities that didn't feel right to accept at the time . . . or ever. I had been offered a significant sum of money to promote a

London-based betting system, and I was presented with an opportunity to appear in a commercial during the Super Bowl, among other corporate offers and reality show cameo opportunities that I didn't think were appropriate. Even the president, after reading a report in the tabloids, asked if I was giving consideration to joining the cast of *Dancing with the Stars*. No, I told him, I didn't think it was a good idea at the time and I let him know that I wasn't a particularly good dancer.

While my initial answer was in the past, I developed a great relationship with Deena. We continued the conversation we began that day at the Hay-Adams. She is kind and caring, yet smart and perceptive—a top-notch professional. She is known for her work on *Dancing with the Stars* (or *DWTS*, as the fans call it), *The Masked Singer, Celebrity Big Brother,* and several other popular shows. Deena has worked in reality TV since its inception with *Keeping Up with the Kardashians,* a show that she played a key role in creating. She not only has an impressive Hollywood career, but she is also known in political activism circles for her work as an organizer of March for Our Lives as well as one of the executive directors of the Los Angeles Women's March Foundation. Even though her political leanings are different than mine, we have always found common interests. As we got to know each other, we developed what I believe to be a meaningful relationship. We could respect each other and be friends despite any political differences, a truly novel idea to many. Since our first conversation in Washington, I had come to lean on her and trust her feedback. I had run ideas and opportunities by her that had come my way, and she always gave me sound and constructive advice. I am pretty sure she steered me away from doing some pretty stupid things that the kid in me thought would be "really cool" but would have been professionally (and possibly personally) detrimental.

During one of my trips to Los Angeles, we caught up over coffee and continued our ongoing conversation about my future. One of those talks revisited the possibility of me joining the cast of the upcoming season of *Dancing with the Stars*. Deena even discussed potential dancing partners for me. I had been very suspect of doing the show as time went on because of my lack of skill and complete lack of any, I mean any, background in dancing. I was literally the guy in the corner at dances growing up and as I grew older the guy hanging at the bar at weddings. In the sixth grade, my music teacher Mr. Mara had stopped music class while I was attempting to play the snare drum and yelled up to me in the back row of the music hall: "Spicer, you have the sense of beat of a steamroller." As harsh as that was to hear as a sixth grader (I dropped out of music and opted for study hall), he had a point. Needless to say, I wondered if this was really something I could pull off. Admittedly, I was also wary of jumping back into the national spotlight in such a public way.

As the weeks went on, the conversation about me joining the cast had become more serious. I discussed it with my wife, and we wondered how it would fit into the long-term vision of what I was trying to accomplish. Rebecca reminded me that we had not really even finished the first dance at our own wedding. We had taken one group lesson and realized that we could get away with a few turns and then head off to cut the cake. For almost two years since leaving the White House, I had done everything that I thought I was supposed to do. I focused on building a business, doing consulting work—and I had been honored to attend several really interesting events. I had even dabbled in the media world as a special correspondent for the show *Extra*. But once in a while, you think you should do something so wildly out of your comfort zone that it would only happen once in your lifetime. I had even been a guest judge of a charity event in the Washington area called DC's Dancing Stars Gala, which consisted of local personalities dancing to raise money for area causes. I realized that as silly as it might sound, *DWTS* could be the last opportunity to do this type of thing. There are only so many times people keep asking before an opportunity is gone for good. I figured that maybe this was the time to do *DWTS*. My son was in favor of it, but my daughter, who has become quite a dancer herself, had seen my dancing up close at two father-daughter dances. She cringed at the idea of me attempting to dance on national TV. She was firmly against having her dad join the show.

Deena told me about the sense of family within the *DWTS* community. Contestants who had appeared together stayed in touch with each other as well as their dance partners. Unlike other reality shows, there was something unique about *Dancing with the Stars*. Your job every week was to do the best job you could while having some fun. You are not trying to tear someone down or disparage the other contestants. There is no cash prize or long-term contract. No one is trying to become a professional dancer. The winner literally gets a mirror ball trophy, which I'm sure would fetch a good price on eBay from *DWTS* die-hards, but it isn't getting auctioned off at Sotheby's. It is that uniqueness that set it apart for me. Furthermore, it was actually a show that I could encourage my kids to watch.

I kept my decision-making circle close. I bounced it off a couple of friends, mentors, and people who I thought could give me some honest feedback. The last thing I needed was for this to get out and become a story that would end up blowing up the possibility before I had made a final decision. One person I thought could give me an honest assessment was Bruce Hough, who had served as Utah's national committeeman to the Republican National Committee during the six years I had worked there. Beyond his service on the RNC, he happened to be the father of *DWTS* alumni Julianna Hough and Derek Hough. "Can you keep a beat?" Bruce asked. "Kind of," I sheepishly replied. "Well, if you can do that, you can get by," he said. Admittedly, saying I could keep a beat was a stretch. Bruce was clear that if I worked hard and was willing to take the instruction, I could get by on the dance floor. I also reached out to Tucker Carlson, who had joined the cast in season three, to get his take about the experience as someone on the right. After weighing the pros and cons, he said, "Why not go for it?"

Slowly, I began to lean into the idea of doing it. I called Deena and told her I was in, but I wanted some reassurances because I suspected there could be backlash. I wanted to know when the going got tough, the tough wouldn't exit stage right. They had told me that over its first twenty-seven seasons, *DWTS* had several controversial contestants, including swimmer Ryan Lochte, who competed on season twenty-three while being the subject of a spate of negative publicity for fabricating a story that he and two fellow teammates were robbed at gunpoint in Rio de Janeiro—which earned him a ten-month suspension from all Olympic and USA Swimming competitions. His first *DWTS* performance was interrupted by a protestor who stormed the stage, prompting the show to cut to an immediate commercial break while security tackled the guy.

I asked Deena to arrange a call with some network executives. On the call, they assured me that yes, they had my back and were prepared for any backlash involving my connection to President Trump. Before I gave my final yes, I asked everyone that we all take forty-eight hours to think hard about this decision. I asked the executives to go as high as possible at ABC to share my concerns about what could come their way in response to my casting, including potential boycotts and viewers targeting advertisers. Two days went by, and I was told everyone understood my concerns and was willing to back their decision to invite me to be part of the show.

With those assurances, I decided to join the cast of ABC's *Dancing with the Stars* and signed the paperwork.

I tried to pry from Deena, who would be alongside me on the show. *DWTS* has a tradition of unveiling its cast and celebrity-dancer pairings live on the air on ABC's *Good Morning America*. This year, one of the twists was going to be that the celebrity-dancer pairings wouldn't be revealed to the cast until the first rehearsal and not to the audience until the first live show. She gave me some hints but nothing I was able to decipher with absolute certainty.

On Tuesday, August 20, I boarded a flight from Washington, DC, to New York City, where I then took a car to the Millennium Hotel in Times Square . . . and that's where it all began. This was it. Any thoughts about backing out were too late. I was in this.

I checked into the hotel and before I even had time to settle into my room and put my bags down, I was told I needed to go down a couple of floors to report to the tailor. It was a whirlwind. The production crew had taken what was a hotel suite and converted it into a makeshift tailor shop. There were garment racks from one end to the other and clothes hanging on rods with different people's initials pinned to them and shoes scattered below them. There were people crammed into every corner of the room feverishly sewing, tearing, and throwing fabric, and taking measurements all at the same time. It was amazing to suddenly be thrust into this.

I was quickly greeted by one of the costume designers who started measuring me up and down and pulling suits on and off, all while telling me that within a matter of hours that they would be working through the night to have this ready for the promotional shoots the next day, where all the male contestants would be wearing some kind of formal wear.

After about fifteen minutes of all the measurements being taken, I headed down the elevator to the Gotham Ballroom to check in for what would be the first meeting for the dancers, the cast, and the network executives. After getting off the elevator, I was greeted by the publicity teams from ABC and the BBC. Interestingly, I learned that *DWTS* was licensed from the BBC, which owns the original basis of the show, called *Strictly Come Dancing,* the British version of the show.

Walking in, I felt like I was at an awkward high school mixer. I looked around at the thirty or forty people scattered across the room, hoping to see some familiar faces. I didn't know who was a dancer, who was a producer, or who was just there for other reasons. Keep in mind, I had not watched *DWTS* prior to this season. I literally could not name a single dancer with the exception of a couple whom Deena mentioned months earlier—and even then it was one thing watching a YouTube clip of someone dancing a routine and seeing them in a cocktail setting like this. Thankfully, Katie Armstrong, who coordinates my various engagements, was with me. She has a keen sense of pop culture, which would help me identify who was in the room. I knew I was going to rely on her to be my guide through this experience.

I looked over and saw one guy who I swore was Chris Kattan, who had been a cast member on *Saturday Night Live* and a *DWTS* contestant on season seventeen in 2013. At that point, I had begun meeting the rest of the cast, and within the first twenty minutes I realized it wasn't Chris, it was actually Sasha Farber, one of the professional dancers. So much for having a clue who anyone was.

Katie had given me a heads-up that Hannah Brown was going to be one of the contestants and that she would probably be getting the most attention of anyone because of the strong following that she had from her recent appearance on both *The Bachelor* and *The Bachelorette*. The show had begun to drop hints on its Instagram page, and Katie had correctly guessed Hannah was going to be part of the cast. Katie and I had a running list of who we thought would be joining the show. Notably, I went 0 for 12. Katie was around 2 or 3 out of 12.

Lamar Odom, the Los Angeles Lakers player who had been married to Khloé Kardashian, was easy to pick out because of his height. I also recognized former Baltimore Ravens linebacker Ray Lewis when he walked up and introduced himself. As a lifelong Patriots fan, I had known who Ray was, considering both teams are in the same conference.

Kate Flannery, who played Meredith on *The Office,* was easy to pick out. I had been a huge fan of the show and always thought her character was hysterical. While a few of the cast members did not make it that night (Christie Brinkley, Mary Wilson, and James Van der Beek), I was basically clueless on who else was going to be on the show.

After about an hour of mingling, we wrapped up and I started to realize that ironically, while I didn't know most of the people who were going to be on the show, most of them probably didn't know who I was, either. One by one I began googling each one to get an idea of who they were.

The following morning at the crack of dawn, we all met in the lobby of the hotel and boarded vans to go only a few blocks to the guest entrance of *Good Morning America*. After entering the building, we were put on a cargo elevator and guided into a room where the guests and dancers waited together (commonly referred to as the greenroom but which is rarely, if ever, green). As we were sitting there, Karamo Brown, who was a cast member of Netflix's *Queer Eye,* approached me and introduced himself. He expressed that he was excited to meet me because he was looking forward to having a conversation about the political divide that exists in our country. So far, it had been a really pleasant start to the day.

Producers split the cast in half, took each group to different sides backstage, and then introduced us on-air one at a time. When it came to my turn they showed me a mocked-up podium, which said "Good Morning America, Times Square" on the front instead of "White House, Washington, D.C." A production assistant signaled me to head out from backstage as the announcer said "Sean Spicer, White House press secretary." I had taken the podium several times at the White House, but somehow gripping this podium and coming out announcing that I would be a *DWTS* cast member on *Good Morning America* was probably more nerve-racking than any time I had done it inside the White House Briefing Room.

We all took our seats, and the *GMA* hosts began asking each cast member questions about themselves and whether they were excited about the season.

Country music star Lauren Alania, who had been on *American Idol,* said that she was starstruck when she met Kate Flannery because she had been a huge fan of Meredith on *The Office*. Amy Robach, one of the *GMA* hosts, jokingly said, that similarly, she was starstruck when she saw me. Then the host of *DWTS*, Tom Bergeron, who was sitting next to Amy and *GMA*'s other host Lara Spencer, followed up by joking that "Sean will be in charge of assessing audience size." I took it in stride at the time, thinking that part of this was about being able to laugh at yourself. It was a way of breaking the ice, and I left it at that.

Shortly after, we were asked to do a short, fun dance on the floor. It was at that moment I realized that the other cast members had some decent—if not good—rhythm and dance moves. I did not.

Immediately after we wrapped up our duties for the segment, we were put back in the same vans that had driven us there. We drove down the street to Planet Hollywood, where a press line of entertainment reporters was assembled. Instead of the *Washington Post*, *Politico*, and others I was accustomed to facing from the White House press corps, I would be fielding questions from *Entertainment Weekly*, *Extra*, *People*, *Variety*, and *Access Hollywood*.

The questions were what I had expected they would be: Do you expect to make this political? Do you think this will be harder than being White House press secretary? I kept remarking that I wanted to do something different and enjoy this new experience that would be a reprieve from politics. I was thinking to myself, "Hey, this is actually going pretty well." Between interviews, I couldn't resist checking my Twitter feed to see how various people—supporters, political reporters, and those who had criticized me along the way—were reacting. So far so good. This appeared to be going well, much better than I had anticipated. Even *Politico*'s Playbook PM newsletter left it at "IT'S ALL

HAPPENING: Sean Spicer will be on the next season of 'Dancing with the Stars,' along with Ray Lewis, James Van Der Beek and Christie Brinkley, because it's 2019."

Shortly thereafter, we all piled back into the vans and headed across town to Milk Studios to shoot a series of promotional photos and videos that were going to be used for reenactment cast photos, some individual shots, and several promotional videos for the show. Between the shoots, we changed outfits and also had a little bit of time to slowly get to know one another. Once again, Katie quietly offered me insight as to who various people were and their backgrounds so I could at least strike up a conversation. The area, which was a large loft, was partitioned off with curtains to break apart the various shoots. Off to one side was an elaborate spread of drinks and finger foods. Everything seemed so "Hollywood" to this East Coast native—decaf, almond milk espressos, and vegan gluten-free food items. There were two large black leather couches we all sat in as we waited for our turn to be photographed. As I was about to take a bite of some kind of cage-free sustainably raised ham quiche, Katie stopped me mid-bite and said, "You're going to want to see this," showing me her phone with a tweet from the show's host, Tom Bergeron, that had a statement he had issued right after the *GMA* announcement. He had taken to Twitter to criticize the producers' decision to cast me, with a title stating, "Some thoughts about today." While he never mentioned me by name, the subtext was clear. His statement read as follows:

A few months ago, during a lunch with DWTS' new Executive Producer, I offered suggestions for Season 28. Chief among them was my hope that DWTS, in its return following an unprecedented year-long hiatus, would be a joyful respite from our exhausting political climate and free of inevitably divisive bookings from ANY party affiliations. I left that lunch convinced we were in agreement.

Subsequently (and rather obviously), a decision was made to, as we often say in Hollywood, "go in a different direction."

It is the prerogative of the producers, in partnership with the network, to make whatever decisions they feel are in the best long-term interests of the franchise. We can agree to disagree, as we do now, but ultimately it's their call. I'll leave it to them to answer any further questions about those decisions.

For me, as host, I always gaze into the camera's lens and imagine you on the other side, looking for a two-hour escape from whatever life hassles you've been wrestling with. That's a connection, and a responsibility, which I take very seriously, even if I occasionally season it with dad jokes.

Hopefully, when [co-host] Erin Andrews and I look into those lenses again on September 16, you'll be on the other side looking back, able to enjoy the charismatic pro dancers, the unpredictable judges and the kitschy charm that has defined DWTS since 2005.

I had been prepared for some backlash. Deena had warned me that the first couple of days—maybe the first week—could be met with some snarky reactions but assured me that it would ultimately smooth over and be fine. I just had no idea that the criticism was going to happen that quickly or come from someone who was actually part of the show.

As I was reading the statement on Twitter, Deena slowly approached. I had a funny feeling I knew exactly what she was coming to talk to me about and it was not whether I liked the quiche. I finished the photo shoots, but then we went down a floor and commandeered a conference room, where we were met by other executives from ABC and the publicity teams from ABC and BBC to discuss the statement issued by the host of the show I was joining. Everyone gathered around the table, stunned and bewildered, repeating countless times that they had been caught off guard and would be discussing the post at the highest levels.

While I think I had met a couple of these folks at the meet-and-greet the previous night, I didn't recognize most of the faces or know each of their roles. I had no clue about anyone's political leanings in the room (except Deena's), but based on the general ideology of the entertainment industry I couldn't help but think how most of these people likely were not pleased to have to be dealing with comments made by the show's host pointedly against a newly named cast member. Not a single person in that room had even a hint of anything short of a professional demeanor, and they were all extremely supportive in their words and expressions. I could already feel the sense of the family Deena had mentioned. But Tom was the longtime host, and I was the guy they had known for ten minutes. Just playing the Hollywood odds, I wasn't convinced that the odds were in my favor.

Immediately, my PR instincts kicked in. Instead of thinking of myself as a cast member, I thought about it as a crisis situation and zeroed in on how we were going to handle this as if I were the client. The responses on Twitter had started to pile up, ranging from Tom should be punished to I should be kicked off the show. Inside the conference room, the executives were all clear that they stood by their decision to include me as a cast member. As we began batting around responses, I made it clear that any punishment or retribution for Tom would only seek to add fuel to the fire. Instead, I said that the first thing that we needed to do was make sure that everybody else around the show, meaning Erin Andrews, the other co-host, and the judges, were aware of Tom's comments and that ABC would be standing firm on casting me. I knew from the get-go I was going to have enough trouble with judges because of my lack of dancing skills, but this was not how I wanted to get to know the judges or anyone else on the show. Talk about tainting the proverbial jury pool. The judges had worked with Tom for years, and the only things they knew about me was that I had been President Trump's press secretary and I was already the center of a controversy. I was concerned that if any of the others weighed in it would only cause more controversy, which would not be good for anyone in particular or the show in general.

I suggested that our response be twofold. First, the show's executive producer, Andrew Llinares, would issue a statement simply sending a positive message that saw beyond partisan politics and offered a more reasonable perspective. Andrew would be the voice of this, saying that he was standing by not just me but the entire cast and how excited they were for this season. It could not just be about me, it had to be how excited they were for the entire cast. After we had some back-and-forth and made a few edits, we ended up with, "We've got a great and diverse cast. We are excited about the season." Plain, simple, and to the point. There would be no further comment from the show.

Second, I suggested that I make a simple statement that would praise Tom for his previous service on the show as a host and discuss my hopes for the show being an example of how we could take the temperature down in this country by bringing people together in a fun and respectful way. I drafted a statement, and Melanie Pritchett Fitzpatrick, the head of *Dancing with the Stars* publicity, helped to share it with some of the entertainment press. My statement said, "I think Tom has been a great host. And I firmly believe when the season is over he's probably going to realize bringing a diverse group of people together, who can interact in a fun, civil, and respectful way, is actually a way we can move the country forward in a positive way. And it will make this show an example of how Americans can disagree about politics and tune in to good entertainment shows and keep their politics at bay."

The approach was simple: keep the response short and positive, and try to move forward.

But Tom's statement had ignited a firestorm. Outrage erupted and a nationwide #boycottDTWS trend broke across all of the major social media platforms. Liberals came out of the woodwork to condemn it, as did some pundits, journalists, and Hollywood elites.

"Don't Let Sean Spicer Tap-Dance Out of Infamy on 'Dancing with the Stars'" was the headline of a column by the *New York Times*' chief television critic, James Poniewozik. "Letting Sean Spicer tango onto prime time this fall is not the largest disgrace of all time. But it's still a disgrace. Period," he wrote in the pages of the supposed "newspaper of record," just after lamenting about how his column is "probably giving Spicer what he wants, which is attention as he takes one more step toward an imagined life in which he's no longer a buffoon, where people shrug off his mendacity."

Vox Media reported that "Sean Spicer is on a post–White House redemption tour, and Dancing with the Stars is his latest stop," noting that, "while the argument could easily be made that few of Dancing with the Stars' contestants are true stars and that appearing on the show is just a shallow fame grab, casting 'controversies' rarely amount to little more than an eye-roll. In Spicer's case, however, joining season 28 was seen as an attempt to help erase his unsavory reputation in the minds of many Americans—and the show's willingness to make him a 'star' was seen as giving him a pass he didn't deserve." Redemption tour? Really? After almost two years after leaving the White House, this was supposedly my latest stop. What were the others and where was I going next? And can I get a T-shirt and some backstage passes for my friends to this supposed redemption tour?

In a commentary piece for CNN, political analyst Anushay Hossain blasted the show for casting me, arguing, "there's no saving a man like Sean Spicer, and there shouldn't be." Following the first episode, she called the montage of my White House podium highlights that *DWTS* aired before my performance "nausea-inducing" and asked why "Sean Spicer gets the chance to try to rehab, rebrand and relaunch a whole new image of himself."

Former E! Network late-night show host Chelsea Handler tweeted, "Sean Spicer joining Dancing with the Stars is proof that America loves giving people second and third chances . . . if they're white," while Scott Dworkin, author and cofounder of the Democratic Coalition, whatever that is, also took to Twitter to air his grievances, writing, "ABC and DWTS are basically helping Trump and the GOP raise money. Disgusting. #BoycottDWTS." How my participation had anything to do with Trump and the Republican Party raising money still baffles me but it's not surprising to see them create outrage without any basis in reality.

Even the showrunner (the Hollywood term for "the head honcho") of one of ABC's biggest series, *Grey's Anatomy*, felt the need to weigh in and proclaim my casting to be a travesty. Krista Vernoff tweeted, "I deeply abhor this decision by the company I work for and truly love" and "This is not cause for celebration or celebrity." She even tagged Disney CEO Robert Iger and ABC's account in a plea to reconsider the decision, writing, "It's not too late to change this plan." By the way, her comments were in response to a tweet I wrote a day earlier saying, "it's time to have some fun. Excited to join a great cast and show."

The day after the announcement on *Good Morning America*, I headed to LaGuardia Airport to catch a flight back to Washington. I kept thinking about what Deena had told me: the first couple of days, maybe the first week or so, would be tough, but then it would get better. So far the prediction was on course, now I just waited for the part where it got better.

On August 27, I drove to a ballet studio in Falls Church, Virginia, where I was scheduled to meet my dance partner for the first time. Rumors had already started to abound about who was partnered with whom based on where the pros had been sighted by fans. One of the dancers, Cheryl Burke, was spotted in Baltimore right before the season began, which gave everyone a pretty good suspicion that she and Ray Lewis were partners. While I wasn't 100 percent sure who mine was going to be, I had a pretty good idea based on a conversation I had with Deena. I had requested that my dance partner be married, and because I'm five feet six, be at least a little shorter than I am. Deena and I agreed that I needed to be paired with a pro who was going to have the patience to work with someone like me with very limited skills. While I saw this whole thing as a fun experience, I knew that for the dancers, it was their career. When the six female pros were announced on *GMA*, coupled with Deena's hints and rumors about other dancers in different cities, I felt pretty confident that Lindsay Arnold would be my partner.

Sure enough, I was right. From day one, I truly felt like I hit the jackpot with Lindsay. She is a professional in every way. Beyond being an amazing dancer and teacher, she possesses the patience and kindness that someone with my level of skill requires. On a personal level, she was thoughtful, kind, caring, funny, gracious, and all-around a class act. I couldn't have asked for a better partner.

Prior to *Dancing with the Stars*, Lindsay was a top four finalist and fan favorite on season nine of Fox's *So You Think You Can Dance*. In 2017, she won the coveted Mirror Ball in season 25 of *DWTS* with singer and actor Jordan Fisher, which, according to ABC, came "after a season full of perfect scores and gushing praise from the judges." Among her other previous dance partners were former MLB catcher David Ross and NFL linebacker DeMarcus Ware. On top of all of that, Lindsay is an amazing choreographer. In addition to traveling to where I was on any given week, adapting to my schedule, and patiently teaching me to dance, each week Lindsay masterfully choreographed a brand-new routine to the music we were assigned. In my case, Lindsay had to choreograph the best dance she could in the assigned style while taking my personal limitations into account. Clearly, she's the real deal, and was accustomed to being paired with athletes and entertainers. But now she was paired with a political lightning rod with zero rhythm. As soon as I met Lindsay, I had a tremendous amount of respect for her as a dancer and as a person. I did not want her to get dragged into the controversy that had erupted around my casting.

Cast members (that is, the stars) are given a choice of where they want to practice. Some use the *DWTS* studio in Los Angeles, but others like me choose to stay close to home and practice where their family lives. In order to stay with my family and keep up with my business obligations, I had chosen to stay in the Northern Virginia area prior to the launch of the show. From that day forward, we would practice up to four hours a day and after moving around from different studios, we began to settle on the third-floor ballroom at the Army Navy Country Club as our home base. The club, which I had joined while I was a lieutenant in the Navy, had been my oasis from all the vitriol I experienced in many public places since I had joined President Trump's White House. During my time at the White House, it was the only place I could have dinner with my family knowing we would not be bothered. I even escaped to rooms in the club to write most of my first book. The membership—which has a significant number of veterans and active-duty members of the military—is respectful, and the staff is caring, kind, and professional.

The first week of rehearsals was spent learning basic steps, and Lindsay slowly began teaching me pieces of the routine. During these early stages, we filmed a series of interviews that would be used for a video package leading up to our first dance. I was anything but surprised when during the first one, Lindsay described my skills as being at "a pre-pre-preschool level," and said that I'm definitely not "natural at it."

A few weeks in, I learned that we would be performing the salsa for the premiere of the show. To be honest, I didn't know the difference between the salsa, tango, or rumba. I didn't even know rumba was a dance, and the closest thing I had come to a salsa was a dip served with chips. Lindsay introduced me to the song we would dance to: Spice Girls' "Spice Up Your Life." Get it? It didn't take long to figure out that someone in Hollywood had realized that this would be kind of a cute way for me to enter. That was the first band-aid that got ripped off. Within a few days, she started to talk about what the accompanying outfit would be. She built it up very slowly first. It went from "you're going to wear a green shirt" to "there's going to be white pants," to slowly "it's going to be a little ruffly." It was initially going to be all pink. She made sure to note that as if somehow a green, ruffly shirt now sounded better.

At this point, I was trying to think of what it actually could look like. Lindsay looked at me and said, "Come on, Sean. You said you were all in and that you wanted to get out of your comfort zone." She was right. I was all in, but a green, ruffly shirt was really far out of my comfort zone.

After four weeks of getting the routine down, we left the East Coast and headed to Hollywood for the premiere of the show. My first stop was a tiny tailor shop on Fifth Avenue in Los Angeles where I would meet the tailor who had sewn costumes for nearly every past *DWTS* season, Mr. Garo and the show's costume designer Steven Lee. It was the kind of shop you would walk by a hundred times without knowing it, but when you walk inside, every space on the wall is filled with pictures of previous seasons' contestants. This was the first time I would be seeing my outfit for the season premiere—and it wasn't tough to spot it as soon as I walked in. Hanging on the hook was the brightest green shirt I had ever seen in my life. What had I gotten myself into?

The next morning, we went to the iconic, twenty-five-acre CBS Television City in Los Angeles, which is known for hosting shows such as HBO's *Real Time with Bill Maher* and CBS's long-running game show *The Price Is Right*. I was shown my trailer, which was roughly six by twelve feet and consisted of a small couch, a desk, and a little bathroom. I had always thought it would be cool to have a trailer in Hollywood, but I was thinking more along the lines of a big RV size. This was much less glamorous than what I had envisioned.

We proceeded to run through each couple's routines onstage for the first time so that the camera crew could appropriately set up camera shots for the show—which is actually live—something they referred to as "camera blocking." At the end of the run-through, I had my next Hollywood experience: my first spray tan. I was pretty certain that nobody would notice how tan I was once I showed up on national television in that lime green shirt. But then I figured that I probably wouldn't have many weeks to soak up these Hollywood experiences, so I went for it and got a spray tan.

The next day, everything started to feel real—very real. Upon arrival at the studio that morning, each couple was assigned a specific time to practice their routine on the floor. Next was the dress rehearsal, which was the first time we actually put on the outfits and the first time the entire cast would all see each other in them. Walking out of my trailer for the first time in a ruffled, lime green shirt, white pants, and white shoes was a moment that I may never forget. As I traveled from my trailer in the lot, down the hallway of the studio, and onto the set there was not a single person who didn't gaze at the shirt. I reminded myself, "I'm all in."

I didn't think it could get much worse—that is until we started the run through and I saw the stairwell that the cast would be cascading down to for the beginning of the show. One problem that never crossed my mind was my absolute fear of heights. So not only was I dressed in this ridiculous outfit, I was climbing up the stairs to a platform that was twenty-plus feet in the air, with an exceptionally small landing that we all crammed onto, experiencing what may have been one of the most nerve-racking experiences in my life. To add insult to injury, everyone thought I was joking about my fear of heights at first, not realizing that I was literally terrified about climbing up and waiting on this platform to walk out. You don't just climb up once and you're done. It's Hollywood, baby, and I quickly got used to the phrase "that was great, let's just do it one more time." And one more time usually means at least ten more times. Yup, one more time climbing those stairs and staring down . . . in a lime green ruffled shirt.

As the final rehearsal had wrapped up and I headed back to my trailer, I bumped into Erin Andrews outside her office. We began to make small talk about football and the Patriots when Tom (Bergeron, not Brady) came down the hallway. He interrupted the conversation I was having with Erin and said something to the effect of "I just want to let you know that it would have been the same statement no matter who it was." I simply looked over to him and said "okay" and immediately went back to my trailer.

I had never brought up that Tom had been very critical of my time in the White House, as evidenced by his past tweets about me that friends had forwarded to me. One was a photo of a man cleaning elephant poop with the caption "Watching Sean Spicer's press briefing." While Tom had tried to pass off his comments as being about not having any politics in the show, it just was not the case. He had tweeted several times about me during my tenure in the White House. In an August 2019 report, celebrity news site Cheatsheet weighed in on the matter, writing, "Like so many, Bergeron, despite wanting to keep politics out of his show, has taken to expressing his views on social media. Additionally, unlike many in his line of work, the host has given money to Democratic causes," citing a Daily Beast report that found Tom has given thousands of dollars to Democratic causes, including more than $3,000 to Barack Obama's presidential campaign alone. For him to act like it was simply a matter of my being a political figure and it wasn't about me specifically was disingenuous, to say the least. As an aside, the avatar for Tom's Twitter handle is "BYE DON." Get it? It's pretty clear he wants to keep politics out of things.

Later when I was asked by *US Weekly* if Tom and I had spoken on set, I used the colloquial phrase "we bumped into each other" in the hallway. *US Weekly* ran a story with that detail in it, but then ScreenRant took that quote and ran the headline "Sean Spicer (Kind of) Got Physical with DWTS Host Tom Bergeron After Backlash," the story went on to say. "The two were said to have had a meeting of the minds during an altercation in the hallway." Not only was this patently false and a total mischaracterization of what happened, it's just another example of the media undermining what I had set out to do with the show. I thought we could prove that people from different backgrounds or with different beliefs could get along, and many in the media did not want to see that happen.

I truly still believed that the show would be a rare reprieve from not only politics and policy, but also from the stresses of day-to-day life. For two hours a week, *Dancing with the Stars* provides families with a unique, family-friendly opportunity to come together, escape, unwind, and relax.

My fellow contestants and I all came from unique and diverse backgrounds, yet the show created a sense of unity. We were all proud of the causes we supported and the policies we believed in, but no one was trying to win anyone over by participating in this show. I continued to understand what Deena had meant by the show being a family. None of us knew each other for long but we all understood the common goal and purpose of the show.

Needless to say, I was holding my breath leading up to the show. I had been scheduled to perform seventh that night and sure enough, my turn came. Tom Bergeron began by telling the crowd, "We got one former White House press secretary and only two former champions left, Emma and Lindsay." The intro video began, officially revealing Lindsay to the audience as my partner and showing clips of our journey thus far. I expressed that my political career gave people a very one-dimensional look at who I am as a person and that I was excited to branch out of that and try something new. Lindsay talked about how "the internet kind of broke talking about Sean Spicer being on *Dancing with the Stars*" but said she's "looking forward to forming my own opinion." That meant a lot to me, and I thought this was a great way to kick off the season despite the media backlash.

I began my routine on the stage in the blinding fluorescent-green blouse, whacking on a set of bongo drums to the Spice Girls. Remember, I hadn't played drums since the sixth grade so this was not exactly graceful. I ended the performance in a knee slide. Knowing I wasn't going to wow the crowd and the judges with my salsa moves, we—okay, Lindsay—thought that a knee slide at the end would add some pizzazz to the performance and just maybe distract from the moves. I was actually really concerned that if I didn't nail the knee slide the whole thing would be off. Unfortunately, we don't get judged on these slides because if we did, I think I actually would've gotten a couple of points on that. When the dance was over, and I had completed the knee slide, I breathed a sigh of relief because it had felt like the longest minute and a half I've ever experienced.

My first critique came from judge Bruno Tonioli, who told me I was "going bonkers on the bongos" and looked like I was being attacked by a swarm of wasps. Ironically, while that was true, I thought it was interesting that I was being judged on my bongo playing rather than dancing, although I'm not sure which was worse.

Next was judge and choreographer Carrie Ann Inaba, who followed up by saying, "I'm going to give you Best Fluorescent Shimmy of the night." I was definitely expecting worse, so this was a pleasant surprise and of course made me laugh.

I wouldn't find out until later that the green shirt had started to trend on Twitter and become a meme.

And finally, judge Len Goodman concluded by saying, "I admire your courage coming on this show" and "as the others have said, you brought fun to the ballroom. Well done." That was pretty much the equivalent of the southern expression "Bless your heart."

To probably everyone's surprise, including my own, I didn't receive the lowest scores of the night. The judges awarded me 12 out of 30 points, just ahead of Lamar Odom, who barely fared worse with a total 11. Luckily, no one gets kicked off on the first night so I knew that I would live to fight another day.

At the end of every show, each couple goes down a press line to talk with various entertainment outlets, and this would be the first of the season. Up until this point, everything was going great. The cast had a blast and the audience was ready for more. Unfortunately, while we had come together, I quickly realized that some in the media sought to pit us against one another.

The types of questions that were asked by reporters after this show and the ones to come revealed just that. While some revolved around my shirt and how my performance was, my fellow contestants and I were routinely asked about the "controversy" surrounding my casting and sometimes about the ramifications of President Trump's administration instead of our dances.

The *Hollywood Reporter,* for instance, didn't hold back when asking my competitors about the "Spicer backlash."

Summarizing a conversation I had with reporters, they wrote, "Even if people can forget the current political turmoil for two hours while they're watching the show," *THR* pointed out, "after it ends they're still faced with the ramifications of the policies set by Spicer's former employer" and "Though *THR* spoke with two other contestants about the Spicer backlash—one claimed (or feigned) ignorance, and another said Spicer was polite to his fellow contestants—a publicist asked that the questions about Spicer be relayed only to him."

Some cast members endured backlash just for having a civil conversation with me. As I noted earlier, I had a very pleasant conversation with Karamo Brown, who is an outspoken LGBTQ advocate and liberal policy supporter, before the season started about how he was excited to engage in a dialogue with me on how to bridge our political divide. When backlash to my casting first ensued, he sent a tweet, saying, "I'm excited to sit down with him and engage in a respectful conversation" and in another interview, he noted that I seemed like a nice guy. This was all he said publicly about me, but it was enough to rile up the left. The backlash was so bad that he deactivated his Twitter account and disabled Instagram comments at the time. He told *Entertainment Tonight* that he and his children even received death threats over it, including one involving his son being chased by someone in a car who was screaming about his father. When the backlash to his comments ensued, he said, "I started this show with people telling me, 'You're horrible, you're crazy, you're stupid.' Because I showed someone who has a different political view than mine kindness."

The irony was that while we had several really pleasant conversations about life, none were ever actually about politics. Imagine that—two people enjoying each other's company and not discussing politics. It was some folks on the left, who preach tolerance and inclusion, who attacked a black LBGTQ contestant for merely hoping to engage in a civil discussion to understand each other.

These attacks were absolutely wrong. For anyone on either side to attack him, let alone his family, for being open to having a conversation with someone is absurd.

You can tell a lot by how liberals in the media think by looking at how they frame situations like this and what they decide to run as "news." *Time* magazine, for instance, felt it was somehow newsworthy that Karamo and I got along, and published an article titled "Post–Dancing with the Stars, Karamo Brown Continues to Support His New 'Friend' Sean Spicer." The second sentence states, "While speaking with reporters, Brown said that he and Spicer have formed a bond despite being politically opposed." The fact that they deem this to be anything other than a normal, civil interaction says a lot more about them than Karamo or myself. It's sad that the idea of two people wanting to engage in a civil conversation is "news."

In many ways this is the problem; the media bemoans the lack of civility but then creates outrage about people being civil. I am happy to engage with anyone who wants to have a civil and respectful conversation. That's my bar. I don't care about your political leanings, who you voted for, or anything else. Notice you didn't see anyone on the right bemoaning me for engaging with Karamo; it was the left attacking him for daring to be decent and kind.

After wrapping up the press interviews, I got in the car to head to a birthday celebration for one of the professional dancers. This was the first time I had gotten a chance to look at my phone and check in with my family to hear what they thought. A good friend of mine, Elizabeth Manresa, had been out with my wife, children, and some of our close family friends to watch the debut of the show. (Elizabeth is responsible for introducing me to Rebecca all those years ago.) She had taken a video of my kids watching my performance and sent it to me. As I noted, my daughter's biggest concern was that I would embarrass her (I can't say it was unwarranted), so I was very interested in seeing what her reaction was going to be. After watching them in the video remark that I had done well, I teared up, knowing all too well that embarrassing eight-year-old kids was probably the worst thing I could have done. Watching the reaction of my two children is a moment that every father cherishes. ABC's viewers may have seen the scores I received from the three judges in Hollywood, but it was my children's reviews that really mattered. In their eyes, I had scored all tens.

As I was exiting the car, TMZ took a picture of me getting emotional and reported that I broke down in embarrassment, assuming somehow that I was ashamed of my performance when in fact, I was actually excited about my children's response, which I explained to them as I got out of the car. TMZ's story was initially headlined "Sean Spicer Breaks Down Crying After 'Dancing with the Stars'" but was later changed to "SEAN SPICER SEEN CRYING AFTER 'DWTS' PREMIERE . . . Not Sad, Tears Of Joy!!!" Notably, their tweet of the initial story wasn't removed, and still states, "Sean Spicer danced his heart out, and then proceeded to cry." The story had already been picked up by several other outlets by the time TMZ's story was somewhat fixed, and the truth about why I had teared up was buried in the body of most of the stories, if at all.

Despite some of the initial reporting, I was optimistic about the rest of the season. I also wanted to use this opportunity to benefit two veterans organizations. I sit on the board of the Yellow Ribbon Fund, which provides resources to the caregivers of our wounded service members, and the Independence Fund, which provides track wheelchairs to injured service members who have mobility issues. I had reserved tickets to the show specifically for these groups. The idea was to give veterans, caregivers, and volunteers a night out in Hollywood to thank them for their service. It was an honor to meet many of these great vets and their caregivers when they came to the shows, including Melody Butler and her family and many others from the Yellow Ribbon Fund Keystone Program SoCal. Meeting these amazing people was one of the highlights of my experience on *DWTS*.

Realizing that the green shirt had trended, I thought it would be a good idea to auction it off and donate the money to these two organizations. I joined *Fox & Friends* to announce the auction, and we raised over $4,000 to be split evenly between Yellow Ribbon Fund and Independence Fund.

The next week was my forty-eighth birthday. My mother, wife, and kids flew out to Los Angeles so they could see the show. I certainly did not want to be eliminated with them in the audience. During the final dress rehearsal that week, the crew wheeled out a giant birthday cake for me. The cast and crew sang happy birthday, and Lamar counted the candles, reminding me how old I was.

This week, I was assigned a tango to the song "Shut Up and Dance" by the band Walk the Moon. I felt like I had paid my dues and I needed to take a much deeper interest in what I would be doing and what my outfit looked like, which ended up being a much simpler white and black jacket with black pants. Phew, no ruffles.

When I faced the judges for the second time I received the following scores: Bruno—5; Len—5; Carrie Ann—6, totaling 16, which put me fourth from the bottom. Keep that in mind—while I still recognize my lack of skill, I was hardly at the bottom despite the emerging media narrative.

The moment of truth came. Announcing who would be saved in no particular order, as they like to say, the judges proceeded to name Lamar Odom and Peta Murgatroyd safe, followed by James Van Der Beek and Emma Slater, Ally Brooke and Sasha Farber, and Karamo Brown and Jenna Johnson. Four couples safe, four to go.

I didn't think I would last long on the show but I wanted to get through at least one elimination. It wasn't lost on me that I had some political detractors who were eager for me to get kicked off early in the season. Furthermore, my early elimination would help feed the narrative being driven by many reporters. As I listened to the names being called, I kept hoping I was safe. Early on in the show, the protocol had been that the eliminated couple left for the airport immediately after the show (they asked every couple to bring a change of clothes to each show) and flew overnight to New York to appear on *Good Morning America* the next morning. I did not want to have to leave my family there in California on my birthday and fly to New York City for my elimination interview.

Thankfully, Lindsay and I were the next couple to be announced safe. The judges' scores combined with the viewers' votes had kept us out of the bottom two. The bottom two couples of the week were Ray Lewis and Cheryl, and Mary Wilson and Brandon Armstrong. When it came down to the judges to choose which couple to save,

Carrie Ann chose Mary and Brandon, followed by Bruno, who chose Ray and Cheryl, and Len, whose deciding vote also went to Ray and Cheryl. That meant Mary Wilson and Brandon Armstrong would be the first to be eliminated. I had gotten to know Mary a little bit, and I was sad to see her leave. We had enjoyed lunch together a few times, where she would regal me with stories about her time with the Supremes. Getting to know her, a true music icon, and listening to her stories was a real highlight for me.

After taking a deep breath, realizing I was saved and would stay on the show for at least one more week, I did another round of the post-show press, and my family and I headed to a local restaurant in the Grove—a shopping area a block from Television City—to celebrate my birthday and for making it through the first elimination.

Hannah Brown's birthday happened to be the next day, so the show surprised us both by bringing out cakes for each of us. Of course, my cake was in the mold of the lime green ruffled shirt, which by that point had become famous on the internet. It was truly a great time and was probably the most attention I'll ever get for a birthday but ironically, little of it had to do with me as much as it did that I was standing next to Hannah Brown as we blew our candles out together. Many of the contestants, dancers, crew, and friends of the show cast were all there. I was excited to see that *Shark Tank* star Robert Herjavec was there with his wife and professional ballroom dancer Kym Herjavec, along with several notable reality TV stars who were friends of Hannah, as well as Sailor Brinkley-Cook and her mother, Christie Brinkley.

The next day, photos of the event in the tabloids showed up and I had people texting me how cool it was that I celebrated with "Bachelor Nation." Huh? I called Katie. "Didn't you know that

Colton Underwood, Cassie Randolph, and Demi Burnett were there? They were all on past seasons of The Bachelor and various spinoffs," she informed me. I clearly had no clue, but apparently everyone else did.

Week three's theme was Movie Night. I would be channeling John Travolta for a disco cha-cha to "Night Fever" by the Bee Gees, a routine inspired by *Saturday Night Fever.* As I flew home after surviving week two, I watched YouTube clips of the movie, trying to get a sense of some Travolta moves. In one clip he bounces down to the floor back and forth on his knees. I texted the clip to Lindsay, writing, "I think I can pull this off," to which she replied, "Sure, we can try." I could almost sense the hesitancy, or maybe it was laughter in her text. As it turned out, I could not even come close to doing it but I did okay when show night rolled around. Len told me I "mastered the roly poly" and gave me a score of 5—as did Bruno and Carrie Ann—totaling 15 out of 30. Not that I'm complaining but compared to the week before I thought I had improved.

I knew from the first day of *DWTS* that I was not going to be a great dancer, but if I had any chance of survival I needed to focus not on the dancing side of the scorecard but the viewer voting side of the scorecard. Considering my background in political campaigns, I decided I was going to work the voting side by engaging directly with viewers (and recruiting potential viewers)—and remind them to vote each Monday night—much like a campaign. I launched a website, spicerarnold.com, where my friend Matt Mazzone made a spoof "campaign ad" that touted the reasons to vote for Spicer Arnold 2019. A voice-over artist narrated the "campaign ad" that said: "For 28 seasons *Dancing with the Stars* has had plenty of great dancers, full of rhythm and moves. This fall, let's finally vote for someone who represents people like us. Whether it's the waltz, cha-cha, salsa, or freestyle, Sean Spicer is the dancer we can be proud of, he will do whatever it takes to bring home that mirror ball. 'I'm going to fight for every American who has been overlooked or forgotten because they lack rhythm or moves.' This fall, vote Spicer Arnold. Call, text, or click. 'I'm Sean Spicer and I approve this message.'" I made up T-shirts, hats, and yard signs (all of which were available for sale and all proceeds went to the Independence Fund and Yellow Ribbon Fund). I had developed a list of high-profile people who have a lot of Twitter followers and email lists and started to get the message out that I would appreciate their support. Specifically, I asked them to please text SEAN to 21523 beginning Monday night starting at 8:00 p.m. Eastern Time. I even released a video of "endorsements" that included actors Scott Baio, Dean Cain, and Kristy Swanson, Patriots Hall of Famer Matt Light, My Pillow CEO Mike Kindell, and country music star John Rich.

Like every campaign, this was going to be about developing core supporters and turning them out on Election Day, or in this case show night. This was going to be a very similar proposition. I needed to know who I could count on, who could rally other folks, and to make sure that not only did they support me or retweet me but that they actually cast all 20 of their votes (10 via text; 10 online). Conservative leaders like Donald Trump Jr., Kimberly Guilfoyle, Dan Bongino, Pete Hegseth, Mike Huckabee, Sara Carter, Arthur Schwartz, Jesse Watters, Sarah Huckabee Sanders, Kristy Swanson, Scott Baio, and many others. I even got my old colleagues involved, like Reince Preibus, who had been the chair of the Republican National Committee and White House chief of staff. All were part of the "core campaign team."

I also met with several young YouTubers and TikTokers through my friend Michael Gruen, including Jason Wilhelm and brothers Maverick and Parker Baker, who wanted to help. I invited some of them as guests to the show, and they posted on their TikTok accounts asking their millions of followers to vote for me. On November 22, just over a week after my elimination on the show, I made my first TikTok with the help of YouTuber and former managing director of an e-sports organization Jason Wilhelm, who has the handle @General. I joked about being new to the platform, saying, "I've got The General here, he's going to give me a tutorial, get the troops in line," but it's safe to say *Business Insider* wasn't laughing. The outlet ran a full-page story on November 23 dedicated to my debut on TikTok, lamenting, "The new account also fits in with Spicer's new 'fun' public persona post-White-House, which has included a three-month stint on 'Dancing With The Stars.'" Here we go again with the criminalization of me having . . . fun? Gasp. As a side note, I have since deleted my TikTok account because of its connection with communist China.

Getting past week three was something I had not planned. In fact, I had been scheduling meetings, speaking engagements, and events for most of October and November, with the expectation that my run on *DWTS* would end early in the season. Instead, I was having to reschedule everything. As my monthly Navy reserve weekend approached I called my commanding officer, Captain Jim Polickoski. "Sir, this may be the oddest request you have ever heard, but I have made it another week on *Dancing with the Stars* and would like permission to reschedule the upcoming drills," I asked. Sure enough, it was a first. Fortunately, he granted permission.

The mock campaigning continued through week four. Lindsay and I performed a paso doble set to "Bamboléo" by the Gipsy Kings. Carrie Ann Inaba said the dance was "not as militant" as the previous week (don't tell that to the *New York Times* columnist who slammed my "militaristic" and "cold brutality" dancing style), and we picked up 21 out of 40 points with the judges' scores: Bruno—5; Len—5; Carrie Ann—5; and guest celebrity judge Leah Remini—6. Leah had been a contestant on season 17 and was a star on the CBS show *King of Queens*. After I finished my routine, she offered some kind words of encouragement, which I really appreciated. At the end of the night, the viewers' votes had come in and saved me from elimination once again.

Week five came in the blink of an eye. It was Disney week. We shot the opening numbers in Disneyland, but we had to work in the overnight hours when the park was closed. It was surreal being in Disneyland at a time when no one else was there. The entire place was shut down, yet all the lights were on. The magic of Disney was alive. The Disney cast joined us as we taped the opening number for the upcoming week. Funny enough, the cast members never broke. You could ask them the most outlandish question at four in the morning and the Peter Pan and Wendy characters still answered as Peter Pan and Wendy.

Each team had been assigned a song from a Disney movie for their next dance. Lindsay and I would be doing the quickstep to "You've Got a Friend in Me" from *Toy Story 3*. I was dressed as Sheriff Woody, and Lindsay was his counterpart, Jessie.

During a pre-show interview, I shared that I would be dedicating the performance to my father, whom we lost to pancreatic cancer in 2016, as well as all fathers who are suffering from cancer but are still being the best dads they can be. A few years ago, Rebecca and I took the kids along with my parents to Disney World in Florida. As a family, we had all ridden the Buzz Lightyear ride and had a blast. It was definitely one of our favorite rides. So *Toy Story* really had a special place in my heart. It was one of the great memories I have with my dad, mainly because I watched him have an incredible amount of fun with my children. My deepest sadness when my father died was knowing that he would not be able to share more moments like those with his beloved grandchildren over the coming years.

While the performance earned our highest scores to that point (our first 6 from Len and Bruno and our first 7 from Carrie Ann) and a positive reaction from the audience, the self-proclaimed dance critics in the mainstream media were not as easy to please. If you thought such a harmless performance would be enough to keep them from spewing divisive political vitriol, you thought wrong.

Vanity Fair Hollywood writer Laura Bradley was so outraged after watching the episode that she wrote, "Spicer's horrific, lime green-clad debut was not enough to send him home, and now ABC is allowing him to tarnish even Sheriff Woody's good name," in an article titled, "Who Let Sean Spicer Play Woody From Toy Story?" Pause. A couple of things here: ABC was allowing me to tarnish Woody's name? I am sure Sheriff Woody is a great sheriff and theoretically a good character, but let's just remember that we are talking about an animated character. Anyway, Laura Bradley's recap of the performance began with a nod to the president's impeachment inquiry. "As the president continues to battle his impeachment inquiry, the man who once routinely lied on his behalf took to the stage Monday night dressed in full cowboy gear, including a sheriff's star, to dance his quickstep to a fast-tempo version of the Toy Story standby 'You've Got a Friend in Me,'" she wrote. "The judges were pleased. As judge Carrie Ann Inaba put it, "You give good Woody!" Spicer ultimately walked away with a 19/30 score. He dedicated the dance to his father, who died of cancer in 2016."

"At this point it seems safe to assume the rest of Disney's most beloved characters are hiding in the vault, praying they won't be next," she concluded. Stop for a moment and think about what she's saying. I thought I had simply dressed up as a Disney character for a reality dance show.

In another article, titled, "Sean Spicer Goes Full Woody From 'Toy Story' in Bizarre 'Dancing With the Stars' Performance," the *Daily Beast*'s senior writer Matt Wilstein wrote that the emotional moment of me getting choked up while paying tribute to my father was "undercut ever so slightly by his preposterous costume."

In a stunning act of bravery, the *New York Times* dedicated an entire column, titled "No, Sean Spicer Really Can't Dance," to my poor dancing skills. Dance critic Gia Kourlas described my final performance as "militaristic," and betraying "cold brutality." Remember, this is the *New York Times* we're talking about— and the dance critic who normally writes about the New York City Ballet and Lincoln Center performances. I actually found some humor that she even wrote about my time on a reality show.

"He hides behind an egregious smile, parting his teeth to make it look as though he's been caught mid-laugh," Kourlas wrote on the pages of the biggest legacy newspaper in the country. "That smile seems meant to distract from his plan of attack. Watching Mr. Spicer try to wipe away some of his disgrace through dancing hurts. Yet here he is, week after week, using dance as a way to redeem his character.

"Bad dancing by a nonprofessional can be disarming. It allows you to see the truth within the body that reveals character. But Mr. Spicer, the former White House press secretary and communications director for President Trump, is something worse: an untruthful dancer," she added. Got that? My dancing is untruthful. At least she likes my smile.

Throughout the season, there was a constant assumption that I was trying to redeem myself—or as the *New York Times* put it, I was wiping away my disgrace through dancing. Unfortunately for them, I was enjoying myself, having fun, and learning something different. I wasn't asking for forgiveness. Have I made mistakes? Yes, I wrote an entire book talking about the ups and downs of my tenure in the White House.

Surviving one more week meant I had another opportunity to dance one more time, but it also gave me another opportunity to recognize someone important in my life. The song Lindsay and I would be dancing to was "Someone to Love" by Queen. This one was a natural pick—this would be a tribute to my wife. After all, our fifteenth wedding anniversary was coming up in a few weeks. Katie and I worked with Rebecca to identify pictures that the producers could use in the pre-dance video. And as the pictures came in, the producers started asking if Rebecca could be on set for the show. It's important to note that Rebecca has a public-facing career, but she's an incredibly private person. She would be the first to tell you that she's protective of our family and we have gone to great lengths to shield our children from the public eye. So, I wasn't sure what her reaction would be to appearing on national television—especially on a reality dance show. But there was another twist—Rebecca was in Lima, Peru, on a work trip, and we had about forty-eight hours to get her to Los Angeles. But before that, Rebecca had to catch an overnight flight from Lima to Miami, fly to DC, drive to our Virginia home, relieve my mother, who had been staying with the kids, attend a school event, drive to a couple of soccer games, dump one suitcase, pack another suitcase, pack the kids' bags, and drive them to friends' homes where they would stay for two nights. If there's one person on earth who can pull it all off—and do it gracefully—it's Rebecca. She landed at LAX around noon the day of the show. She went straight to our hotel, dropped her luggage, unpacked her outfit for the show, and headed over to get hair and makeup, in true Hollywood style.

It was such a whirlwind that I barely got to see her before she was whisked to her seat in the audience.

Prior to the show, I stopped by a flower store across from the SLS Hotel where I was staying, to pick up a dozen roses. I let the producers know in advance that at the end of the dance I would like to present them to Rebecca on camera. The producers thought it was a great idea, but they thought my twelve roses would look rather wimpy on television and asked if they could swap them out for two dozen stunning long-stem roses. Of course I agreed, and prior to the start of the show I hid them under the seat of Robert Brown, Hannah's father, who was going to be sitting by Rebecca.

Lindsay and I danced a Viennese Waltz to Queen's "Somebody to Love" and received straight 7s; our highest score. Thankfully, we stayed out of the bottom two again, and I got to have a night out after the show with Rebecca.

After making it past week seven, Lindsay and I flew back to Virginia because I wanted to make sure I was home with my family to trick-or-treat with my kids on Halloween. I didn't have to worry about finding a costume—I wore my Sheriff Woody outfit from the prior week. I hadn't asked the folks at *Vanity Fair* for permission to dress up again as Woody, but I figured I would risk it. My family ended up at a neighbor's house for a Halloween dinner as we have the last few years, and much to my surprise the hostess had dressed up as me—lime green shirt and white pants. We had a good laugh, and I reminded her to vote on Monday night!

Halloween was on a Thursday. That morning, Lindsay and I practiced at the Army Navy Country Club ballroom. While practicing, I learned that Lindsay's mother-in-law had been taken to a hospital in Africa after falling ill during a trip with her father-in-law. She thought everything would be okay and decided to fly back to Utah to be with her husband.

Friday morning I had a scheduled 7 a.m. flight to LA to get back in time for practice that afternoon. Upon arriving at Reagan National Airport in DC, I learned my flight was canceled. Realizing if I didn't get back to LA in time I would lose an entire afternoon of practice, I feverishly tried to find another flight. I was able to find a 9 a.m. flight from Dulles airport that landed at 2:00 p.m. Pacific time and was able to rush to the studio to get a few hours in. Lindsay had flown from Utah to LA early that morning. As we wrapped up practice, she had a feeling things were looking up for her mother-in-law.

We had planned to wake up that Saturday morning and practice our dance to Styx's "Come Sail Away" and film a promo shoot aboard the USS *Iowa,* a decommissioned Navy battleship. When I saw Lindsay called at 7 a.m., well before the time we were supposed to go, I wondered what was up. I called her back, and Lindsay told me that her mother-in-law had tragically passed away and that she was on her way to LAX to fly home to Utah to be with her husband

and family. I could not even imagine what she or her husband were dealing with. I had had the opportunity to say goodbye to my father and tell him how much he meant to me. Knowing how sudden and tragic this was for Lindsay and her husband was something I could not fathom. Within hours, Deena and others from the show were trying to figure out what the way forward would be. I went through the promo shoot alone, concerned about Lindsay and her family and not knowing what was going to happen.

Finally, the decision was made that Jenna Johnson, who was Karamo Brown's partner and had been eliminated a week earlier, would be stepping in to partner with me for the week. She was Lindsay's childhood best friend and there was no one better to take on the role. Like Lindsay, Jenna is an amazing professional, a great teacher, and an all-around good and kind person. I hit the jackpot with Lindsay, and here I was hitting it again with Jenna.

Nonetheless, it was still a challenging week. Getting thrown a new partner on Saturday before Monday's live show might rank just below putting on a lime green shirt on week one. Not only was I being introduced to a new partner, but that Saturday we had an entire group of new dancers who were being added to the routine. As if it could not get more challenging, I spent the rest of the day sick to my stomach, having gotten some kind of food poisoning. As sick as I was, I managed to keep it together to attend the Saturday vigil mass at the church across from my hotel. After Mass, a woman approached me. "You're Sean Spicer right?" she asked. Sick to my stomach, I replied, "I am," thinking of all nights, please just let me get back to my hotel. "I have seen you here every week, and I wanted you to know I am a lifelong Democrat. I don't agree with anything your former boss stands for. That being said, I have enjoyed watching you on *Dancing with the Stars* and have been voting for you every week. You seem like a good sport and I appreciate the fact that you stay through the end of Mass each week." I did not see that coming. Of all my "moments" in Hollywood, this is one of the most impactful. It reassured me that despite our differences, we can find common ground and be kind and respectful to each other.

Knowing how many curveballs had been thrown at me at this point, Sunday morning Jenna and I went back to the rehearsal studio early to get another few hours of practice before the camera blocking session at the studio that afternoon.

When Monday finally rolled around the scores came in as follows: Carrie Ann—7; Len—7; Bruno—6; which gave me a final score of 20 out of 30. Len had remarked, "we keep throwing you out of the boat and the viewers keep throwing you a life preserver." He was right. The judges very clearly wanted me gone, but the viewers had kept me alive. I actually gave the judges credit for not trying to hide anything.

In addition to my dance with Jenna, we were scheduled to do a dance-off in a style we had performed earlier in the season. I would be facing Kate Flannery and her partner Pasha, and we were tasked to perform a salsa to C+C Music Factory's "Gonna Make You Sweat." It's important to note that during my second week with Jenna as my partner, Lindsay, despite her family situation, was still actively involved in choreographing the routine. She never ceases to amaze me. (Since leaving the show, she has announced that she and her husband, Sam, are expecting a baby girl. I can say without equivocation that she will be an amazing mother.)

In addition to rehearsals with my new partner, I did what I had done every other week, asking supporters to vote. During the show, all the contestants and dancers hang out at the end of the dance floor in the "Star Lounge." Don't get any ideas of grandeur about the lounge; it's literally an elevated platform with a railing where the couples gather and chat with Erin Andrews before or after their dance. I had two phones in my hand, making sure my "campaign" was in full swing. As the show entered its second hour, I saw that President Trump weighed in for the first time, tweeting, "Vote for Sean Spicer on Dancing with the Stars. He is a great and very loyal guy who is working very hard! #MAGA."

A short time later, Lindsay called from Utah to make sure I was doing okay. At a moment that should have been about her and her family, there she was making sure I was okay. While she didn't say it, I knew she was wondering if that would be my last show. But at the end of the night, Jenna and I were the first couple announced safe, meaning I would return for yet another week, thanks completely to the voters. Both Lindsay and Jenna were thrilled when the results came in. Jenna was so astonished that she made a face that became a viral meme. Much was said about her expression, but she truly was shocked and excited. So was I.

Kate Flannery was the star who was eliminated that night. Ironically, I had lost to her in the dance-off that night. That's when *DWTS* purists reached a boiling point.

The rules had been changed in season 28 to limit voting to text and online—eliminating the toll-free 800 telephone option and further limiting all voting to occur only during the live airing of the show in Eastern/Central time zones. Fans in Mountain and Pacific time zones could still technically vote but they would have to do so while it was airing in the earlier time zones, meaning they were voting before actually viewing the show. In prior seasons, the lowest-scoring couple would be eliminated the following week after their judge's score was combined with a week of fan scores. No more. Now, with voting limited to the two hours of the live show, the fans' votes would be combined with the judges' scores and the bottom two would face the judges. In order to correct the "injustices" of past seasons, where the more popular contestant had moved on over better dancers, now the judges would save one of the two bottom couples. This additional rule was an attempt to give the judges more sway in keeping the better dancers moving on. In the previous season, country music DJ Bobby Bones had taken home the Mirror Ball despite not being the best dancer according to the purists. Bobby has a massive following on his radio show and longtime fans of *DWTS* complained he had won because of fan votes—not because of his dance moves.

Kate Flannery and Ally Brooke ended up in the bottom two in week eight despite both having higher judges' scores than I had, and in Kate's case, she had additionally beat me in the "dance-off" that week. As they faced the judges, Carrie Ann said, "I just want to say it's confusing for me at this point why these are the bottom two. I'm just a little confused and a little irritated." Bruno nodded in agreement, adding that Flannery did not deserve the bottom two slots. "Again, I'm in the same position as Carrie Ann," he said. "You know, I have to do my job. You shouldn't be here."

"Confusing," "Shouldn't be here"? How could these two veteran judges be confused about a format that had existed since the show's inception? The entire reason the formula was changed was exactly because fans had advanced contestants in the past who were not the best dancers. They may not have liked the result but they should not have been confused. Yes, both Kate and Ally were better dancers but the formula was not just based on the judges. Because viewers had voted for me, I had enough votes to offset the judge's scores. Thinking I could win a pure dancing competition is like thinking I could win a slam dunk contest. (Remember, I'm five six.)

Carrie Ann made another comment when speaking to the media after the show expressing her frustration with my continued presence because she felt other people were "working hard." I had said from day one that I'm not the best dancer—or anything close to it. I knew I would have to work twice as hard to overcome a lack of training or talent. I have never had a problem with the judges' critique of my abilities, but this struck a nerve. The implication was that I was not taking the show seriously or working as hard as the other contestants, which was truly insulting.

Trevor Noah of *The Daily Show* was so appalled with my continued presence on *DWTS* that he dedicated 8 of his 22 minutes of his air time expressing outrage over how far I had gotten in the contest. "Because you see, he's harnessed the full support of the conservative world," he said. "I know Sean Spicer isn't technically breaking any rules. I mean, he's breaking a ton of dancing rules and just general rules of physics about how the human body is supposed to move," Noah said, before accusing me of "ruining" the show for "a lot of its fans."

The ratings told a different story. On October 15, 2019, IMdB noted that "ABC managed to net the most viewers last night with solid numbers from Dancing with the Stars. The reality dance competition series celebrated Disney Night on Monday and continues to do well for the network, growing week-to-week." Likewise, the *Hollywood Reporter* ran a story on September 17, 2019, headlined, "TV Ratings: Sean Spicer Helps 'Dancing With the Stars' Premiere Tick Up."

Despite the show's ratings, calls for me to quit grew louder. But I realized that it wasn't just about me. This was the livelihood of Lindsay and Jenna. For them to take someone as bad as I am and then make it to the quarterfinals was a true testament to their strength as talented dance partners and teachers. They earned this as much as I did. Additionally, I had asked people to take time out of their Monday nights and text and log in to vote for me. I owed it to these people to keep going. People have countless things going on Monday nights—making dinner, helping with homework, getting kids ready for bed, and the list goes on—and yet they took time to watch, or at least took time to vote for me.

After Jenna and I made it into the quarterfinals, *USA Today* ran a cover story on its Life section on November 8, 2019, titled "Spicer Prevails Despite Rule Change On 'DWTS': fan support swamps intent of shift to lessen power of popularity over skill." In the story, reporter Bill Keveney wrote, "A change to 'Dancing with the Stars' elimination rules meant to value skill over popularity is the subject of widespread complaints—unless you're part of the legion of voters saving Sean Spicer's spray-tanned hide every week." I guess the spray tan did get noticed after all.

The rules changes had given the judges more say but as he noted, it was meaningless if people like me had such overwhelming fan support. Keveney noted, "that's exactly what's happened with Spicer, as the president in recent weeks has urged his 66 million Twitter followers to vote." The only problem with his description was that the first time the president had tweeted for people to vote for me was late in the previous week's show. Don't get me wrong, I greatly welcomed and appreciated the president's support. His son Don Jr. and so many others had been supporting me each week. But to make it seem like the president had been actively tweeting for the previous eight weeks was not true. As the president would say . . . Fake News.

Week nine would be the end of my run—I had beaten the odds and made it to the quarterfinals. At the outset I knew this week was going to be tough. I had two different events to attend that week, one in Erie, Pennsylvania, and one in Mexico. Neither location had a convenient flight route from LAX, but I had agreed to speak at the Global Summit of the Jefferson Educational Society of Erie as a favor to my friend Steve Scully of C-SPAN and couldn't cancel either event. When these events were scheduled before the show started, I thought there was no way I would be in the quarterfinals. At this point in the competition, I had gotten used to traveling across the country while rehearsing, but for the first time this week, we would have to perform *two* original dances. One performance had been tough enough; two was going to be a real challenge.

Jenna and I traveled to Pennsylvania, and we practiced in a local facility called "The Little Dance Studio" before and after I gave my speech. It was owned by the Little family, and they were fans of the show and great hosts. When we traveled throughout the season, from Newport, Rhode Island, to Erie, Pennsylvania, the *DWTS* team, especially Eric Biermann who always made sure we could work around my travel schedule and always found a great local studio where we could practice.

My first dance that week was an Argentine tango to "Bills, Bills, Bills" by Destiny's Child, which received a total score of 26 out of 40. In what would be my final chance to rebound, Jenna and I took the stage for the last time to perform our second dance, which was a foxtrot to One Direction's "Story of My Life." This time, we received straight six marks from the judges and totaled a score of 24 out of 40.

It was right after the dance that President Trump weighed in on Twitter again. "Vote for Sean Spicer on Dancing with the Stars,

He is a great and very loyal guy who is working very hard. He is in the quarterfinals—all the way with Sean! #MAGA #KAG." But this time with the difference between my score and everyone else's, the votes weren't enough to keep me out of the bottom two.

I had always known that if I wound up in the bottom two, I was cooked. The judges could never save me. As Len had said, they wanted me out of the boat. And that was certainly the case. It was down to Lauren and Gleb. I looked at Lauren and I think she was about as safe as someone could feel in an elimination. For the first time all season, I was facing elimination. Carrie Ann and Bruno both decided to save Lauren and Gleb, which meant I was out. So were Jenna and Lindsay.

Jenna had stepped in and made the transition as seamless as she could, but talking to Lindsay that night I could tell she wished she had been able to be there. I told Lindsay I missed her and I wished I had done better. Lindsay had still choreographed the dances that week and recorded them with her sister to send to Jenna and me. Even though she couldn't be there, she thought the Argentine tango was my best dance yet. It included a lift that I never thought I would be able to do, but about halfway through I missed a step and at that point in the competition there was no room for error.

I had mixed emotions as the show was coming to a close, concluding the unforgettable experience by saying, "Thanks to everyone who supported me. Thanks to my family for everything they did. I've loved being on this show. Thank you for making me a part of it. God bless you all. Happy Veteran's Day."

Going home that week meant that I would be able to celebrate my fifteenth wedding anniversary with Rebecca. She had been juggling everything back at home—her own career, homework, lunchboxes, sports, house repairs, and everything else that families balance—for three months so I could have this experience. I had told Deena that I was "all in." So was Rebecca. Every Monday night she feverishly texted and emailed every person she could think of to ensure they submitted all twenty votes—family far and wide, coworkers, school friends, neighbors, college friends, and her high school friends in Nashville. On the night I was eliminated from the show, she stayed up late into the night to make sure she personally thanked everyone who had been voting: "Thanks everyone for the support the past 9 weeks. Never could have imagined stretching this ride into Nov. sweeps ('ratings period' for non-tv people). It's amazing to think how much fun he had and how far he came … especially if you had seen the first dance at our wedding reception—which was 15 years ago this Wednesday! Thank you, thank you. It's been incredible."

I had said all along that *DWTS* is a family show, and I knew that my children had been staying up late to watch it every Monday night. Evidently, that was painfully apparent the next morning while Rebecca was trying to get everyone off to school and work. But the kids had really become engaged and asked if they could watch with me that Monday I was home. All four of us watched together that night. It reminded me of an earlier time in my life when families had appointment viewing and would all gather to watch favorite shows. There was a certain peace to watching the show, surrounded by my family, knowing the pressure was off me now. I also knew that we would be back in California for the show finale. It seemed a bit ironic that there was only one week out of the entire season that I would not be on set.

That night, we all watched with amazement as James Van Der Beek danced what we thought was another outstanding performance. It was always fun to watch James—he had a natu-ral ability and flair that I simply didn't have. He's also a very kind person who puts family first. I had some deep, solid conversations with James throughout the season, and I am truly glad I got to know him. That night, as my family watched his pre-dance video package, we learned that James and his wife, Kimberly, had sadly experienced an unspeakable loss. She had miscarried, and they shared their very personal, emotional story on national television.

I have mentioned several times the "family" environment that forms over the course of the season with the cast. That night, as I watched with my own family at home in Virginia, my heart broke for James—as if we were family. It's a very stark and painful reminder that we may not all see eye to eye on everything. We can have very different backgrounds. But we can—and do—share in each other's pain and loss.

Later that night, my family sat speechless as James wound up in the bottom two along with Ally Brooke—another amazing per-son and dancer. This was not a selection that anyone should have to make. There were a few weepy eyes in my family room as the judges decided to eliminate James—and Ally promptly begged if she could go home instead of James. That is just the family bond that grew over the season.

When I flew back the following week for the show's finale, I had the opportunity to catch up with James and express my con-dolences in person. He summed up the ending of the season pretty perfectly. "Who would have ever thought you would have made it to the quarterfinals and I would be eliminated in the semifinals?" he joked. No doubt about it—James is one of the good people in Hollywood. He is a kind and caring person who always sees the best in people, brings out the best in people, and genuinely wants to make the world a better place.

I was grateful for the experience and for the fans who kept voting for me week after week, so that I could defy the odds and keep having fun. From the beginning, I didn't think I would make it further than a couple of weeks, but I made it to week nine of the competition thanks to the support of so many people across this country.

But leave it to CNN to capitalize on my elimination. In a November 12, 2019, article, Fox News noted that "CNN senior media correspondent Brian Stelter was blasted for offering breaking coverage of former White House Press Secretary Sean Spicer's elimination on ABC's 'Dancing with the Stars' while staying quiet on the growing Jeffrey Epstein scandal that has plagued the Disney-owned network." Just to be clear, Stelter was covering my elimination from *DWTS* on a major network, when there were real consequential events to be covering.

"Stelter, an outspoken critic of President Trump and frequent defender of the left-leaning media, has been notably silent about the bombshell allegation—made by ABC News anchor Amy Robach in a leaked video—that her network killed her story about convicted pedophile Jeffrey Epstein three years ago. The controversy expanded after ABC News reportedly worked with CBS News to find the alleged leaker who had recently switched networks. That led to her firing despite her strong denial last week that she leaked the video."

Indeed, on November 11, six days after the video of Robach leaked, Stelter tweeted, "Trump gave Spicer a big boost, but tonight it wasn't enough. Spicer has been voted off 'Dancing With the

Stars.'" Less than ten minutes later he weighed in again, writing, "After Spicer was voted off "Dancing," @realDonaldTrump deleted his 8:33 pm tweet urging people to "vote for Sean." Trump had written, "He is a great and very loyal guy who is working very hard." Now he's posted a new message: "A great try by @seanspicer. We are all proud of you!" So essentially, the president went from telling everyone to vote for me to replace it with a "we are proud of you" message after I was eliminated in the quarterfinals. That somehow became a scandal in Stelter's eyes. Early the next morning he wrote, "President Trump took the 'Dancing' competition seriously, tweeting out support for @SeanSpicer and urging the MAGA universe to cast votes for a man who has remained loyal during a perilous time for the president. But every dance party ends eventually. . . ."

Conservative pundit Stephen Miller reacted to his rant, tweeting, "@brianstelter has officially tweeted more about a dance show than two mainstream networks colluding to fire a female employee for exposing a network anchor revealing her story about a high profile pedophile was spiked."

Fox News noted, "Moreover, Stelter did not tackle the subject on his Sunday show 'Reliable Sources,' a program purportedly focused on the media. During the entire week since the video leaked, it was not mentioned once on either CNN or MSNBC. None of the broadcast networks, including NBC News, CBS News or ABC News, addressed the story on their morning or evening telecasts."

CNN's website also published a lengthy report by Stelter on the matter of my elimination, which, as Fox News pointed out, is "something he has yet to do on ABC News' Epstein scandal."

"Spicer capitalized on his former role as White House press secretary by doing the tango and the foxtrot for millions of ABC viewers. His former boss President Donald Trump seemed to take the competition seriously, tweeting out support for Spicer and urging the MAGA universe to cast votes for a man who has remained loyal during a perilous time for the president," the so-called media reporter wrote for CNN.com.

"Frankly, the surprise is that Spicer lasted this long, in the face of persistently low scores from the judges. It seemed like he received a significant boost, week after week, from Trump supporters who swarmed ABC with votes," he continued.

Politico and other mainstream news outlets also noted my elimination. Interestingly, at the onset of the show, the odds of me getting eliminated immediately were overwhelming. Sports Betting Dime, a sports betting website, published an analysis of the season in August 2019, titled "Dancing with the Stars Season 28 (2019) Odds & Props: Ray Lewis Favored, Sean Spicer Given Worst Odds," with the following predictions:

Ray Lewis. . . . . +400
James Van der Beek . . . . +450
Karamo Brown . . . . +550
Ally Brooke . . . . +600
Kel Mitchell. . . . . +600
Lauren Alaina. . . . . +700
Christie Brinkley . . . . +1200
Mary Wilson. . . . . +1200
Hannah Brown. . . . . +1400
Kate Flannery . . . . +1400

Lamar Odom . . . . +2500
Sean Spicer . . . . +5000

There I was at the bottom of the list with my odds of winning 5,000 to 1, which was double the odds of Lamar Odom, whom they put second to last with odds of 1 in 2500. Even though I truly beat the odds for nine weeks, that never was the story. It wasn't until the day I got eliminated that the stories suddenly broke through. You have to ask, is this the same oddsmakers as the one at the *New York Times* who had the odds of Trump losing 93 to 7?

It was hard to imagine how such depressing and divisive reactions came from something so fun and lighthearted. For these reporters to paint such harmless dance performances as some sort of crime is something worth exploring.

What amazed me week after week was that people seemed genuinely shocked about my advancements to the next rounds. How dare this happen? How could this possibly occur? It was almost like the 2016 election all over again. Many in the press and on the left were in a state of bewilderment, wondering who these people were who could possibly be voting for Sean. Is it the Russians? Who is it? Who's voting for him? Because to them, all of their colleagues and peers didn't like me and certainly didn't like Trump, so, how could I possibly be advancing? There's almost a sense of disgust that these people exist. They want to wish them away. They think if they write another article or send another tweet, somehow it'll all be right.

My experience on *DWTS* is not one I ever thought I would have, but it is one that has reaffirmed my suspicions about our current state of politics and has opened my eyes to just how vital it is for conservatives to maintain a presence in every sector of society—and that certainly includes TV and entertainment.

I truly enjoyed my time on the show. Deena had been right—the beginning was tough but in the end, it was worth it. She had also been right about it being a family. It wasn't just the contestants and professional dancers, though. It was the entire crew—producers, publicists, tailors, makeup artists, hairstylists, and designers. They are the backbone of the show. They also are the soul of the show. And I am grateful to each and every one of them for their work and their friendship.

CHAPTER 3

★ ★ ★ ★ ★ ★ ★

LIGHTS, CAMERA, ACTIVISM

One of the highlights of my time on *Dancing with the Stars* was having President Trump weigh in on my performances. To many people, this was an outrage. Why would the president of the United States bother to weigh in on a silly Hollywood show? After all, he's the leader of the free world . . . shouldn't he be busy appointing judges, reviewing legislation, or dealing with foreign leaders? Perhaps. But taking a few seconds to show support for a former staffer seems like it should be seen as a positive attribute.

The Donald Trump I know understands that the world we live in is multidimensional, with every industry playing an integral role in shaping society as we know it. If there's one thing he learned during his time as one of the "Hollywood elite," it's that the industry wields tremendous power—power that many are just starting to recognize in the wake of today's culture war.

It's easy to forget that Donald Trump's rise to political power began with him weighing in on various hot-button issues while still a Hollywood celebrity and businessman. As far back as the 1980s, Donald Trump took to interviews with stars such as Larry King and Oprah to lament how other countries were ripping us off on the world stage. In one 1980 interview with gossip columnist Rona Barrett, when asked why he wouldn't dedicate himself to public service, he told her, "I would dedicate my life to this country but I see it as being a mean life, and I also see it in somebody with strong views, and somebody with the kind of views that are maybe a little bit unpopular, which may be right, but may be unpopular, wouldn't necessarily have a chance of getting elected against somebody with no great brain but a big smile. That's a sad commentary for the political process."

Barrett replied with the question, "Television in a strange way has ruined that process, hasn't it?" to which Trump agreed, saying, "It's hurt the process very much. I mean the Abraham Lincolns of the world. Abraham Lincoln would probably not be electable today because of television," adding that "that's a shame, isn't it?"

What Donald Trump is telling us here is that Hollywood matters. All the elements that go into television and entertainment productions—from personality to presentation—matter. As many political thought leaders have famously said, politics is downstream from culture. In order for conservatives' ideas to win out in the end, they have to win not only a political battle but also a cultural battle. The left gets that, which is why they have long used Hollywood as a tool to influence culture. Trump understands how to promote conservative ideas the way the left promotes liberal ideas.

There's no question that conservative ideas have been under attack by Hollywood for decades. Patriotism and capitalism are demonized, Judeo-Christian values are mocked, and the few conservatives who manage to find their way into Hollywood circles are eventually smeared or blacklisted.

The few conservative-leaning friends and colleagues that I have who at some point in their lives headed out to Hollywood quickly transformed their thinking and joined the left in large part because it was easier to get along than swim against the tide. Like them, I am one of the few conservatives who can say I went to Hollywood and lived to tell the tale. Okay—maybe that's a slight exaggeration—but what I can say is that I am one of the few who came back more conservative than when they entered.

Donald Trump can say the same. He is one of the few politicians who experienced Hollywood liberals from the inside, making him the ultimate outsider from the inside. When I first started working for him in 2016, I wondered how someone so deeply intertwined in elite Hollywood circles could hold such low regard for the industry—and do so outspokenly. Then I experienced it for myself—and believe me, that changed everything.

While it's arguably a known fact that Hollywood leans liberal, most people don't realize just how risky it is for individuals on the inside to hold conservative views. Doing so automatically puts a target on their back as they quickly realize they are risking not only their social standing but also their career.

What's worse, I've seen firsthand how Hollywood elites will put their own interests aside for the sake of advancing their political agenda, valuing ideology over what makes good business sense. They know what will get them ratings and make money, but they would rather sacrifice those things for what they believe to be a noble cause.

Political writer Derek Hunter explains this idea perfectly in his book *Outrage, Inc.: How the Liberal Mob Ruined Science,*

Journalism, and Hollywood. "Most of these movies and shows aren't produced with profit in mind; they have a message they want to convey," he wrote. "Only audiences don't show up to hear it.... Entertainment, like sports, serves a purpose: an escape from the stresses of everyday life. But escape isn't allowed anymore; everything is political because, to many, politics is everything."

That in mind, if you've ever wondered why conservatives rarely make appearances on late-night shows, it's not because they choose not to. More often than not, it's because the late-night shows' hosts and producers refuse to have conservative guests on their show. One major reason for this is that they want to keep conservatives, who might help their show's ratings and grow their audiences, from, ironically, growing their own audiences.

In 2017, I experienced this dynamic firsthand when comedian Jimmy Kimmel had me on his ABC show, *Jimmy Kimmel Live!* for a sit-down interview. It earned the show its top TV rating in three months as well as a rare win over Jimmy Fallon's competing late-night show. If it weren't for NBA championship lead-ins at the time, it would have been the highest Wednesday TV ratings in eight months. Don't get me wrong—I don't think it was all about me. It was about the people who supported the president who were finally tuning in to see a guest who supported him, too. With that in mind, wouldn't you think the producers would be inclined to invite other conservatives on the show? Shouldn't Kimmel be chomping at the bit to talk to another conservative on-air? Perhaps a Republican senator? Nope. The backlash from the left is too much to handle.

All late-night show host Samantha Bee had to do to garner unprecedented media attention was mention a conservative on her Wednesday TBS show, *Full Frontal.* She dedicated an entire segment to attacking Dennis Prager's "dangerous" conservative organization, PragerU, for "reaching a new, younger audience" with "conservative propaganda" and "colorful graphics and social media." PragerU is a YouTube channel where Dennis and others on the right post short videos to explain topics from religion to politics. But, as it turned out, her warning backfired and earned PragerU an expanded audience on top of unprecedented revenue. According to *CNS News,* "Bee was the one to get stung by the segment," as PragerU reported in a tweet that Friday: "THANK YOU, Samantha Bee @FullFrontalSamB! Over $35,000 raised and counting to ensure we continue to reach more people with our 'dangerous' videos. Please make a tax-deductible donation in Samantha Bee's name to help us continue our impact!"

This was the worst-case scenario for a liberal late-night host who literally believes that conservative ideas are a danger to society. Of course, she didn't think it was a danger to society when she used her opening monologue to call Ivanka Trump a "feckless" C-word. That incident drew public ire and resulted in the show losing advertisers and support—in what must've been a first for a left-leaning show. It seemed to be a misguided redemption stunt a few months later when TBS announced plans to transform the show into *"Full Frontal 2.0,"* shifting the focus to politics and the midterm elections. So let's recap: Bee says something incredibly inappropriate and insulting and instead of getting canceled, she got a reboot. Lesson learned. Attacking the right is good for business.

Around the time I was on my book tour for *The Briefing,* I was a natural target for the new and improved agenda-driven show. Right after the book launched, family and friends of mine had put together a private book event in the Rhode Island town I grew up in at a private club. While greeting teachers, old neighbors, and friends from the window overlooking the water, we noticed a few people dressed as "a unicorn, riding a unicorn over a rainbow"—quoting an excerpt from my book describing how president Trump defied all political expectations. As we later discovered, under the costume were members of Samantha Bee's crew who had followed me to the event. Her crew also crashed my first book signing at Barnes & Noble in New York City, trolling me with questions during the audience question-and-answer period, such as "Is it weird now to watch Sarah Huckabee Sanders do the press conferences? Do you feel like, a little, 'Oh man, I wish I was up there tricking the press'?"

I didn't take much of an issue with it at the time. I thought it was fair game for a comedy show to do, and so long as no one was hurt or threatened, there was no need to respond. I later learned that it was part of the show's political transformation, which included the launch of an audience engagement app, that, according to Bee, was a result of a year-long exploration of the question "Could we gamify the midterm elections?" It all made sense. The book tour stunt was the perfect fodder for the politically revamped show.

What didn't make sense at first glance was why the show doubled down on divisive politics when divisive politics is exactly what got the show into hot water in the first place. On second thought, it did make sense. While initially getting a faux punishment, she was ultimately rewarded with a new show.

Time and time again, late-night shows make decisions that push left-wing politics at the expense of losing loyal viewers. You would think the producers and hosts would take note and change their woke tune to stop alienating their conservative audience members. But that is seldom the case. They practically do the exact opposite. Hardly any shows regularly offer a conservative perspective. It's a parade of left-wing guests night after night. For that reason, I was admittedly surprised when I received my invite onto *Jimmy Kimmel Live*. But more than that, I was hopeful that maybe this dynamic could slowly start to change. Unfortunately, the events that transpired afterward killed any hope I had for that.

Kimmel has strayed so far from traditional comedy since then that he now frequently uses his prime-time comedy show to slam President Trump and lecture his audience on hot-button political issues ranging from gun control to health insurance. He said that the reason he decided to delve into political comedy and advocacy was as a result of "a real serious concern for the future of this country" and claimed that most late-night hosts like himself are liberal because the job requires "a measure of intelligence." When CBS correspondent Tracy Smith asked for his thoughts on his show's plunging Republican viewership due to his political rants in place of comedy, he proudly waved his hand goodbye to his Republican viewers and said that he "probably won't want to have a conversation with them anyway." It's safe to assume that I won't be invited back onto his show.

Jimmy Fallon's new comedic philosophy seems to be cut from the same fabric as Kimmel's. During one of his many damning critiques of President Trump, he told his audience it was his "responsibility to stand up against intolerance and extremism as a human being."

I'm not sure when exactly moral arbitration became the responsibility of comedians, but that's where we are today. There has been such a momentous shift since the days of Jay Leno and David Letterman, who dominated late-night for decades. On those shows, while both supporters of the left, they took shots at politicians, but it was funny as opposed to vindictive and personal.

There has been a shift in what's considered funny now. The hosts seek to appease the left more than they seek to entertain.

It's unfortunate to see how this mindset has plagued so much of the comedy world, especially considering its traditional role as an escapist form that brings people together through laughter and lighthearted entertainment. Today, humor has turned into hostility, and comedy has turned into condescension. Many of the country's most loved comedians have allowed politics to captivate every part of their lives.

Shortly after my departure from the White House in 2017, Stephen Colbert invited me to open the Emmy Awards show with him. If you didn't watch it, you'd think it was some sort of an abomination based on the headlines that ran the next day. After Stephen had jokingly opened the show and asked how we could judge the size of the viewing audience, I surprised the audience and pushed a podium on wheels out from behind the curtain to exclaim that it would be the "largest audience to witness an Emmys." The audience went crazy. Afterward, and well into the after parties that lasted into the night, celebrities and others approached me to comment on how funny they thought it had been and what a good sport I was to poke fun at myself. By morning, the tone and response changed quickly.

One *Washington Post* article, entitled "Sean Spicer's cameo at the Emmys was yucky," lamented that I "got a turn on one of Hollywood's glitziest stages" in an "attempt to rehabilitate" my image. Brian Stelter's CNN headline echoed the *Post*'s outrage, asking, "Why did the Emmys help Sean Spicer rebrand?" Rebrand? Yeah, pushing a podium out and saying a line was all about the new and improved me. The *New York Times* probably had the most dramatic take of all in its column, "The Shameful Embrace of Sean Spicer at the Emmys." Staff writer Frank Bruni slammed Colbert for having "abetted Spicer's image overhaul and probably upped Spicer's speaking fees by letting him demonstrate what a self-effacing sport he could be." You can't make this stuff up. Oh, and let's not forget when CBS host James Corden was forced to apologize after he was pictured giving me a peck on the cheek after the show. It reminded me of what happened to Jimmy Fallon after he was accused of the horrible crime of "normalizing" then-candidate Donald Trump by simply tousling his hair on his show.

Just as James Corden was, comedians are often forced to choose a side and are shamed into apologizing if they don't. The left can forgive so many incidents but ones that involve the act of simply "normalizing" conservatives are completely intolerable. As Alexandra Desanctis of the *National Review* put it, "Though there is no shortage of vitriolic commentary across the political spectrum, it is increasingly partisans of the Left who demand ideological conformity, and total condemnation and rejection of those who fail to champion the progressive agenda." There is this consistent narrative from the left-leaning media like CNN and the *New York Times* that conservatives are in search of being "normalized" or "forgiven," which is just plain false.

When we talk about bridging the divide and listening to the other side, we have to be willing to actually listen and accept the other side. But often what happens is that the left will approach the conversation with an ultimatum that goes something like this: "If only you believe my opinions are right then I can see you as a decent person." They're willing to accept someone on the right so long as that person is willing to accept the left's superiority or cave to their demands. Their idea of "everyone getting along" looks like everyone agreeing with them.

The all-time low ratings of award shows that we're seeing today are indicative of the cultural battle that is brewing. Americans are voting with their remote controls. While the self-proclaimed intelligent liberal hosts are shrinking their audiences, conservative and even moderate comedians are finding tremendous success. For me at least, I used to tune in to awards shows to see if a band, show, or movie I liked won. I attended concerts to listen to music I liked. Now, it's almost commonplace that every event, every concert, every performance not just exists to entertain but proclaims and advances their progressive cause or, as has been increasingly the case, denounces the right.

The 2019 Golden Globe Award show was certainly an exception, as comedian Ricky Gervais shocked the country with an epic takedown of Hollywood hypocrisy.

"Apple roared into the TV game with *The Morning Show,* a superb drama about the importance of dignity and doing the right thing made by a company that runs sweatshops in China," he said from the stage. "So you say you're 'woke,' but the companies you work for, Apple, Amazon, Disney . . . If ISIS had a streaming service you would be calling your agents."

Later in the night, he mocked the stars for their close relations to the late sex offender Jeffrey Epstein, who he claimed didn't kill himself—to the dismay of the audience. "Shut up, I know he's your friend but I don't care," he joked. Probably my favorite line of all, he warned the stars not to make any political or "woke" statements when accepting their awards, saying, "you're in no position to lecture the public about anything. You know nothing about the real world. Most of you spent less time in school than Greta Thunberg."

The left was outraged. A viral column published the following day by the *Los Angeles Times* lamented that "The #GoldenGlobes mood was already sober thanks to an impeachment, threat of war with Iran and Australian bush fires. The last thing anyone needed was Ricky Gervais there, telling them they sucked." Now compare that to the public's response. Gervais gained over 300,000 followers in one day following his wildly popular speech. To say his performance was a breath of fresh air for the American people is an understatement. He wasn't even preaching conservative politics—he was simply straying from the left's typical virtue-signaling stunt speeches during award shows. But they couldn't handle it. Somehow poking fun at the left is just not considered funny in Hollywood.

The interesting thing is that there is clearly a late-night audience on the right, as evidenced by Gervais's widely popular performance. We see the same with Fox News' conservative comedian host Greg Gutfeld, who pulls in more viewers on his show, *The Greg Gutfeld Show*, than many leading late-night hosts, including HBO's Bill Maher, NBC's Seth Meyers, TBS's Samantha Bee, CBS's James Corden, and HBO's John Oliver, according to 2019 Nielsen Media Research reports. That's a huge and overlooked accomplishment considering the reach of those networks. This shows that despite the evidence that there's an audience for this kind of conservative comedy, most networks are willing to overlook it. They are literally willing to sacrifice ratings and profit because it doesn't align with their politics.

Other conservative-leaning comedic voices don't typically have the same luxury as Greg Gutfeld to circumvent the comedy gatekeepers. Despite consistently high ratings, ABC canceled the conservative-leaning sitcom *Last Man Standing* with Tim Allen after six notably profitable and popular seasons. The last season alone pulled 8.1 million views and was the second most popular comedy on the network. It took ABC three months to come up with an excuse for killing one of its highest-rated shows, which they claim had nothing to do with politics. Allen was "stunned and blindsided" by the decision, as was the rest of America, but it didn't take much digging to see what really led to the show's demise.

Entertainment publication *Deadline Hollywood* described Allen's character as a "political conservative and devout Christian adhering to traditional American values" in a show that "appeals to viewers in the Heartland, a constituency that helped elect Donald Trump as president and has been energized post-election as evidenced by the ratings success of new USA drama Shooter."

That right there tells you everything you need to know about the basis for its cancellation. Ask yourself a simple question. If the show was doing that well, why was it canceled? And after it was canceled, why didn't anyone else pick it up? I think Hollywood hated the idea that they were helping to promote a show whose lead character represented everything they despise. Here's the secret: they are going to do everything they can to ensure that the public only is exposed to liberal ideology and will do nothing to showcase anything positive about conservative people, causes, or values. It's really that simple.

Further, Allen's character doesn't seem far off from his off-camera self. He has been outspoken about his refusal to conform to Hollywood politics and even went on Jimmy Kimmel's show to discuss his attendance at President Trump's inauguration. Allen was immediately put on the defense as to why he was there and explained he was there for a veterans event but "you gotta be real careful around here. You get beat up if you don't believe what others believe. It's like 30s Germany." Oops, he just revealed the secret. You have to believe what others believe or you get beat up. I know, or at least I hope, that he wasn't really talking about getting beat up but you get the point. Agree with the prevailing ideology in Hollywood or you're out. Literally out.

In both roles, both on and off the screen, Allen epitomizes what the left hates most: the normalization and relatability of a Hollywood television personality who holds political beliefs and values opposite of their own. The show, which featured a wide variety of characters who got along despite their political differences, echoed that same sentiment.

The left's backlash to the show was similar to the backlash I faced on *DWTS* and other shows on liberal-dominated networks. They couldn't stand having me on because it gave America the chance to see and hear from me directly, which made it harder for the media to paint me as a crazy right-winger.

It was the same reason they had a meltdown over Ellen DeGeneres's friendship with former president George W. Bush. Ellen's sin was simply sitting next to him at a Dallas Cowboys football game. Pictures of the supposed national travesty quickly circulated on social media, as the left voiced their deep concerns at the fact that she was seen smiling and conversing with someone of a different political background.

The backlash prompted Ellen to address the incident during her show the following week. "During the game, they showed a shot of George and me laughing together, so people were upset," she said. "They thought, why is a gay Hollywood liberal sitting next to a conservative Republican president?

"Here's the thing," she continued. "I'm friends with George Bush. In fact, I'm friends with a lot of people who don't share the same beliefs that I have. We're all different, and I think we've forgotten that that's okay, that we're all different. But just because I don't agree with someone on everything, doesn't mean that I'm not going to be friends with them. When I say be kind to one another, I don't mean only the people that think the same way that you do. I mean be kind to everyone." Be kind to everyone. I don't hate anyone because of their political beliefs. In fact, I don't hate anyone unless they have done something terrible to deserve it. And in almost all cases, I'm willing to forgive those who do bad things but ask for forgiveness. Unfortunately, many on the left do not share this sentiment.

All of this was a far cry from what we typically hear from Hollywood liberals like *Saturday Night Live* cast member and 2018 Emmys host Michael Che, who declared "the only white people that thank Jesus are Republicans and ex-crackheads," or actor Will Smith, who suggested we cleanse America of Trump supporters. Yes, you heard that right. He took to a press conference for his movie *Suicide Squad* in Dubai to alienate half the country, saying, "As painful as it is to hear Donald Trump talk and as embarrassing as it is as an American to hear him talk, I think it's good. We get to hear it. We get to know who people really are and now we get to cleanse it out of our country."

Here is the ultimate irony. The left, the people who preach tolerance and inclusivity, are the ones who shout down anyone on the left talking to anyone on the right. In all of my experiences, it's not those on the right, whom the left portrays as the intolerant ones, that go nuts when someone on the right engages with some on the left. Weird, right?

This can only be acceptable because the reality is that in Hollywood, politics always takes precedence over civility and profit. We see this same dynamic at play within the films and other productions that come out of Hollywood. While virtue-signaling celebrities and movies with a "message" dominate the award shows, they seldom dominate the box office.

Rotten Tomatoes, the self-proclaimed "most trusted measurement of quality for Movies & TV," puts out consensuses that regularly show a divide between the media class and regular people. A pro-free-speech film by conservative host Dennis Prager and comedian Adam Carolla, titled *No Safe Spaces,* reveals exactly that. As of February 2019, audience critics lauded the film with an average score of 99 out of 100, while mainstream Hollywood critics slammed the "obnoxious" film with an average score of 45 out of 100. Similarly, Hollywood critics gushed over Congresswoman Alexandria Ocasio Cortez's Netflix documentary *Knock Down the House* with a perfect 100 percent while the audience gave it 35 percent. For comedian Dave Chappelle's anti-politically correct comedy show *Sticks and Stones,* the audience gave him a near-perfect 99 percent approval compared to 29 percent from triggered establishment critics. The gap between critical and public receptions in movies is increasing by the day.

The success of movies like *American Sniper, Unplanned, Soul-Surfer,* and *Last Temptation of Christ* shows how people are craving something different from what's incessantly shoved down their throats. *Unplanned,* a film that tells the true story of a Planned Parenthood clinic director turned anti-abortion activist, became a smash hit in the box office despite roadblocks, and an undeserving R-rating by the liberal entertainment media. The faith-based movie *Overcomer,* which tells the Gospel story, raked in a whopping $8.2 million during its opening weekend.

Both with their reviews and pocketbooks, Americans are sending a clear message to Hollywood about what they want. There is undoubtedly a massive demand for wholesome content that depicts traditional American values, but Hollywood continues to push their lunacies instead. This wasn't always the case. When I was growing up, the amount of G-rated, family-friendly movies to pick from was plentiful. Now, it's hard to find movies that don't have profanity or sexual content.

Take the *Fifty Shades of Grey* trilogy, for instance. The books-turned-Hollywood-movies are known for their graphic sex scenes featuring violence, bondage, dominance, and sadism. The *Fifty Shades Freed* movie was released just after the world watched Hollywood elites dress in all black for the 2018 Golden Globes in protest of the sexual misconduct and scandals in the industry that most of them turned a blind eye to for decades. "Is violence against women really the message Hollywood should be sending right now, even if it is portrayed as consensual?" asks Lauren DeBellis Appell, a Virginia mom, and writer, in a column for Fox News.

"As parents, we're trying to raise responsible kids, with the end game that one day our independent little free birds will fly the nest and stand on their own two feet. We are counting on the fact that we're getting just enough of this parenting thing right so they won't be living in our basements until they're 35, and that they'll be ready to walk into adulthood equipped with the tools they need to make good judgment calls."

It may seem harmless to give your children full access to Netflix or drop them off at the movie theater with their friends, but parents need to realize the gravity of the messages that Hollywood is trying to send and the values they are trying to instill. Hollywood undoubtedly continues to be responsible for the cultural and moral demise of our society.

Interestingly, in an essay for *American Spectator*, novelist and screenwriter Lou Aguilar writes, "There is a huge paying audience for traditionalist entertainment, especially that which includes traditional romance—which is more real and commercially successful than the fantasies Hollywood keeps trying to fabricate—but they have nowhere to go, other than literature. According to the Romance Writers of America, the romance fiction industry is worth $1.08 billion a year, about the size of the mystery/thriller and sci-fi/fantasy genres combined, [but] this type of entertainment is shockingly rare in film and television."

These types of novels regularly top the leading bestseller lists such as the *New York Times, USA Today,* and *Publishers Weekly,* which have massive, loyal audiences of readers. But the left is going after those, too. The *New York Times* bestseller list is known to be hostile to conservative authors and routinely either ignores or deflates their book's rankings on the list. The list is not based on sales and they won't reveal their formula, which is ironic, that an industry that is so adamant about fighting for the truth and transparency creates a list that is not based on actual sales. Can we really trust the *New York Times* when they decide what books are more important than others? According to rumors on how the list is derived, a book purchased at an independent book store on Manhattan's Upper West Side is valued more than one purchased on Amazon or at a Costco.

Upon an in-depth analysis that compared the *New York Times* bestseller list to Nielsen BookScan, the largest book wholesaler in the country, the New York–based entertainment outlet the *Observer* made the following conclusions:

If you happen to work for *The New York Times* and have a book out, your book is more likely to stay on the list longer and have a higher ranking than books not written by *New York Times* employees.

If you happen to have written a conservative-political-leaning book, you're more likely to be ranked lower and drop off the list faster than those books with a more liberal political slant.

That might help us to understand the curious case of Jordan Peterson's book *12 Rules for Life,* which was the number one hard-cover nonfiction book on the *Publishers Weekly* and *Wall Street Journal* lists (meaning it sold the most books that week) but completely absent on the *New York Times* bestseller list. We should all stop and ask how it could be possible that someone who actually sells the most books in the country in this category does not find himself on the top 20 list in the *New York Times.* One can only conclude that those who control the list want to suppress the success of right-leaning authors and the ideas they express. When David Horowitz released his bestselling book *Blitz,* he sold the eighth-most number of books in the country in the nonfiction category, yet the *Times* ranked his book 14th. Former Speaker of the House Newt Gingrich had a similar experience the same week with his book *Trump and the American Future: Solving the Great Problems of Our Time.*

Beyond the basic principle of fairness, one of the reasons that these book lists matter is that they are often intertwined with Hollywood films. The Fifty Shades of Grey and Harry Potter trilogies, for instance, can thank their tremendous book ranking successes for making it to the big screen. But don't hold your breath if you think fairness means anything to those in charge of rankings and lists. In the same way that the leftists in the mainstream media toss their principles aside when politically convenient, Hollywood elites abandon their so-called commitment to honesty and fairness to advance their causes. The levels of hypocrisy that they are required to stoop to in order to do so know no bounds. One major way we see this is in the way they constantly lecture us on how we should behave but turn a blind eye when one of their own breaks their sacred rules.

Case in point: NBC kept *Will & Grace* actress and liberal activist Debra Messing after saying "a black vote for Trump is mental illness" and calling for a blacklist of Trump supporters, but canceled Roseanne Barr's show *Roseanne* months earlier after she made a racist comment about former Obama adviser Valerie Jarrett. I'm not excusing the behavior of either one of these actresses, but it's amazing to see the contrast in how they are both treated.

Despite Roseanne's show having unbelievably high ratings, NBC kicked her out. They went to great lengths to banish Roseanne, taking away her ownership of the show, kicking her off the cast, and renaming it. On the other hand, Debra Messing's comment was unreal . . . I can only imagine the outrage that would ensue if a celebrity on the right publicly implied that all black Americans think alike.

"Will Fake News NBC allow a McCarthy style Racist to continue?" President Trump asked in a tweet responding to the double standard.

CBS also showed its hypocritical colors when giving Alec Baldwin his own show after he was charged with assault in January 2019 for hospitalizing a man over a parking space dispute. The *New York Times* reports that Baldwin "has a history of losing his temper," noting that he was suspended in 2013 as host of an MSNBC talk show after shouting a homophobic slur at a photographer and that a year later he was arrested for disorderly conduct after flipping out on police officers who had stopped him for riding his bicycle against one-way traffic on Fifth Avenue—or otherwise just doing their jobs. In 2011, his temper was so bad that American Airlines kicked him off a flight for refusing to get off his phone when asked. The airline posted a statement to Facebook claiming Baldwin "slammed the lavatory door so hard, the cockpit crew heard it and became alarmed, even with the cockpit door closed and locked," and was "extremely rude to the crew, calling them inappropriate names and using offensive language," according to ABC News. And let's not forget the 2007 voice mail that surfaced in which he called his own daughter, who was eleven years old at the time, a "rude, thoughtless little pig." But hey, his mean-spirited *SNL* impersonation of Trump must go on so we must look the other way, right?

Bill Maher, who hosts a weekly comedy show on HBO, is another Hollywood darling with a long history of offensive remarks. Similar to the Roseanne Barr incident, he compared President Donald Trump to an ape, but of course, it was classified by the left as a joke and he was not fired. *Insider* reports that he has a long history of "fat-shaming" while Fox News reports that he has long been criticized for using racially charged language on his show. For instance, in 2017, he blatantly used the n-word during an interview with Senator Ben Sasse on a live broadcast, and again in 2019, he lobbed a clearly racist joke to black CIA veteran and GOP congressman Will Hurd, asking him if he gathered tips and intel out "by the Popeye's Chicken" during an interview. Tellingly, there's rarely any backlash for going on his show.

But take a wild guess what actually did prompt backlash from the left: Maher's decision to invite conservative provocateur and former Breitbart writer Milo Yiannopoulos on his show for a debate in 2017. Maher drew instant condemnation from the left, which included an HBO petition, a #BigotBillMaher hashtag, and even a declaration from Jeremy Scahill, a journalist who's appeared frequently on Maher's show, that he refuses to appear as a panelist because of Yiannopoulos and his views. "He has ample venues to spew his hateful diatribes," Scahill wrote. "There is no value in 'debating' him. Appearing on Maher's show will give Yiannopoulos a major platform for 'his racist, anti-immigrant campaign.'"

In a column published in the New York *Daily News* in February 2017, *Deadspin* writer Chuck Modiano described Maher's "shameful mainstreaming" of Milo, noting that "The *Washington Post* called it 'a bromance,' the *New York Times* called it a 'largely docile, chummy affair,' the *Daily Beast* a 'lovefest,' and the *Huffington Post* a 'mutual admiration society.'" *Jezebel* was succinct: "Bill Maher is a Monster." He criticized the "format" of Maher's show, which began in the 1990s when his ABC show, *Politically Incorrect,* routinely hosted both liberals and conservatives to discuss hot-button political issues. One of those guests was conservative author Ann Coulter, whom he developed a mutually respectful relationship with over the years. Modiano, appalled by this, writes, "Coulter is more than a TV foil. Maher regularly refers to Coulter as 'my good friend,' and she calls Bill her 'true loyal friend,' as well. They go out to dinner. Is it worth asking how a self-proclaimed liberal could ever be good friends with a woman as bigoted and vile as Coulter?"

It's the same intolerant ideology we see behind the Ellen DeGeneres/George Bush controversy. The left cannot tolerate the mere idea of conservatives and liberals living civilly with one another. It has to be one side winning and stomping out the other. And here's one more thought for the left: If you truly believe your leftist ideas and politics are better and all of us in the right need to be "normalized" and "humanized," wouldn't you think the best way to do this would be to engage more with us so we could see the virtue of the left? The problem is they can't defend their ideas so they cancel out and shout down the right. To them, like Brian Stelter, we aren't even human (hence the need to be humanized) and we aren't normal (hence the need according to them for us to be normalized).

"For Maher's format to succeed, he must regularly invite more Coulters, more Milos, and more hate," Modiano continued. "Even less outrageous Republicans are being held hostage to Trump—and won't dare defy Trump's 84% approval rating amongst Republicans. This comes at a time when real progressives are not trying to dialogue and legitimize a fascist and racist agenda. Real progressives are in the streets and in town halls forcefully condemning it."

"Real progressives"? What happened to progressivism being all about inclusivity and tolerance? Modiano threw that concept out the door entirely, concluding that "progressives should already be leaving Maher's contaminated liberalism in droves."

Don't expect this writer to say the same of progressive darling Jane Fonda, who earned the nickname "Hanoi Jane" during the Vietnam War after posing on an anti-aircraft gun used to shoot down American pilots. She was honored as an award presenter at the 2020 Oscars and the Emmy Awards show and was previously inducted into the National Women's Hall of Fame. Because she is now a staunch advocate for leftist causes—as seen by her four-week streak of being arrested during climate change protests on Capitol Hill last year and her rants about the evils of capitalism—her slate is wiped clean and the media gush over her "bravery." I find it very interesting how someone who has so publicly attacked our service members is so well regarded by the Hollywood elite.

The same forgiveness was not granted to Kevin Hart when he was forced to step down from hosting the same Oscars show that Fonda presented at after his decade-old anti-gay jokes resurfaced on Twitter. Ironically, the backlash was led by Hollywood celebrities like Jamie Lee Curtis and C-list bit actor Billy Eichner, who claimed Hart's apology was not worthy of acceptance. It's easy to see what happened here. Hart constantly pushes the left's boundaries while Fonda fights on their behalf. It was never about past remarks made by either of the celebrities; it's about what side they benefit now.

Hollywood elites love to lecture America about morality, but for more than one hundred years their industry has been the epicenter of sexism, abuse, and discrimination. They constantly lament the gender pay gap but its own male stars significantly outearn females.

I think it's very telling that Showtime snubbed Melania Trump from its *First Ladies* drama series that was announced in the summer of 2019. Michelle Obama, played by Viola Davis, was chosen to be the star of the show, while Eleanor Roosevelt and Betty Ford were depicted by other stars. It's shameful that our first lady, who not to mention speaks five languages and is an incredibly accomplished businesswoman, model, and mother, was excluded from a show that would have undoubtedly gushed over her if she was a liberal.

Two thousand nineteen also brought us the movie *Bombshell*, which gathered every little bit of dirt the producers could gather on the Fox News sexual harassment suits, but don't hold your breath if you're expecting them to do the same for the NBC sexual harassment scandal/cover-up. Of course, these are the same people who knew about Harvey Weinstein and Matt Lauer and chose to sweep it under the rug. It's ironic that Hollywood is both the greatest offender and greatest judge of who is deemed worthy of public acceptance. They glamorize drugs, guns, promiscuity, adultery, sex, and violence yet take no responsibility and are absolved from any accountability from the public. For all the virtue-signaling about gun control from Hollywood celebrities, they sure don't seem to have a problem with guns when it lands them high ratings and starring roles. They'll tell you that President Trump, the NRA, gun-toting American patriots, and conservative media are to blame for mass shootings, but conveniently ignore the fact that they are the greatest transgressors of promoting and glamorizing gun violence.

Consider this: the Media Research Center reported that four top-grossing movies from the week leading up to the mass shooting in Las Vegas, including *Kingsman: The Golden Circle, American Assassin, mother!,* and Stephen King's *It,* featured 589 incidents of violence; 212 of them involved guns and at least 192 of them featured gun-related deaths. One study by the Parents Television Council reported that the degree of gun violence on prime-time TV has increased in the last five years following the Sandy Hook Elementary School shooting. The hypocrisy is palpable.

Like the media, Hollywood liberals live by the rule "do as I say, not as I do." But their second rule puts them in a class of their own. That is: If you can't fight something that works in practice, smear it in fantasy. The left does an incredible job in this department. In fact, they do such a good job that their industry shapes our opinions and influences popular culture and politics without us even knowing. Agenda-driven TV shows on streaming services cannot be overlooked. The narratives and messages are seeding a subconscious mindset in viewers, especially young ones.

Take the popular show *The Handmaid's Tale*, which pushes a narrative that if conservatives had their way, the United States would be run by an oppressive dictatorship that treats women like cattle. A June 2018 *Elle* magazine headline, for example, reads "The Creepy Ways 'The Handmaid's Tale' Resembles Trump's America." The intro reads as follows:

"Hulu's The Handmaid's Tale presents a bleak vision of America in the not-too-distant future—when the USA has been re-named Gilead, and is run by an oppressive dictatorship of religious fanatics. But one thing viewers of The Handmaid's Tale have pointed out consistently are the distant but disconcerting parallels between Gilead's upheaval of America, and America under Donald Trump—painting a fictional, exaggerated picture of how things could go wrong." The article goes on to list "a border crisis," the "oppression of LGBTQ+ people," "a rise in conservative populism," and even a "decline in birth rates" to draw fear-mongering parallels between the show's plot and the current state of the United States today. The *New York Times* writes of other journalists who have drawn comparisons between the show and the current political climate in a piece titled "A Handmaid's Tale of Protest," noting, "In *Vanity Fair,* one critic explored whether it was an allegory for the Trump era. In *The New Yorker,* a reviewer discussed its 'grotesque timeliness'; another at the same publication said that already 'we live in the reproductive dystopia' the show presents."

Those words carry weight. Just look at the thousands of viewers and abortion advocates who took it a step further by dressing up as handmaid characters in long red cloaks to stoke fear while protesting abortion legislation. "As symbols of a repressive patriarchy, the crimson robes and caps—handmade, repurposed or ordered online—have become an emblem of women's solidarity and collaboration on rights issues, similar to the pink knitted hats worn during the Women's March after President Trump's inauguration," the *Times* added.

This is a classic example of how leftists in Hollywood lecture open-mindedness and inclusivity yet they only tell one side of the story while depicting the other in a negative light. We also see this when it comes to the debate over capitalism and socialism, which, despite the fact that it is increasing in popularity and intensity by the day, is only portrayed one way in Hollywood.

Consider *First Man*, Hollywood's 2018 movie about man's first trip to the moon that deliberately left out the iconic scene of Neil Armstrong planting the American flag on the moon. The *Telegraph* writes that the film "has chosen to leave out this most patriotic of scenes, arguing that the giant leap for mankind should not be seen as an example of American greatness." Yes—you read that correctly—the AMERICAN FLAG was left out of a historic Hollywood film about one of the proudest and most integral moments in American history. Makes sense.

It's interesting that these people in the Hollywood sphere live and die by box-office sales in America, yet they frequently preach socialism and anti-Americanism.

Further, at the 2020 Oscars, the director of an Obama documentary Julia Reichert quoted Karl Marx and *The Communist Manifesto*, urging "workers of the world to unite." But those were just words. Netflix actually signed a $100 million deal with the Obamas' production company, essentially giving the former president editorial influence over the massive entertainment platform. Further, former Obama administration official Susan Rice sits on Netflix's board of directors while Netflix founder Reed Hastings slammed Peter Thiel for supporting President Trump, accusing him of using "catastrophically bad judgment" and "not what anyone wants in a fellow board member." Clearly, Netflix is taking a multifaceted approach to push a leftist agenda, but the reasons to be concerned about the platform extend far beyond the board. *LifesiteNews*, a pro-life news website founded in 1997 by Campaign Life Coalition, lays out several compelling reasons to think twice about allowing Netflix in your household, including:

1. Netflix was first out of the gate to bully and threaten the Georgia economy over the heartbeat law.
2. Netflix executives Ted Sarandos and Reed Hastings have subscriber-paid salaries of $30 and $36 million. Both Sarandos and Hastings personally support radical leftist politicians and PACs.
3. Netflix streamed a show by "comedian" Michelle Wolf titled *Salute to Abortions,* which concluded with a blasphemous closing song, "God bless abortion."
4. Netflix allowed child pornography when it defended the Argentinean film *Desire.*
5. Netflix produced the animated series *Big Mouth,* specifically aimed at teenagers, that celebrates pedophilia, abortion, masturbation, and which the creators themselves describe as "a perverted *Wonder Years.*"
6. Netflix has also jumped on the drag-kid bandwagon to exploit children and groom them for pedophiles with the series *Dancing Queen.*

7. The Netflix original series *13 Reasons Why* continues to air even after a study from the *Journal of the American Academy of Child and Adolescent Psychiatry* found a 29 percent increase in suicide rates among the demographic that views the show, immediately after the release of the show.

Even if you're trying to avoid left-wing content on Netflix, the platform shoves movies and shows at the top of the viewer's feed as soon as they turn it on with a feature that automatically plays previews. If you pay attention to what is promoted, it's almost always something that pushes a left-wing agenda.

HBO isn't much better. Consider this: the network chose none other than Brian Stelter, the CNN host/spokesman, to be the executive producer on a documentary on the rise of fake news. I thought I was reading the *Babylon Bee* when I first got wind of it. If you need a refresher on why it's absolutely absurd for Stelter to be given any authority over what is deemed fake news, just wait for my chapter on media. Further, HBO's new show *Euphoria*, which is geared toward teens, glamorizes drugs, sex, and pornography, with one episode that features twenty explicit shots of male genitalia—because the original eighty were deemed too excessive, according to a *New York Post* story. Why in the world would that need to be included in a show for kids?

In one of the most egregious cases of Hollywood liberal lunacy, in the fall of 2019, controversy ensued over the film *The Hunt*, in which liberal elitists hunt conservative "deplorables" for sport. It was initially met with enough backlash to be pulled from theaters, as it followed a politically motivated mass shooting in Texas, but Universal Pictures later reversed their decision. They appeared to lean into the controversy, touting the film as "the most talked about movie of the year" that would release on none other than the superstitious Friday the 13th.

Trump was right when he weighed in on this controversy, telling reporters that Hollywood is doing a "tremendous disservice to our country" through their outright bias and hostility toward conservatives. "Liberal Hollywood is Racist at the highest level, and with great Anger and Hate!" he tweeted earlier in the day. "They like to call themselves 'Elite,' but they are not Elite. In fact, it is often the people that they so strongly oppose that are actually the Elite. The movie coming out is made in order . . . to inflame and cause chaos. They create their own violence and then try to blame others. They are the true Racists, and are very bad for our Country!"

It's unfathomable that a movie with this type of story line would be released at a time when politically charged violence is on the rise. Then again, Hollywood elites have a habit of fantasizing about violence against President Trump and his supporters.

For all the actors and actresses who talk about concerns over guns and violence, here they are:

Many A-listers expressed their grievances with President Trump early on with depictions of a bloody, decapitated commander in chief. During the 2016 primaries, singer Marilyn Manson released a disturbing music video that features a beheaded Trump-like figure on a cement floor, while comedian George Lopez tweeted a photo depicting former Mexican president Vincente Fox brandishing Trump's decapitated noggin, with a caption that read "Make America Great Again," according to the *Ledger*. Clearly having learned nothing, Lopez joked in 2019 about killing President Trump for half of the $80 million bounty that Iranian leaders had placed on Trump's head following the killing of their military leader, Qasem Soleimani. "We'll do it for half," Lopez commented.

Not to be outdone, left-wing comedian Kathy Griffin posed for her graphic photo in 2017 holding what looks like President Trump's bloody, severed head, and later bragged in an interview on *Rising* that it was ultimately "worth it" because it opened doors for her on the international stage. TMZ reported that President Trump's son Barron was watching TV at home when the photo appeared on the screen and sent him into a panic.

Madonna, the singer who was so overcome with her hatred of then-candidate Donald Trump that she offered oral sex to people who supported Clinton's campaign, took to the 2017 Women's March in Washington, DC, to admit she thought "an awful lot about blowing up the White House." But not to worry, CNN came to her defense, running a story that was actually headlined "Madonna: 'Blowing up White House' taken out of context," writing that the singer "was just trying to express herself." Seriously? Tell that to the Covington boys.

Comedian Larry Wilmore joked about wanting to suffocate Donald Trump with "the pillow they used to kill Scalia" (referring to former Supreme Court justice Antonin Scalia) during a segment on his former Comedy Central show. "I don't want to give him any more oxygen. That's not a euphemism, by the way. I mean it literally. Somebody get me the pillow," he said. Is this funny? This is the same kind of rhetoric that creates crazy people. Let's not forget that while all the talk of right-wing violence comes from the left, it's almost always their side that actually commits acts of violence. Remember the Bernie Sanders supporter who shot up the Republicans' congressional baseball practice in Alexandria, Virginia, leaving Congressman Steve Scalise in a wheelchair? The left certainly doesn't want you to.

In a segment on Bill Maher's HBO show, writer Fran Lebowitz suggested that Trump should be turned "over to the Saudis" to face the same gruesome fate as *Washington Post* columnist and activist Jamal Khashoggi, who had just been reported to have been dismembered and murdered in the Saudi consulate. Maher joined the audience in laughter and later dismissed the backlash as people getting mad over a joke. "What happened? You said something and they're mad at you. I know this feeling. What, the thing you said about the Saudis? You were making a joke and it went too far, we're sorry. Is that where we are?" When the left claims to joke, we all have to get over it. But when it's someone on the right, they must be banished and canceled.

Robert De Niro fantasized about giving Trump repeated blows to the head, once during a live segment on ABC's *The View,* while his fellow Hollywood actor Mickey Rourke said he'd like to give the president a "Louisville slugger" before spitting unprovoked vitriol at Melania Trump just for being married to him.

Trump's youngest son, Barron, was not off-limits, either. Actor Peter Fonda envisioned a deeply disturbing form of violence against him, suggesting, "We should rip Barron Trump from his mother's arms and put him in a cage with pedophiles." I don't care what your politics are, that's wrong on so many levels.

Then, of course, we had actor Jim Carrey suggest that Republican Alabama governor Kay Ivey should have been aborted, painting a horrific picture of her head being sucked out of a womb with an abortion tool.

For all their outrage over President Trump's demeanor and verbiage, one needs to look no further than Hollywood to see the worst of the over-the-top, visceral language coming from within.

President Trump knows this well and is all too familiar with the hypocrisy. It's why he didn't hold back when speaking to the press about Hollywood, calling the industry racist and dangerous for our country. Like President Reagan, he knows the importance of Hollywood. In his book *Movie Nights with the Reagans*, former Reagan speechwriter Mark Weinberg points out that Reagan understood the importance of the movie business while most Americans thought it to be frivolous. "I remember him pointing out on more than one occasion that the export of American culture and values—primarily through movies—was how many countries got to know and form opinions of the United States," he wrote. Trump understands this about Hollywood, which is why it's imperative that we follow his lead in calling out the corrupt industry.

Beyond consistently calling out Hollywood for its blatant hypocrisy and discrimination, one major and overlooked way we can do this is by supporting conservative work. One of the reasons conservatism is mostly absent from the arts is that there is a widely believed notion that there's hardly a market for it. But that's not necessarily true.

Chuck Konzelman, co-director of the pro-life film *Unplanned,* recounted the major financial hardships his team faced during production. "Days before we had to start shooting, we needed a million dollars," he said. His team had investors pull out after several meetings and MyPillow founder Mike Lindell stepped in to help finance the film. It is outrageous to think they weren't able to easily fund one of the only pro-life films made in recent years. Conservatives should be ready and willing to counter the far-left secular industry in whatever means they can. And like President Trump, conservatives should be the first to promote and purchase work from our own side, whether it be books, films, music, or other productions.

Consider *The Chosen*, a new series about the life of Jesus, which has become the largest crowdfunding media project after 16,000 people invested over $10 million into the show, according to an April 2019 Fox News report. The episodes are available through VidAngel, a Christian entertainment app, allowing the producers to circumvent the Hollywood gatekeepers. The concept pilot for the show was first released on social media to gauge potential interest and ended up exceeding expectations by amassing 20 million views worldwide.

In a February 2020 interview with *The Federalist*, the show's creator, Dallas Jenkins, explained the implications this could have for conservatives who are increasingly alienated by institutional leftists that dominate Hollywood, Big Tech, the media, and academia. "If Christian content creators want to reach audiences directly," he says, "they're going to have to make a choice if they're going to compete in the big pond with all these other big streamers that aren't really interested in faith-based content on a significant level, or if it's fine to create a whole new paradigm."

In many ways, Trump's presidency serves as a blueprint for creating this type of "new paradigm." His entire rise to power was dependent upon his ability to bypass massive institutional roadblocks meant to keep conservatives off a level playing field.

He utilized his Hollywood experience to beat the left at their own game. You can see this at any one of his campaign rallies, which are arguably his own form of art.

The president is going around Hollywood to deliver an experience to the American people. All the production elements are there, from massive audiences to music to merchandise, but most important, he's delivering a message—one that absolutely terrifies the left.

The right has spent years clamoring for their own to engage in culture, social media, and Hollywood, but the moment someone does, it's viewed as "undignified." Many on the right didn't like the fact that I joined *Dancing with the Stars*, while many on the left didn't like the fact that President Trump supported me. I would argue that now more than ever, conservatives should unite in an effort to take on the left from all angles at every opportunity—even if that means cheering on a stiff dancer doing the salsa to the Spice Girls in a lime green ruffled shirt. While we should look to build our own shows and platforms, that doesn't mean we should cede the current ground to the left.

CHAPTER FOUR

★ ★ ★ ★ ★ ★ ★

THE RISE AND FALL
OF LEGACY MEDIA

n my previous book, *The Briefing*, I emphasized the importance
of focusing on specific issues we have with individual news stories as opposed to painting the entire media with a broad "fake
news" brush. I will always stand by this belief; however, there are a
handful of media outlets that have increasingly grown to deserve
the label. I'm talking about the outlets that, rather ironically, have
virtuous mission statements about truth-seeking and making the
world a better place. To understand the unique media landscape
we see today, and more important, to be able to successfully push
back against it, we must first look at the traditional "legacy media"
outlets that for decades have shaped our country's narratives and
in turn shaped our society.

"FACTS FIRST"

Many of us remember when CNN blessed us with their "Facts
First" campaign ad in 2017. For a while, you couldn't even fly

without seeing it thanks to the network's airport monopoly—which reportedly costs them more than a hefty $6 million every year just to retain, ensuring American travelers are subjected to their political agenda.

The thirty-second ad, launched amid the mainstream media's battle with President Trump over his "fake news" accusations, features an apple with a narrator making the case that an apple is an apple, even if people call it a banana. "They might scream banana, banana, banana, over and over and over again. They might put banana in all caps. You might even start to believe that this is a banana. But it's not. This is an apple," it declares. It was ripe for parody considering the network's extensive list of misleading reporting in recent years, from the endless Trump-Russia collusion scoops to their opinion commentary routinely disguised as hard news.

Every Sunday, CNN's "essential media news" (that's of course according to them) show *Reliable Sources* with Brian Stelter, who lectures the public on media bias as it "examines the media world," tells "the story behind the story," and reveals "how the news gets made." Everything about the show—from the concept to the host to the tone-deaf commentary—is concerning.

I don't have any personal problems with Stelter, but his show epitomizes the head-in-the-sand mentality that has permeated many newsrooms across the country, and therefore I think is worthy of reflection.

Stelter claims, "journalists shouldn't advocate for an outcome," yet his anti-Trump agenda is apparent in his reporting, from the guests he has on the show to his routine questioning of Trump's mental health and fitness for office to the segments that are devoted entirely to Trump's Twitter typos. His coverage is far from harmless; he had a guest on his show who said on live television that Trump is responsible for more deaths than Adolf Hitler, Mao Zedong, and Joseph Stalin—and Stelter refused to push back on it. Think about that for a second. A guest on his show accused the president of the United States of being responsible for more deaths than history's cruelest dictators, and Stelter did not correct them—or even ask a follow-up question about it—and is still on a network that claims that "facts come first."

Stelter also rushed to the defense of Christine Blasey Ford, the woman who accused Trump's Supreme Court nominee Brett Kavanaugh of sexual assault right before and during his confirmation hearings. He urged his viewers to put themselves in her shoes and imagine TV pundits who "sound so confident, like they want to know the truth, like they do know the truth. But only you know your truth," he said. "All of a sudden, all these smears, all these hoaxes from people who are pretending like they know you." Ironically, Stelter routinely makes claims as if he knows through his sources the motivations of the people he is reporting on.

It was also his colleagues at CNN that pretended to know the "truth" about the intentions of the Covington Catholic High School students, among them Nick Sandmann, whom they immediately framed as the aggressors during an interaction with a Native American activist in Washington, DC, the following year. The kids were wearing "Make America Great Again" hats. Of course, many in the media love to tell you that children are absolved from criticism yet they are the first to use kids as political pawns. For instance, in response to the U.S. Treasury secretary Steven Mnuchin saying climate activist Greta Thunberg should go study economics, CNN anchor Chris Cuomo tweeted, "Why do these trumpers think it is ok to go at a kid?" Fair point, and in this

case I actually agree. Ironically, this was right after his own network had to settle a massive lawsuit with Covington Catholic High
School student Nick Sandmann for falsely smearing him as a racist. They were quick to defend Greta, but the Covington Catholic
High School kids were the subject of their attacks.

In December 2019, I attended the annual Army-Navy football
game in Philadelphia with my family. (Or the *Navy-Army* game, as
the scoreboard would prove at the end of the game.) Although we
are a Navy family, we showed our support for both services—sitting
the first half with our Army friends and second half in the Navy
section. While I was excited to see Navy win, in the hours after the
game a "scandal" ensued because someone had noticed some of
the midshipmen and cadets making an upside-down okay symbol
with their fingers as the television cameras captured the postgame
festivities. The media picked up on the online outrage that this was
somehow a secret symbol of white power and made it a top story
questioning the students' motives. No one asked any questions. It
was simply lazy, copycat "reporting" based on assumptions and
no facts. The reports smeared these young men and women who
have chosen to serve our nation. After each school did a thorough
investigation, it turned out that it was a silly game called the "circle
game." According to dictionary.com, "the circle game is an activity where one person makes a 'circle' with their fingers and holds
it below their waist, convincing a second person to look at it. If the
second person looks, they receive a punch to the shoulder." Instead
of asking questions, doing a quick internet search, or asking a student for details (I know, that's far fetched), those so-called journalists could have gotten the facts and could have avoided painting
these young patriots as racists. Could have . . . but didn't because
that wasn't convenient for the media.

Earlier in 2019, CNN confidently reported their "truth" about *Empire* actor Jussie Smollett and rushed to his defense after he sparked a national media firestorm with his false allegation that he was attacked by two Trump supporters who beat him, doused him in bleach, and placed a noose on his neck before eventually running off yelling "this is MAGA Country." CNN—including Brian Stelter's show—refused to concede that the overwhelming evidence produced by the Chicago Police Department suggested that Smollett had not been attacked but rather had filed a false police report. Stelter claimed, "we may never really know what happened," after the Chicago Police Department, according to *National Review,* announced after a twenty-three-day investigation "that it had uncovered overwhelming evidence to suggest Smollett staged the attack." In fact, "Two Nigerian brothers, one of whom worked on Empire, were arrested in connection with the attack and told the police that Smollett paid them by check to stage the crime. Police then recovered the check Smollett issued in exchange for their services, as well as surveillance footage of the brothers purchasing the items used in the staged attack."

Notice how the media demands empathy only when the person in question plays into their narrative, but demands *evidence* when they don't. If you go along with the anti-Trump narrative, you are assumed to be credible and believed, but you won't be granted the same "benefit of the doubt" if you stray from the media's agenda.

Christine Blasey Ford, Kavanaugh's accuser, was deserving of every ounce of empathy CNN could muster up—because she was a Kavanaugh accuser and Kavanaugh threatens their agenda. Stelter went as far as lamenting "all week long, actual news outlets have had to chase down and debunk lies about Ford." He condemned "the right-wing smear machine" for digging up "misinformation" such as her RateMyProfessor.com page and accused the right of using "more subtle" tactics that were really about "sowing doubt" and "creating uncertainty" over the thirty-five-year-old alleged incident.

In another display of hypocrisy, former White House press secretary turned CNN analyst Joe Lockhart admitted to fabricating a conversation between GOP senators during President Trump's Senate trial. Lockhart tweeted:

"Overheard convo between two Republican Senators who only watch Fox News: is this stuff real? I haven't heard any of this before. I thought it was all about a server. If half the stuff Schiff is saying is true, we're up shit's creek. Hope the White House has exculpatory evidence."

Washington Post blogger Jennifer Rubin shared his fabricated quote with her nearly 400,000 followers and it quickly went viral. Lockhart later admitted to making the whole conversation up but kept the tweet up anyway. The lie got nearly twelve times as many retweets as the admission—a common problem we see when the media spreads disinformation and *quietly* corrects it later. So much for CNN's commitment to facts first.

"DEMOCRACY DIES IN DARKNESS"

In February 2017, the *Washington Post* introduced its "Democracy dies in darkness" slogan in what seemed to be a response to President Trump's routine remarks about the "fake news media."

It didn't take long for the jokes to begin. In October 2017, the *Post* was slammed by conservatives for burying a damaging story about Amazon being slapped with a massive $300 million tax fine by European officials. This was a bombshell tax evasion story in every regard. In fact, Trump had repeatedly warned of something like this. In December 2015, he tweeted, "The @washingtonpost loses money (a deduction) and gives owner @JeffBezos power to screw public on low taxation of @Amazon! Big tax shelter." In July 2017, he wrote, "Is Fake News Washington Post being used as a lobbyist weapon against Congress to keep Politicians from looking into Amazon no-tax monopoly?" and "So many stories about me in the @washingtonpost are Fake News. They are as bad as ratings challenged @CNN. Lobbyist for Amazon and taxes?"

A few months later, Matt Drudge—founder of the Drudge Report, one of the most influential news aggregate sites in the country—called out the hypocrisy in a rare tweet: "$300M fine against AMAZON for tax dodge in EU . . . Nothing on washingtonpost.com front page? Democracy Dies . . . with monopolistic Bezos!!"

You have to appreciate the irony here. The "Democracy dies in darkness" slogan was coined right after the election of Donald Trump, and it was Donald Trump who had been the one to repeatedly warn the public of the paper's questionable dealings.

So, yes, democracy certainly dies with buried stories, but it also dies with misleading stories.

As Bongino Report pointed out in a tweet in December 2019, "It took eight days of being corrected before *The Washington Post* corrected a glaring error in a recent article about education spending." The article referenced was titled, "The one education reform that would really help? Giving public schools more money," with the subheading, "The one thing we haven't tried in the past 30 years is sufficiently investing in our schools." Why would the *Washington Post* knowingly mislead people into believing we haven't increased funding for public schools in thirty years but also refuse to correct the statement when called out? The long-overdue correction, which was issued only after Twitter users and other commenters disputed it for an entire week, read: "An earlier version of the piece stated that public funding for schools had decreased since the late 1980s. That is not the case. In fact, funding at the federal, state, and local levels has increased between the 1980s and 2019."

This was an important distinction given that the piece was an obvious plea for more government funding for academia. Without that premise of decreased funding, there was nothing left on which to base the article. It deserved a complete retraction, or at least a correction, but the *Post* kept it up—along with the misleading subheading.

In one of the more obvious displays of zero self-awareness, *Washington Post* reporter Rachael Bade tweeted a picture of herself along with several of her colleagues at a restaurant seemingly "celebrating" the Democrats' impeachment of President Trump. Her caption read: "Merry Impeachmas from the WaPo team!" So much for Nancy Pelosi's "somber" impeachment effort.

The examples of the *Washington Post*'s misdeeds are endless, but one thing remains certain: these examples of reporters mischaracterizing, ignoring, and even celebrating partisan political victories is what democracy dying in darkness looks like. On rare occasions, we hear it directly from one of their own. In her November 17, 2016, column, *Washington Post* media columnist Margaret Sullivan gave us insight into the newsroom's philosophy when she called for the press to "scrutinize, not normalize" the Trump administration. In her April 28, 2017, column, she bragged that "Eons ago—yes, way back before Jan. 20—I urged the American press to scrutinize, not normalize the actions of the new administration," adding that "Given the unusual background of

President Trump, and his campaign pledges to tear down government as we know it, that seemed a necessity."

A few years earlier, while she was still a public editor for the *New York Times*, Sullivan was asked if the paper had a liberal bias during a *Reliable Sources* interview on CNN, to which she replied: "modified yes with lots of nuances." Her predecessor, Arthur Brisbane, was not as subtle, writing in his last column that a progressive worldview "virtually bleeds through the fabric of the Times."

"THE TRUTH IS MORE IMPORTANT NOW THAN EVER"

Speaking of the *Times,* not to be outdone, the paper came up with their own revamped slogan in 2017: "The truth is more important now than ever." Once considered one of the most trusted newspapers in the world, the *Times* is now arguably the head cheerleader for the political and cultural left. It's hard to find a single edition without blatant bias, factual errors, or misleading stories.

Remember that this is the publication that spent over two years peddling the Russian collusion conspiracy theory that sent the nation into political disarray and published an article falsely accusing the Trump campaign of having "an overarching deal" with "Vladimir Putin's oligarchy." As First Amendment lawyer Harmeet Dhillon put it in an article for conservative news site Townhall:

> The *Times* peddled a wild, baseless conspiracy theory, yet the author, who spent nearly a decade as the Times's executive editor, simply presented his politically-motivated assumptions as unassailable fact. It was a classic example of the "collusion delusion" that gripped the political left

throughout the first two-and-a-half years of the Trump administration. The newspaper's editors should have known that the shocking allegation was false—not to mention defamatory—but they published the article, taking yet another shot at the Trump campaign. Not only did the *Times* ignore evidence contradicting the statements it published, but according to the lawsuit, it did so without even bothering to contact the campaign for comment. This failure to even attempt to verify its reporting is particularly damaging for the *Times*, demonstrating its neglect of the most rudimentary rules of responsible journalism in its rush to publish this hit piece.

As Harmeet pointed out, the author of the piece spent nearly a decade as the publication's executive editor. Political assumptions had been framed as unassailable fact, and the editors had turned a blind eye to the false and defamatory allegation. It certainly doesn't sound like "truth is more important now than ever" inside the walls of the *Times*.

In August 2019, the *Times* ran a lengthy story headlined: "Trump Allies Target Journalists Over Coverage Deemed Hostile to White House," expressing outrage over the "conservative operatives" who sought to hold reporters accountable for misleading the American people. Allies of President Trump had decided that if a reporter was going to attack a member of the president's team or a supporter, this group would simply point out how the reporter had engaged in similar behavior. The point was to call out hypocrisy. It showed not only how they have different rules for themselves but also how they truly see themselves as better than everyone. It was a window into the mind of the elitist mentality that so many of the legacy media groups collectively have.

These are the same people who will tell you that attacks on the press undermine the First Amendment and democracy but are the first to cheer on the mainstream media attacking Fox News or conservative media. In their eyes, appearing on Fox News compromises their credibility as "objective journalists," but sitting alongside the likes of extreme leftists like MSNBC hosts Rachel Maddow, Chris Hayes, or Joy Reid is just fine. In fact, they see that as *adding* credibility. Likewise, attacks on government institutions and intelligence community members are intolerable unless of course, Immigration and Customs Enforcement (ICE) agents are at the center of them. In each case, the media gets to make the rules, and they are always the first to be absolved from any accountability when they break them.

It's easy to see why 91 percent of the news coverage about Trump is negative. The extreme one-sided narrative does far more to sow discord and division within our country than the topics they obsess over. But it is also the reason these legacy newsrooms are failing. The American people are waking up to their hypocrisy and bias.

A recent Pew Research Center poll reveals that "Republicans have grown increasingly alienated from most of the more established sources, while Democrats' confidence in them remains stable, and in some cases, has strengthened. These results reflect similar findings from a Morning Consult survey last October [2019], which found that the gap between how Republicans and Democrats view national media brands like CNN and Fox News continues to widen." While Republicans have grown less comfortable with legacy media, one could equally make the case the legacy media has tried to cater increasingly to the left.

If you get twenty-dollar cocktails with Don Lemon on Fifth Avenue in New York City, you are probably very happy with his coverage of important world events on CNN. If you are more inclined to drink a beer at your neighborhood bar on wing night, you probably aren't.

Cable news has a compulsive need to promote dramatic narratives and intentionally manipulate national narratives to suit their view of how things should be. Many in the media are not only often bent on distorting the story, but they are also equally as determined that you will only hear their version. Legacy media giants have traditionally enjoyed a monopoly on the megaphone. Most print, broadcast, and digital media were, for years, guarded by the same spin masters that are crafting the next poorly sourced speculative attack on the president and others on the right.

In 2015, then-candidate Trump changed the game. It's safe to assume that more people see his tweets than watch CNN, more people have attended his rallies than follow Brian Stelter on Twitter, and more people have watched his press conferences than watch *The View*. President Trump has broken through the traditional media outlets—communicating directly to the American people (or anyone he wants to reach) by instantly sending his messages over Twitter. The traditional media no longer controls the national narrative or the means by which their carefully curated reports are communicated—which means the media no longer controls the minds of their viewers, listeners, or readers. The landscape is rapidly changing thanks in large part to a commander in chief who is happy to pave the way. If President Trump wants to push back against any of the wild accusations of a power-starved media, all he needs to do is tweet, hold a rally, or live-stream a briefing, and his message will jump right over the legacy media's gate.

Very simply, candidate Trump disrupted the political institutions in this country, and President Trump has disrupted the media landscape. By disregarding the traditional avenues of presidential communication, President Trump is paving the way for a new era of how our elected officials communicate with us. Gone are the days of pandering to the media in the hopes of being thrown a positive headline or softball interview. Now the people expect their politicians to shoot straighter and walk taller than ever before. When they see President Trump out in front telling it like it is, they feel emboldened, they feel inspired, and most of all they see authenticity.

CHAPTER FIVE

★ ★ ★ ★ ★ ★ ★

ADVOCATE NEWSROOMS AND THEIR TEAM RULES

The enemy of the people" is a phrase that's been thrown around quite a bit over the past few years. While I've always said I disagree with this statement, I do believe that in many ways some in the media are the enemy of civil discourse. The efforts they have undertaken to fundamentally and permanently transform America and demonize anyone who gets in their way have violated the spirit and the letter of the First Amendment. They are consciously trying to advance their own agendas—politically and socially—and cancel anyone who doesn't embrace their ideology and walk in lockstep with them.

The reality is that most journalists don't start out with this cynical mindset. As journalism school graduates transition from the classroom to the newsroom, wide-eyed and eager to change the world, their distorted view of journalism is reinforced. They settle into their new echo chambers of newsrooms in New York, DC, Chicago, Los Angeles, and other cities, believing they are advancing a noble cause. Unlike seasoned members of the legacy media corporations, I find young journalists to have an element of naïveté and innocence in their pursuits. That is, until they learn the rules of the game.

Many people may not understand the unspoken team rule-book in most media operations. As long as you agree to the team rules, act accordingly, say the right thing, cover the right stories, and promote the right agenda, you're safe and absolved from any accountability.

By sticking to these rules members of the media have created an institution that has further polarized the country.

RULE #1: COVER YOUR EYES WHEN IT'S OUR GUYS

Privileged liberal journalists—and that's exactly what they are—love to whip up outrage when a conservative member of the media does something they deem to be wrong, but they rarely hold themselves to the same standards they set.

In response to the "Merry Impeachmas from the WaPo team!" fiasco that I discussed in the previous chapter, then White House press secretary Stephanie Grisham perfectly said, "And on cue some reporters will circle the wagons & defend their colleagues at all costs. Calling out reporters for inappropriate behavior is labeled (by the media) an attack on the free press. Reporters claim they 'hold the powerful accountable.' But who holds them accountable?"

This is the question every American should be asking.

In one of the most glaring examples of media hypocrisy, let's look at the way the media responded to the case of Megyn Kelly, who went to NBC after a long stint as a right-leaning opinion host at Fox News. She was fired from her weekday show on NBC after asking a question about whether a blackface Halloween costume is inherently racist if the person is dressing up as an admired character. She asked this question during the on-air discussion, and after issuing several apologies and reiterating how horrible she thought the act was, she was quickly pushed aside and fired.

Now let's consider the myriad of celebrities and public figures who got a free pass from the left when not discussing, but actually dressing up in blackface. The same NBC that quickly dismissed Megyn Kelly, as well as the NBC staff members who were very concerned about her remarks, had nothing to say about NBC's very own show host Jimmy Fallon, who dressed in blackface not once, but twice. He dressed in blackface the first time in a *Saturday Night Live* sketch years ago and then a second time to impersonate Chris Rock at the network's 2016 Golden Globes. ABC host Jimmy Kimmel also dressed in blackface when mocking NBA Hall of Famer Karl Malone on Comedy Central's *The Man Show*. Other famous culprits include Robert Downey Jr., Howard Stern, and Billy Crystal. Again, not a peep from anyone. Ironically, when photos emerged of Joy Behar in blackface, *The View* co-host explained she was dressing as a "black woman who she admired for Halloween." So let's get this straight . . . ABC kept Joy Behar, who was doing the very thing NBC fired Megyn Kelly for asking about.

When videos of Kimmel in blackface resurfaced in June 2020 and hashtags to cancel Kimmel trended, he finally released a statement. "I have long been reluctant to address this, as I knew doing so would be celebrated as a victory by those who equate apologies with weakness and cheer for leaders who use prejudice to divide us. . . . I know that this will not be the last I hear of this and that it will be used again to try to quiet me. . . . I won't be bullied into silence by those who feign outrage to advance their oppressive and genuinely racist agendas." Even a headline in the *Los Angeles Times* referred to this so-called apology as "lame." When Megyn Kelly asked a question about blackface, she was fired, but when a late night host that expresses hatred for the right is caught doing it, the outrage is, you guessed it, the fault of the right.

Mary McNamara, culture columnist and critic for the *Los Angeles Times,* wrote of Kimmel's statement, "if you're going to apologize for using blackface, apologize for using blackface. Don't call it a 'thoughtless moment' because, dude, you wrote the sketches, you rehearsed the sketches and you sat in the chair while someone put brown makeup *all over you* more than once."

"Kimmel, Fallon, (Tina) Fey and other white entertainers who have used blackface as entertainment say that racist mockery was not their intent but, frankly, that's as tough a sell as 'My Confederate flag only represents my regional pride.'"

The only difference between Megyn Kelly and all the others, besides being the only one who didn't actually *appear* in blackface, is her political background. She did not play into the liberal team agenda; therefore she didn't have the same protections. Plain and simple. Her biggest mistake was thinking that going from Fox News to NBC would allow her to fit in and be part of the group. She was never one of them.

In October 2018, homophobic tweets of CNN reporter Kaitlin Collins surfaced. In one she wrote, "prologue to Canterbury Tales, you fag." In another, she noted that she had no interest to "room with a lesbian." The response was swift. She apologized, and her CNN colleagues rushed to her defense to claim that she was a good person who had matured since writing the tweets. Fair enough. We all make mistakes and hopefully learn from them and mature as a person. But we can all wonder if this had been another reporter at a right-leaning outlet, would the outcome have been quite different?

After MSNBC dumped longtime liberal host Chris Matthews stemming from allegations that he had made inappropriate sexist comments, they chose Joy Reid to replace him. Interestingly, according to Aidan McLaughlin of the left-wing media site Mediaite, "there remains an unresolved controversy in Reid's career, mentioned only in passing in coverage of the good news: her dubious claim that offensive posts on her old blog were planted by nefarious hackers." In 2018, Mediaite had uncovered what it called a "slew" of homophobic posts on a blog she had written.

In a statement to Mediaite, Reid claimed, "in December I learned that an unknown, external party accessed and manipulated material from my now-defunct blog, The Reid Report, to include offensive and hateful references that are fabricated and run counter to my personal beliefs and ideology." Her response went on to say, "The manipulated material seems to be part of an effort to taint my character with false information by distorting a blog that ended a decade ago." Through her lawyer, Reid claimed the FBI was investigating the hack.

As offensive materials became uncovered, Reid issued another statement, noting, "there are things I deeply regret and am embarrassed by, things I would have said differently and issues where my position has changed."

In its own statement regarding the posts, MSNBC came to Reid's defense. "They are not reflective of the colleague and friend we have known at MSNBC for the past seven years. . . . Joy has apologized publicly and privately and said she has grown and evolved in the many years since, and we know this to be true."

There are two issues here. The first is the same as it was for CNN's Kaitlin Collins. Inappropriate posts surface, reporter says they are sorry, network backs them up and says they have matured. Life goes on.

The second issue, which Mediaite's McLaughlin notes, "is that Reid insisted, quite forcefully, that she was hacked. Her lawyer said there was an FBI investigation into the alleged hack. That is a serious allegation. Given NBC's long standing silence on those two claims, the industry assumption is that the network knows the hacking claim is an invention. NBC declined to comment when reached by Mediaite. Now Joy Reid is set to ascend to one of the top jobs on cable news. She will be hosting a news and opinion show, according to the *Journal*. Offensive old blog posts are one thing and could have been answered for in 2018. Doesn't the journalist owe an explanation for her highly dubious attempt to explain those posts away?"

Yes, she does. But aside from Mediate, no other outlet cares. Why? The answer is simple. The media (in this instance, I am speaking of the left-leaning majority) are quite forgiving if you are part of the team.

In July 2019, *Fourth Watch*, a media watchdog newsletter founded by veteran media insider Steve Krakauer, called out NBC medical contributor Dr. Joseph Fair for claiming that he had contracted COVID-19 when, in fact, he had several negative tests proving he was not positive for coronavirus. For weeks, NBC had tracked their medical expert's battle—which included broadcast coverage from his hospital bed—but the doctor and the network failed to report that he never actually had the highly contagious virus. *Fourth Watch* published this information:

"And now we know Dr. Fair never had coronavirus, despite nearly a dozen appearances on NBC and MSNBC where he talked about having it or recovering from it. In the end, NBC's viewers were left with two very alarming—and false—impressions. First, that an expert virologist can take every precaution but can still catch COVID-19 through his eyes. False. Second, that tests can be so untrustworthy that you can have multiple negative tests and still have coronavirus. Craig Melvin described them as 'false negative tests' in that initial report on May 14. Hoda Kotb said, 'every time it came back negative, but clearly you have it.' False. Anti-science. And truly damaging."

The left frequently calls the right out for being "anti-science," but in this case where the facts are clear, crickets.

Some of the biggest culprits of turning a blind eye to their own can be found in print media. Look no further than the "paper of record," the *New York Times*. Technology writer Sarah Jeong got a free pass from the *Times* Editorial Board after her extremely offensive tweets, mostly between 2014 and 2017, surfaced following her hiring as an opinion writer.

These tweets include Jeong bragging that she was "equating Trump to Hitler before it was cool," and described an "unending cascade of vomit" that flows from her face when attempting to "politely greet a Republican." She also wrote, "it's kind of sick how much joy I get from being cruel to old white men." She has also said, "white people genetically predisposed to burn faster in the sun, thus logically being only fit to live underground like groveling goblins," opined that white people would be extinct soon, used a #CancelWhitePeople hashtag, declared "cops are a-holes," and suggested we "kill more men."

The *Times* stood by Jeong and painted her as the victim who was merely adopting the language of her online harassers, and the media turned a blind eye.

"Her journalism and the fact that she is a young Asian woman have made her a subject of frequent online harassment," according to the statement issued by the paper. "For a period of time, she responded to that harassment by imitating the rhetoric of her harassers. She sees now that this approach only served to feed the vitriol that we too often see on social media. She regrets it, and the *Times* does not condone it." When I was growing up, my mother always said that two wrongs don't make a right, but I guess the *Times* doesn't share that view.

I despise cancel culture. Rarely do I agree with anything the outrage mob demands, especially when it comes to digging up old tweets and trying to get someone fired or ousted from the public sphere. Jeong has since left her full-time position at the *Times* and is now a contracted contributor for NYT Opinion.

Beyond the reporters and analysts, part of the problem with the media also has to do with the left-leaning contributors of the networks themselves.

Following the Iowa Caucus in February 2020, which saw a record turnout for an incumbent president, Team Trump posted a photo on their flight home of their smiling faces in bright red hats that read "Keep Iowa great." Former senator turned MSNBC contributor Claire McCaskill tweeted the picture, writing: "One of these things is not like the others. Hint: they made him squat in the aisle so he was visible." The obvious insinuation was that Secretary Ben Carson, who was the person McCaskill was referring to, is just a "token black" being made to squat for a photo op.

McCaskill not only ignored the other minorities featured in the photo, but she also neglected to note that the reason for his squatting in the center of the photo was that he was actually sitting in first class with the Trump family and had walked to the back for the photo. As if calling the renowned neurosurgeon and a cabinet secretary a "thing" wasn't bad enough, her condescending tone reveals that she can't fathom that Dr. Carson makes basic movements without being commanded to do so. By NBC's standards, this type of cynical rhetoric should have been intolerable. I have no doubt that if it were a Republican who made this assertion, they would have publicly shamed her with assertions that she is on the "wrong side of history" with her bigotry and racism.

Ironically, the morning after tweeting this and drawing a sharp rebuke on Twitter and across the internet, she appeared on the *Today* show with Savannah Guthrie for an interview regarding the status of the Democratic presidential race, during which McCaskill was never asked about her statement. She was given a free pass on something that was certainly relevant and newsworthy.

The reason is simple: if you're on the left, the media networks will only highlight the good things about you while ignoring the bad.

Just ask Jimmy Kimmel. The comedian recently posted a photo on Instagram introducing former senator Al Franken as a "comedy legend to U.S. Senator to podcaster." Interestingly, he left out the very thing that earned the disgraced Democrat the most headlines—the eight credible allegations of sexual misconduct against him. Kimmel wasn't the only liberal to ignore this glaring detail.

The View host Joy Behar said a "political hit" was the reason for his resignation while her co-host Whoopi Goldberg slammed the rush to judgment and apparent aversion to due process for him in the #MeToo era.

In October 2019, Ronan Farrow's bombshell book *Catch and Kill* was released, sparking national controversy over sexual assault allegations against then–NBC host Matt Lauer and reports that a Hillary Clinton staffer protected Hollywood producer Harvey Weinstein from being exposed as a serial sexual predator. As damning details emerged, MSNBC hosts Rachel Maddow, Brian Williams, Chris Hayes, and Lawrence O'Donnell and CNN hosts Anderson Cooper and Chris Cuomo all neglected to mention anything about the book, Weinstein, Lauer, or Clinton during their shows, leaving their viewers completely in the dark. An October 10 Fox News report noted the following:

> Farrow has been extremely tight-lipped about the highly anticipated book, so the media industry was all ears when Variety, The Hollywood Reporter, and The New York Post revealed news-making excerpts.
>
> "Anderson Cooper 360," "Cuomo Prime Time," "CNN Tonight" and "White House in Crisis" failed to mention Lauer, Farrow, and Weinstein, according to a review of transcripts by Fox News.
>
> Allegations included everything from a heavily-disputed claim that former "Today" host Matt Lauer anally raped an NBC News colleague during the 2014 Olympics in Sochi to a report that a Hillary Clinton aide tipped off Harvey Weinstein that Farrow was attempting to expose him as a sexual predator.
>
> NBC's cable news sister, MSNBC, ignored the story during primetime. "All in with Chris Hayes," "The Rachel Maddow Show," "The Last Word with Lawrence O'Donnell" and "The 11th Hour with Brian Williams" failed to even mention Farrow, Lauer or Weinstein, according to a review of transcripts by Fox News.

An MSNBC spokesperson directed a request for comment to NBC News' senior vice president of communication, who did not immediately respond. MSNBC skipping the story shouldn't shock media watchdogs, as Farrow reportedly believes that he is blacklisted from his former organization, and NBC News chairman Andy Lack is a target of his reporting. But fellow liberal cable news CNN also ignored the story during primetime.

It's interesting how so many left-leaning networks and organizations claim that (a) women should always be believed and (b) that reporters shouldn't be attacked. Yet, once it was their own who was on the receiving end, both of those truisms went out the door. Many didn't believe Farrow while others plainly questioned his reporting. Isn't it interesting how these same people are so sanctimonious up until the point when their own work is being attacked?

Of course, the "cover your eyes when it's our guys" rule only applies until a member of the media diverges from the agenda.

RULE #2: CONFLICTS OF INTEREST ARE NOT OF INTEREST

Just before the 2020 Democratic primary debate season kicked off, the Democratic National Committee announced its decision to bar Fox News from hosting a primary debate. DNC chair Tom Perez had the audacity to point to "the inappropriate relationship between President Trump, his administration, and Fox News."

This was laughable at best. Have you ever noticed that the left tends to accuse the right of the very crimes they themselves are most guilty of committing? Those on the left are always keen to point out relationships that exist between politicians, their families, the media, and corporations. Interestingly enough, it's very rare that they do it themselves.

If you listen to many in the media, every politician is supposedly influenced by every donation they take. Most reporters and pundits are quick to point out the connection between a donor, a donation, and a vote passed or an action taken; however, they will swear that their editorials, op-eds, and advertisements have no influence on them. Does anyone actually buy that? Ask yourself this: If you see that some industry or association is buying a $10,000+ ad in the middle of a newsletter or story, wouldn't you be skeptical of whether or not it has some bearing on current or future topics the outlet will cover? It's amazing that we're supposed to assume that politicians have to be corrupt but media outlets are as pure as the driven snow.

The media frequently calls out conflicts of interest with respect to politicians as well as politicians' families and personal friends. However, they certainly ignore the giant revolving door that exists within their circles. It's a perfect illustration of "do as I say, not as I do."

We're supposed to think it's cute when CNN's Chris Cuomo has his brother, New York Democratic governor Andrew Cuomo, on his weeknight show. The relationship between the brothers undoubtedly influences the network's coverage of Governor Cuomo and the crisis. During the height of the initial COVID-19 outbreak, the younger Cuomo would have his brother on his show almost daily. Rarely did he challenge him on the accusations regarding his brother's poor handling of the soaring number of deaths in New York's nursing homes. At one point, Chris even admitted on-air he could not be objective when it came to covering his brother. He was simply amazing. But let's make sure we are clear, Fox and President Trump have an "inappropriate relationship" but Cuomo on Cuomo is nothing but straight-up news for the very network that defines itself as "the most trusted name in news."

There are also many former Democratic staffers who now work in the media and others who have long family ties to the Democratic Party.

NBC senior political analyst Jonathan Allen left *Politico* to work for DNC chairwoman and congresswoman Debbie Wasserman Shultz, and then he went back to *Politico*. Former MSNBC host Chris Matthews had worked for President Jimmy Carter and worked for six years as chief of staff to Democratic House Speaker Tip O'Neill. CNN's Jake Tapper worked for Democratic congresswoman Marjorie Margolies-Mezvinsky (who now happens to be Chelsea Clinton's mother-in-law) and the left-wing group Handgun Control Inc. ABC's George Stephanopoulos worked for President Bill Clinton. Chuck Todd, NBC's political director and host of *Meet the Press*, worked for the 1992 presidential campaign of Democratic senator Tom Harkin of Iowa.

Stop and think about this for a minute. The very people who are covering the politics of the day have partisan backgrounds. Some are more transparent about their political proclivities than others. Matthews, who was admittedly an opinion host, has always been clear about his Democratic background. But it's safe to assume that most viewers or readers are not aware of the political bias that goes into so-called unbiased journalism.

Furthermore, there are several other reporters and hosts at mainstream news outlets whose spouses have connections to prominent Democratic figures.

One prominent host is married to a former advisor to a Democrat presidential candidate. Another host's wife has an extensive and ongoing history of raising money for Democrat candidates while a third has a long history of advocating for far left-leaning causes. Do they ever note that conflict? I hope you aren't surprised when I say no. If you are going to grill a Republican candidate on abortion and your wife has actively lobbied on behalf of organizations that promote abortion, that might be an issue. Or it might be worth noting if your spouse has done fund-raising for a certain guest appearing on your show.

Beyond that, several of these folks have hopped into government. Most people would have no idea that a prominent cable news host was a political appointee in the Obama administration. In his book *Unfreedom of the Press*, Mark Levin writes, "the *Atlantic*, a progressive media outlet, reported that there were at least twenty-four journalists who transitioned from media jobs to working in the Obama administration. . . . You would be hard-pressed to find a similar extensive relationship between numerous major media organizations and recent Republican Administrations."

These are the first people to point out the lack of disclosure and transparency among people in public office, and yet when it comes to their own lives, they look the other way.

Now think back to the fake outrage over Fox News' supposedly problematic relationship with President Trump. If Fox News is "State TV," as CNN calls it, what do they call interviewing your own brother and tossing softball questions? Oh yeah, that's just TV.

RULE #3: BIAS THROUGH SILENCE

When the media is not blatantly expressing bias, many show their leftist colors by simply ignoring news that doesn't fit their agenda.

This is especially true when it comes to violence. The media is often silent when it comes to violence that is aimed at conservatives, but expresses all kinds of outrage when it's aimed at the left.

When a crazed man attempted to drive a van through a tent of Trump supporters who were registering voters in Jacksonville, Florida, in February 2020, there was scant attention paid by the media. Despite the incident occurring in the early afternoon, none of the evening shows on ABC, CBS, or NBC cared to mention it. It wasn't until the next day that NBC gave it a pathetic twenty-five seconds of air time.

It wasn't the first time the three legacy networks ignored a politically motivated attack on Republicans. Right before the 2018 midterm elections, they ignored the disturbing story of a brand-new Republican county headquarters in Wyoming that was intentionally set on fire. NBC's evening broadcast felt it was more important to air a "spotlight" on Cher's career, while ABC gave air time to a giraffe attack. The following month, another Republican facility— this time the Volusia County, Florida, GOP headquarters—was shot multiple times. The outrageous incident wasn't even worth a mention on any of the three networks the following day. They were too busy criticizing Trump.

Ignoring or downplaying violent attacks on Trump supporters is not only dangerous to society, but it is also a dereliction of duty on the part of the self-proclaimed "guardians of democracy."

They continuously turn a blind eye to violent attacks by Antifa, the militant group responsible for routinely destroying property, defacing statues, and savagely beating conservative citizens and journalists. When one of Antifa's members threw a firebomb at an Immigration and Customs Enforcement facility in 2019, the media largely ignored it. The scarce coverage it did receive was framed in a way that sympathized with the terrorist, who was shot dead by a nearby police officer before he was able to carry out his plan to kill hundreds of people. When a group of his fellow Antifa loyalists gathered to honor him, the local ABC affiliate reported: "Protesters gathered outside a Washington State Detention Center to demand the shutdown of the facility after a man was killed by police after he apparently lit a car on fire and attempted to ignite a propane tank."

Advocates of conservative issues rallying on the National Mall in Washington, DC, are right-wing zealots but these folks are pro-testors. Got it.

When Second Amendment supporters gathered in Richmond, Virginia, in January 2020 to protest gun-control bills being pushed by Democrats, the thousands of peaceful protesters who showed up defied the media narratives that it would quite literally be the start of the second civil war. I kid you not . . . The *Washington Post* ran a fear-mongering front-page story before the event say-ing that the rally was, "in the words of some, to fan the flames of a civil war." NBC published a story about how residents feared that "militia groups" at the event "will turn violent." Interestingly, a Fox News report says that the rally was so peaceful that the protesters even picked up their own trash when they were done. The media created its own narrative out of thin air. Contrast this narrative to their gushing support over the Women's March—which is known for actually being vitriolic and divisive.

Whenever a group of right-wing protesters gather in pub-lic, there's almost always a guarantee that the media will make a mountain out of a molehill. In instances when very small groups of protesters deemed to be far-right gather for nonviolent protests, the media goes nuts. Think about that double standard. When the media doesn't like something they deem to be far-right, they equate it to violence and danger. When the left actually engages in violent acts, they frame it as heroic.

So much of the problem in today's media is what is *not* covered. You would be hard-pressed to find media pundits discussing the numerous, decades-long lawsuits and allegations over Mike Bloomberg's sexism and workplace abuse. As recently as 2016, a lawsuit filed by one of his female employees claims he encouraged "sexist and sexually charged behavior" and reflects on "Bloomberg's notoriously sexist and hostile work environment," which has been "well documented and has been the subject of myriad lawsuits prior to this lawsuit."

ABC News reviewed court cases detailing at least seventeen women who filed similar complaints over the past three decades. One claim, dating back to 1997, accuses Bloomberg of telling a sales manager who had just announced she was pregnant to "kill it" and describes a "locker room atmosphere" that was "sexually harassing." Another lawsuit alleges wrongful termination of a woman who was dismissed from his company while undergoing breast cancer treatment.

Apparently, the serial sexism claims and allegations of using nondisclosure agreements to silence women are not enough to get Bloomberg canceled by the left in the #MeToo era. What's worse, the media largely refused to acknowledge this stunning double standard, that is until he dropped out of the Democrat presidential primary race and it was no longer politically convenient to ignore it. Abby Huntsman, formerly one of the two conservative hosts on *The View*, was one of the only media personalities willing to confront him. She cited his "lewd and sexist comments" and the "frat-like culture" that he allegedly fostered at his company and asked him why he refused to release his female accusers from their nondisclosure agreements.

I have no doubt his response would have ignited a media firestorm if he were on the other side of the political aisle. In an unapologetic defense, he replied, "We don't have anything to hide, but we made legal agreements. Just because you signed a nondisclosure doesn't mean you can't talk about other things." Thanks to the liberal media's selective outrage and full-blown hypocrisy, he doesn't even have to pretend to act remorseful or make excuses. Silence is an effective weapon. As long as he funds anti-gun and other left-leaning causes, the media will continue to give him a pass.

Perhaps nothing highlighted the utter shamelessness of the media more than the way they selectively turned a blind eye during the coronavirus crisis.

Highlighting a March 2020 ABC News/Ipsos poll that showed an unusually high 55 percent approval rating of Trump's coronavirus management, Mollie Hemingway wrote that the media went through the first stage of grief: denial. After all, they spent months trying to convince the public that Trump was to blame for literally anything that went wrong.

"Things got worse when additional polls showed Trump receiving high ratings at the same time that the media received poor ratings," she writes. "A brand new Gallup study—'Coronavirus Response: Hospitals Rated Best, News Media Worst'—was particularly bad news. When Americans were asked about nine different institutions and political leaders, they gave majority approval to all but the media. President Trump has a 22-point net approval rating while the media's net approval rating was negative 11 points. The RealClearPolitics approval average for Trump was its highest during his entire presidency. In response, the media were angry and depressed and began blaming his press conferences. Their theory seemed to be that the more Americans saw Trump, unfiltered, they liked him and the more Americans saw the behavior of the media, they didn't like it. This flies in the face of what many in the media assumed for years. They pushed for daily White House press conferences so that they could have the opportunity to be on camera and pressure the Trump administration. Now that they had daily press briefings with the president, no less, they weren't happy. It was a weird response for a group of people whose ostensible job is to simply report the news of the day."

On April 11, 2020, as the pandemic was expanding, CNN posted a story with the headline "President Trump is wrong in so many ways about hydroxychloroquine studies. Here are the facts." Trump had been promoting the potential benefits of the drug and had even admitted to taking it. CNN was vicious in their attacks on Trump for both promoting and taking it. They had claimed that by promoting it as something people should be asking their physicians about, he was putting people in danger. Then on July 2, 2020, they posted another story but the tone was much different. "Study finds hydroxychloroquine helps coronavirus patients survive better." Huh? No mention of Trump this time or their previous reporting.

Throughout the COVID-19 crisis, President Trump has used the press briefings around the virus as a way to push back on false, incomplete, or misleading narratives and get his own message out directly to the American people. This has clearly annoyed the press. His TV ratings were huge and even ticked up because people craved information on what the government was doing. So

what did the media do next? CNN and MSNBC stopped covering the briefings. On many occasions, they were cutting him out
and dipping back in when they felt it was worth covering another
government official. They so detested covering his briefings that
some outlets went to every extreme, such as adding banners on the
screen about him being "frustrated," "angry," and "unhinged." So
much for objective journalism.

Newsweek correspondent Andrew Feinberg complained that
Trump "wants to hijack everyone's television with another briefing instead of letting people go a single day without him on their
screens," while MSNBC's Mika Brzezinski said, "The President's
need to be on camera, forces his coronavirus team to scram-
ble to prepare for a briefing in which they have no news, drain-
ing HOURS from their 24 hour a day struggle to contain this. . . .
Trump's need for attention is costing precious time." NBC News/
MSNBC contributor Gabriel Sherman also weighed in, tweeting,
"Trump is literally turning all three cable news networks into State
TV. Live daily campaign rallies for the president to strengthen his
hold on power. Unprecedented departure from American norms."
Just to be clear, President Trump held a press conference and the
cable networks (at least initially) covered them of their own free
will. How is that State TV?

The *Washington Post* ran an article by Margaret Sullivan
that was literally titled: "The media must stop live-broadcasting
Trump's dangerous, destructive coronavirus briefings." When the
media networks complied with the demand, the *Post* celebrated
with another article titled, "CNN, MSNBC refused to carry full
Trump coronavirus briefing. Yay!"

Going dark on critical information from the president during a
pandemic, then shamelessly cheering it on, certainly must qualify

as democracy that "Dies in Darkness." I'm confused, though. First, it was a travesty that there weren't any press conferences, then there were too many, and they must be denounced. It's so hard to keep the demands of the media straight.

This wouldn't be the first time members of the press showed selective outrage over press briefings, or lack thereof. During Stephanie Grisham's tenure, the press dragged her over the coals for not holding briefings. In fact, as reported by Fox News, ever since President Trump took office, one of CNN's longest-running complaints was that the White House had broken norms when it no longer held regularly scheduled press briefings. But when Kayleigh McEnany replaced her and began regular briefings, CNN and MSNBC decided not to air them. Even former CNN producer Steve Krakauer called out this absurdity, writing in a column for *Fourth Watch,* when McEnany held her third briefing. "CNN and MSNBC didn't cover a second of it. It was a curious, pathetic display—after months of calls to restart the briefing, what possible reason would the media have to avoid airing it?" he asks.

Could it be that, as author and attorney David Limbaugh suggested in a Fox News column, "The media's attitude is purely adversarial, yet they act appalled that McEnany returns fire, albeit calmly, respectfully and eloquently? They uniformly dismiss this Harvard Law graduate as green and over her head, but she is remarkably polished, and it is driving them mad." I'd say it's likely.

Following media backlash to President Trump's handling of the coronavirus crisis, the White House showed a four-minute video during a daily coronavirus briefing highlighting the media's hypocrisy. It included a timeline of the president's response, clips of multiple reporters suggesting the virus was no more dangerous than the flu, and Democrat governors who had praised him over his actions.

The instant media reaction was a meltdown. Hysteria. How dare the president have the nerve to fight back at the false portrayals of his actions in this fight against the virus? This was just not to be done!

In a classic move, CNN ran the following banners on the screen that read as follows:

"Angry Trump Turns Briefings into Propaganda Sessions"

"Trump Refuses to Acknowledge Any Mistakes"

"Trump Uses Task Force Briefing To Try To Rewrite History On Coronavirus Response"

"Trump Melts Down In Angry Response To Reports He Ignored Virus Warnings"

Substitute "media" for the word "Trump" and a dead-on accurate portrait of what was really going on at this briefing emerges:

"Angry Media Turns Briefings into Propaganda Sessions"

"Media Refuses to Acknowledge Any Mistakes"

"Media Uses Task Force Briefing To Try To Rewrite History On Coronavirus Response"

"Media Melts Down In Angry Response To Reports It Ignored Virus Warnings"

As I noted in my book *The Briefing*, the White House press briefings have morphed from less of an exchange to get information and into more of an opportunity for reporters to gain fame and earn a contract as a cable news pundit. In a July 9, 2020, column for *Columbia Journalism Review*, Bill Grueskin wrote about an exchange between *Politico*'s Ryan Lizza and Kayleigh McEnany. Lizza asked a two part question concluding with "Does President

Trump believe that it was a good thing that the South lost the Civil War?"

Grueskin wrote that "McEnany, who had been rifling through her notes during the first part of Lizza's question, appeared stunned by the Civil War reference. Then, she looked at Lizza the way a schoolteacher might glare at a student who had just belched loudly during class. Without much of a pause, McEnany responded that Lizza's 'first question is absolutely absurd. He's proud of the United States of America.' McEnany was right: it *was absurd*—an instance of performance art, rather than a journalistic effort designed to elicit information."

He went on to note that "A. Craig Copetas, a longtime reporter at the *Wall Street Journal* and *Bloomberg News*, sees it as a broader problem. 'Theatrical spectacle has replaced the craft of journalism,'" he wrote. Some reporters have turned into "performers, operating in a social media universe that tells them they're not alone in the way they feel about themselves."

He hit the nail on the head when he stated that "reporters have often been accused of using these briefings to flaunt their own agendas. Most journalism takes place outside the public view. Reporters research stories while hunched over their desks, and often conduct interviews without a camera rolling; the public usually sees only the finished product. But televised press briefings flip the script, which risks turning reporters into *dramatis personae*, as they compete for attention and air time."

At their core, most media elites look down on the average American. They see them as a "basket of deplorables" who should listen to them, the enlightened. To many in the media, President Trump represents the little guy whom they despise. With his "tell it like it is" style, they see the average American, standing in front of them, calling them out for their hypocrisy. What is even worse for the media class is that Trump has been a master at circumventing the "enlightened" gatekeepers of cable news to go directly to the American people. Ironically, this is what infuriates the media elites the most: the fact that Trump does not need them. President Trump has served as both a beacon and a battering ram for the average person in this country who had, for decades, felt like professional talking heads in the media were not reflecting the daily life, concerns, and desires of normal everyday people.

Speaking of silence, it was amazing how the media's concern over public gatherings during the coronavirus crisis was nonexistent during the massive protests in cities throughout the country in the wake of George Floyd's killing yet a single Trump rally in Tulsa, Oklahoma, was potentially the source for a resurgence of the virus (Okay, that may be overkill, but you get my point). A July 2020 story in the *New York Times* literally read, "Are Protests Unsafe? What Experts Say May Depend on Who's Protesting What." Seriously, that's not satire from the *Onion*. So if you are protesting for a liberal cause, coronavirus will pass you by. But if you attend a Trump rally or March for Life, you will likely get sick and spread the virus. And conservatives are the "science deniers"?

RULE #4: USE OUR DICTIONARY

There's a lot to be said for the way the media uses words to frame issues. Words elicit an emotional response. Politicians and special interest operatives know this better than anyone, and they have been using it to their advantage for decades. It's not necessarily wrong, but it's important to recognize when the media does it, specifically when they do it to frame narratives around news and hot-button issues.

In his book *Words That Work,* communications consultant, pollster, and political pundit Dr. Frank Luntz writes, "It's not what you say, it's what people hear. You can have the best message in the world, but the person on the receiving end will always understand it through the prism of his or her own emotions, preconceptions, prejudices, and preexisting beliefs. Words that work, whether fiction or reality, not only explain but also motivate. They cause you to think as well as act. They trigger emotion as well as understanding."

Dr. Luntz offers the following example of: "Americans would prefer greater energy efficiency to increased conservation because 'efficiency' suggests getting more for less while 'conservation' has a tone of sacrifice to it. For that same reason, 'renewable' energy is more popular than 'alternative' energy."

With that in mind, consider a February 2020 report on pro-life legislation by CNN, in which they described a baby who survived an abortion as "a fetus that was born." Yes, you read that right. A fetus that was born. This article came out just ahead of a Senate vote in February over legislation that would protect babies who survived abortions as well as babies who could feel pain after twenty weeks: the Pain-Capable Unborn Child Protection Act and the Born-Alive Abortion Survivors Protection Act. When covering the vote, the outlet called the bills "abortion restriction bills" despite the fact that the latter bill solely refers to newborn babies outside of the womb.

See the framing here? The left loves science and biology except when the terms don't fit their agenda. They know if they were to use the accurate term, "baby," instead of "a fetus that was born," it would elicit a more emotional response from the reader and therefore reflect negatively on the left's agenda.

A well-known rule in political communications is that a party should be defined by what it stands for rather than what it stands against. Why is it then that the media calls the pro-life movement "anti-choice"? To use the talking points of the Democratic Party and frame the narrative, of course.

We see the same thing when media pundits tell us that the GOP is waging a "war on women's health" as opposed to "defending the rights of the unborn" as well as when they call the "Right to Work" movement "anti-worker" and "tax reform" legislation "tax cuts for the rich."

Axios, an online newsletter based in Washington, DC, recently sent out its daily morning email news brief in which it discussed how immigrants have to trust the federal government during the coronavirus outbreak, which has made it harder for them to stay in the country. President Trump's policies "could scare immigrants away from getting medical help as the coronavirus spreads," *Axios*'s Stef Kight reported. Really? Immigrants or illegal immigrants? Note how they now group them all in one bucket. There would be no reason for *legal* immigrants to fear medical help from the government.

Oftentimes, the words and phrases used by the media are the same words and phrases used in the school system when teaching young people about important issues. Think "anti-fascist"—the popular term used on college campuses to describe the violent left-wing activism group Antifa, which claims to fight fascism—of course, the "fascism" they seek to destroy is America itself. The carefully crafted words are then echoed by the media, reinforcing left-wing narratives around political topics in the malleable minds of young people. Repetition and reinforcement are key here.

This concept is true even with the most basic words we use to describe our political affiliations. Think about the word "progressive." Dr. Luntz writes that many on the left have argued strongly for the rebranding of "liberals" as "progressive" because the word "progressive" not only lacks the negative baggage of "liberal," but it also suggests "progress" and is therefore future-oriented. What young person doesn't want to be part of making progress? It's a flashy, appealing word that conservatives know is misleading, but young people buy into it.

When it comes to using words to frame President Trump in a negative light, the media truly knows no bounds. Consider this observation by Brent Bozell, president of the media watchdog Media Research Center, in his book *Unmasked*:

> [The media] often used highly-charged words to paint [President Trump] as unhinged or out of control. Viewers heard Trump variously described as "furious" (17 times), "fuming" (14 times), "outraged" (8), "venting" (5), "infuriated" (5), "livid" (3), "enraged" (3), "seething" (2), or just plain old "angry" (23).
>
> When Trump communicated he was said to be "lashing out" (53 times), on a "tirade" (8), "blasting" (5), or "erupting" (3). The president was also "on the warpath," "volcanic," "unglued" and "spoiling for a fight" and even "went ballistic" according to reporters at various times that year.

Of course, these numbers have certainly increased since Brent's book was released in 2019, and you can bet the media has expanded their list of favorite adjectives.

We see this far beyond the walls of newsrooms and classrooms. In San Francisco, for instance, thanks to a resolution by the city's Board of Supervisors to use "person-first" language in the criminal justice system, "convicted felons" now must be called "justice involved persons." Likewise, a drug addict must be called "a person with a history of substance abuse" and a "juvenile delinquent" is now a "young person with justice system involvement." You can't even use the terms "convict," "inmate," or "prisoner" anymore.

Donald Trump Jr. highlights more examples in his book *Triggered*:

> But in today's climate, words have completely lost their meanings. When conservatives speak, it's called "violence." When liberals react to that speech by beating people up and throwing rocks through windows, it's called "self-defense." When a conservative says "America is a good country" or "God bless America" that's called hate speech. When a liberal says "all white people should be extinct," as Sarah Jeong from the *New York Times* said, that's called "ironic protest."

Don is spot-on: words matter, but the mainstream media is now redefining words and how we use them with a clear bias.

The left is strategic about the words they use to describe themselves and their causes, and we should be, too. Again, we can look to President Trump as an example of how we can use words to our advantage.

President Trump defines his opponents, whether it be "Crooked Hillary" or "Sleepy Joe." In the same way, he defines his political positions with slogans—think "America first"—which he intentionally repeats as a constant reminder that he fights for our country's interest above all others.

A 2018 article in the *Guardian* titled, "Trump has turned words into weapons. And he's winning the linguistic war," laments that "from 'spygate' to 'fake news,' Trump is using language to frame—and win—debates."

"Liberals lecture conservatives on the 'tone' of their rhetoric while engaging in some of the vilest rhetoric ever to exit a human's mouth," as Derek Hunter puts it in his book *Outrage, Inc.*

RULE #5: FRAME AND BLAME

Nothing paints a picture of media bias and framing like the front covers of *Time*. In addition to finding that an astonishing 89 percent of mainstream media coverage of President Trump during his first one hundred days in office was negative, the Media Research Center studied every *Time* cover since he took office and displayed dozens of side-by-side comparisons between covers depicting President Trump as cartoonish and angry and others depicting Democrats as inspiring, hopeful, and reassuring. Former 2020 Democratic contenders such as Bernie Sanders are portrayed as forward-thinking, smiling leaders. The headline reads, "Building a Better Bernie," while Elizabeth Warren's flattering cover quotes her favorite platform plank, "I Have a Plan for That." Pete Buttigieg received the ultimate treatment for his "First Family" edition, which featured a portrait of him with his husband on the cover as well as a fawning spread of praise for him in the pages—amounting to a multi-paged free campaign ad. Former presidential hopeful Kamala Harris's cover reads, "Her Case," and says she "fights for a path forward." Congresswoman

Alexandria Ocasio-Cortez is labeled "The Phenom" beside her stoic portrait. Of course, President Obama was always depicted as a brave, optimistic leader.

In contrast, President Trump has been portrayed as a self-obsessed king, a melting face, a figure drowning in disarray, a man screeching with his hair on fire, and a head on the end of three giant wrecking balls. One of *Time*'s most recognizable covers features a misleading photo of a two-year old Honduran child looking up at a smug Trump in tears, with the headline "Welcome to America." The child was believed to have been caught up in the Trump administration's border security policy and snatched from her parents by a U.S. Border Patrol agent, but it turned out she was never separated from her parents and the media used the image to spread their anti-Trump narrative. When exposed for their deception, *Time*'s editors pulled the "factually accurate but morally true" card and stood by it. Pause. Did you catch that? When caught manipulating a picture and creating a false scenario, they respond by saying that while it's technically not true, it's "morally true."

It was truly one of the most nefarious examples of the media propagating a false narrative.

Derek Hunter writes:

Until journalists fully remove their masks, it's important to know what you're seeing is what they want you to see— stories they deem newsworthy, presented in a way most favorable to their sensitivities. Media bias is more than just how a story is reported, it's which stories are reported. The power to ignore, to pick and choose, is the most pernicious power journalists have, and they exercise it regularly.

This framing is nothing if not intentional. Mark Levin writes in his book *Unfreedom of the Press*:

George Mason professor Tim Groseclose, formerly of the University of California, Los Angeles, developed an "objective, social-scientific method" in which he calculates how the progressive political views of journalists and media outlets distort the natural views of Americans. It "prevents us from seeing the world as it actually is. Instead, we see only a distorted version of it. It is as if we see the world through a glass—a glass that magnifies the facts that liberals want us to see and shrinks the facts that conservatives want us to see. The metaphoric glass affects not just what we see, but how we think. That is, media bias really does make us more liberal. Perhaps worst of all, media bias feeds on itself. That is, the bias makes us more liberal, which makes us less able to detect the bias, which allows the media to get away with more bias, which makes us even more liberal, and so on."

It is not just the stories, though. It's also the headlines. It's been said that a headline is worth a thousand words. In today's digital age, editors know that most people won't even read beyond a headline. Some reports show that most people don't read a full article before they share it on social media. This makes headlines all the more important. It should mean the media has a greater responsibility—an obligation—not to mislead the public with clickbait, but unfortunately the opposite is true. I believe that many in the media will purposely misconstrue facts in rage-baiting headlines in hopes that people won't actually read the full story.

Dr. Deborah Birx, the White House Coronavirus Task Force response coordinator, explained it this way: "I think the media is very slicey and dicey about how they put sentences together in order to create headlines. We know for millennials in other studies that some people may only read the headlines. And if there's not a graphic, they're not going to look any further than that," she said when asked about the media's coverage of the coronavirus outbreak on *Watters' World* on Fox News Channel.

"I think we have to be responsible about our headlines. I think often, the reporting may be accurate in paragraph three, four, and five. But I'm not sure how many people actually get to paragraph three, four, and five," she continued. "And I think the responsibility that the press has is to really ensure that the headlines reflect the science and data that is in their piece itself."

In June 2020, the *Washington Post* ran a story with the headline "Trump keeps claiming that the most dangerous cities in America run by Democrats. They aren't." Pretty straightforward, right? President Trump made a claim and the headline makes it clear he was wrong. The problem is that Trump was right. The cities with the highest crime rates are currently—and mostly have been for a while—run by Democrats. Reading only the headline paints a very distorted view of reality.

In August 2019, the *New York Times* published a factual headline for their lead story about shootings in Dayton, Ohio, and El Paso, Texas, reading, "Trump urges unity vs. racism." It perfectly encapsulated what President Trump expressed in his remarks the day prior to the story. Following backlash from prominent Democrats like Representative Alexandria Ocasio-Cortez and Senator Cory Booker, the *Times* changed the headline to something more in line with the left's talking points: "Assailing hate but not guns."

As former Arkansas governor Mike Huckabee put it, "That's not reporting; it's political lobbying. The fact that the editors of *The New York Times* were willing to rewrite the headline in response to the manufactured outrage of high-profile Democrats should lay to rest any doubts about the extent of liberal bias in the mainstream media. Legacy outlets such as *The New York Times* play both defense and offense for the Democratic Party. As a result, they've given up their role as journalists and become little more than extensions of the Democratic National Committee. They are practically indistinguishable from Party press officials."

Last year, we saw the same thing with a *Politico* headline that, following backlash from the left, changed from "Senate passes USMCA in major win for Trump" to "Senate passes USMCA, but much work remains." How dare they almost mislead the public with an accurate headline that makes Trump look good!

The *Daily Caller* pointed out another noteworthy headline change, this one from CNN over a story regarding financial aid during the coronavirus pandemic. An April 9, 2020, story published at 10:36 a.m. was headlined, "Democrats Block GOP-Led Funding Boost for Small Business Aid Program." Because it appeared critical of Senate Democrats, it was edited within an hour to read, "Senate at Stalemate Over More COVID-19 Aid After Republicans and Democrats Block Competing Proposals." Seriously? They're not even trying to hide it anymore.

Consider this other cringeworthy headline CNN crafted as news broke that Iranian general Qassem Soleimani was killed by the United States in January 2020: "Trump dined on ice cream as news of the airstrike broke." Talk about a scoop. First of all, who cares what the president is eating? Reading only that headline—which does not even attempt to give any context—makes the reader assume that President Trump is either clueless or inattentive, which is clearly the goal when considering they could have written about how American lives were saved because of the president's bold actions.

Back in the summer of 2017, CNN devoted significant airtime to *Time* magazine's report that President Trump was served two scoops of ice cream during a dinner with journalists, while one of their banners on the screen called the extra scoop an "executive privilege." As Fox News media reporter Brian Flood pointed out, "Ice cream isn't the only food that CNN uses as an attempt to shame the president," noting that in 2016, the network criticized Trump's Diet Coke intake, literally lining up cans of the beverage on Brooke Baldwin's anchor desk to demonstrate the amount of soda the president reportedly consumes. Meanwhile, CNN's Jeanne Moos broke some truly critical news during a segment pointing out that "Trump was possibly served a different salad dressing than his guests and that he sometimes eats fast food." A different salad dressing? Fast food? The horror!

On Thanksgiving Day 2019, *Newsweek* reporter Jessica Kwong posted a story with a headline that read "How Trump is spending his Thanksgiving? Tweeting, Golfing and more." First of all, the president is free to spend Thanksgiving however he wants. So not only is the basis of this "story" completely bogus, but Kwong was entirely wrong: the president was actually in Afghanistan dining with U.S. service members.

One *Washington Post* headline characterized the Islamic State leader who was killed in a U.S. raid as an austere religious scholar in this headline: "Al-Baghdadi austere religious scholar at helm of Islamic State, dies at 48." Further, consider this *Washington Post* obituary headline for a terrorist Iranian general: "Gen.

Qasem Soleimani, Master of Iran's Intrigue and Force, Dies at 62". Compare that to the obituary headline the *Times* posted just six hours later for former NFL coach Sam Wyche: "Sam Wyche, who was the last coach to lead the Cincinnati Bengals to the Super Bowl, but who was later fined by the National Football League for barring a female reporter from the team's locker room, has died." Just reading the headlines, who wouldn't necessarily know who the real bad guy was?

NBC News provided live coverage of terrorist general Qassem Soleimani's burial and urged viewers to "watch live coverage as Gen. Qassem Soleimani is buried in his hometown of Kerman, Iran." Promoting the burial of a ruthless terrorist who killed more than six hundred Americans was apparently more important than covering the burials of any of the U.S. troops he killed. CNBC framed his killing as America taking out "the world's No. 1 bad guy." By many estimations, this is a fairly accurate description. Backlash ensued from the far left and CNBC caved. They offered a "clarification" and changed the phrasing to "America just took out a man many considered the world's No. 1 bad guy." Days later, MSNBC aired Iranian propaganda, claiming that nearly thirty Americans had been killed in Iranian-led missile attacks on American troops, while NBC's Tehran bureau chief shared a video on Twitter that he claimed revealed the explosive footage from the attack. It was actually a video of a drone attack on Saudi Arabian oil refineries from a year earlier.

Beyond the headlines, the media routinely profile people they deem to be "good," those who support left-wing causes like the former head of Planned Parenthood Cecile Richards, and demonize people who diverge from their agenda like Vice President Mike Pence and Congressman Dan Crenshaw, a former Navy SEAL who had lost an eye on the battlefields of Afghanistan. We all remember when *Young Turks* commentator Hasan Piker described Crenshaw as a "Brave . . . Soldier F***ed His Eye Hole" and the *Saturday Night Live* cast member Pete Davidson said of him, "You might be surprised to hear that he's a congressional candidate from Texas and not a hitman in a porno. I'm sorry I know he lost his eye in war . . . or whatever." Everything in me wanted Crenshaw to call him out for not recognizing the service to our nation that had taken his eye.

In his bestselling book, *Fortitude*, Crenshaw writes extensively about outrage culture and his *SNL* experience and his response to Davidson. "Outrage culture has contorted our ability to seek redemption and recover from failure, which in turn has contorted our sense of shame. Not only do we feel no shame for being outraged, but that same outrage incentivizes a lack of shame for just about anything—lies, dubious news reporting, scandals, even simple cases of clumsy commentary. . . . It would have been easy to call for Pete Davidson to be fired after his infamous joke about my appearance in 2018.

"One of the reasons I didn't demand an apology was that everyone deserves some space to seek redemption and forgiveness. . . . Maybe, just maybe I didn't have to act offended (I wasn't) and demand that he atone for his transgressions."

Months later, when Davidson had fallen into a bad place mentally after his relationship with pop star Ariana Grande ended, Crenshaw reached out to him to make sure he was okay. Through all of this, though, the media gave Davidson a pass. Mocking the service that had cost Crenshaw a good part of his vision was not an issue because Davidson and *SNL* are champions of the left and antagonists of anyone on the right especially anyone who supports President Trump. Interestingly, Representative Crenshaw notes in his book that when Shane Gillis, a young comedian, was announced as a new *SNL* cast member, recordings surfaced of him using racial slurs on a podcast during a comedy routine. *SNL* quickly terminated him. Davidson was spared, Gillis was not. As an aside, after Pete Davidson apologized for his jokes about Crenshaw, he took back his apology months later . . . likely in obedience to the mob that didn't approve of their friendly, civil relationship.

Throughout the entire ordeal it was Crenshaw who took the high road. I have learned a lot about forgiveness, humility, and humor from Dan Crenshaw. He is a true patriot and a leader on the battlefield, in Washington, and for our country. We need more people like him.

Clearly, the media's framing game is not subtle, but you don't have to take my word for it. A *New York Times* staff meeting transcript that was leaked in August 2020 literally laid out their Trump coverage agenda shifting from "collusion" to "race" and "division." Dean Baquet, the *Times* executive editor, conducted the meeting in front of a newsroom in disarray after the Democrats came up short with their Russia witch hunt, noting that, "We built our newsroom to cover one story, and we did it truly well. Now we have to regroup, and shift resources and emphasis to take on a different story." As Baquet himself admitted, the *Times* would be deliberately emphasizing Trump's "racism" as the main thrust of the newspaper's coverage "went from being a story about whether the Trump campaign had colluded with Russia and obstruction of justice to being a more head-on story about the president's character."

The media's framing is also evident in their obsession with identity politics. Reporters routinely ignore, mock, and portray conservative women as weak-minded and self-hating—all while those same reporters claim to be the champions of women's rights.

Time's Women of the Year award, for instance, allowed just three conservatives over the past one hundred years—former British prime minister Margaret Thatcher, Congresswoman Margaret Chase Smith, and Supreme Court justice Sandra Day O'Connor. *Glamour*'s Women of the Year honored eleven Democrats and zero Republicans. Michelle Obama and Hillary Clinton were on several *Vogue* covers while Barbara Bush and Melania Trump had none.

The White House Correspondents Association Annual Dinner was used as a platform to mock Sarah Huckabee Sanders's appearance, and comedians have called Kellyanne Conway "Satan's trophy wife." One *Washington Post* headline read: "Melania Trump's Christmas decorations are lovely, but that coat looks ridiculous." So much for women's empowerment.

The media's obsession with identity politics corners them and leaves them scrambling for excuses when the results don't turn out their way. It was easy for CNN senior political reporter Nia-Malika Henderson to claim conservatives attack Ocasio-Cortez because she is a "charismatic" Latina, or for CNN's Don Lemon to claim on the air that "the biggest terror threat in this country is white men." But pushing identity-driven narratives isn't so easy when inconvenient facts contradict them. For instance, *Politico* reported "the next debate stage will be the smallest, whitest one yet" when all of the nonwhite candidates drop out of the 2020 Democrat primary race. Liberals constantly lament how the Republican Party is racist yet black Americans chose Biden over black candidates like Kamala Harris and Cory Booker. This is the constant dilemma they find themselves in but routinely ignore. It's why in response to reports that black support for Trump is rising, CNN commentator (and self-defined "never-Trumper") Ana Navarro tweeted, "Zero chance this is accurate. Zero. The poll must have only been conducted in the homes of Ben Carson, Kanye, that sheriff guy with the hat and those two Cubic Zirconia & Polyester-Spandex ladies."

The coronavirus pandemic pulled off the masks of many left-wing journalists and advocates in a way that had never been done before. CNN seemed to grasp at anything to keep the focus off Trump's effective response, even writing an article titled, "Coronavirus task force another example of Trump administration's lack of diversity." Of course, they would never dedicate an entire article to the lack of racial diversity within any left-leaning organization. Further, I would love to know why this matters in the wake of a worldwide pandemic.

Politico found its own unique way to deflect from any coverage that could be deemed positive to the Trump administration. In an April 2020 report, Vice President Mike Pence was said to have "looked" uncomfortable at the White House coronavirus task force briefing. A few weeks prior the outlet said White House health advisor Dr. Anthony Fauci looked the same. How is this reporting? Guessing at how someone is feeling without ever asking, with the goal only being to further a negative narrative.

Trump was "angry," according to CNN, at one of the pressers. What? How do they have any clue what people think and feel? They don't. But in order to further their liberal anti-Trump narrative, they decide. This happened to me during my tenure. Reporters would openly claim to know how I felt or thought. They rarely asked. Complaining was futile. It would only create further controversy and get them to resort back to their unnamed sources that apparently knew what I thought and felt. One way I knew I was truly dealing with "fake news" was that I had learned early on that, unfortunately, I couldn't share my thoughts or feelings with anyone because of the constant leaks and attacks. Unless they had been able to get my wife to spill the beans, I knew it was untrue.

For the media, everything must be about Trump, because their world is about Trump. They must find a way to tie Trump to anything negative while dismissing anything positive. Virus from China ravaging the world? Must be Trump's fault! Record-breaking economic prosperity? That's Obama! It's ridiculous to watch, but as predictable as the sun rising in the east. It doesn't take decades of political and media experience to see how the media "subtly" changes the narrative.

RULE #6: CHANGE THE RULES . . . WHEN POLITICALLY CONVENIENT

In their relentless pursuit of negative coverage of President Trump, the media have called into question the very existence of journalism standards and ethics as we know them, and even more concerning, they've done so with virtual impunity.

I'm old enough to remember when journalists could be trusted to abide by the rules and principles that they themselves put in place, some of which include impartiality, truthfulness, fairness, accuracy, transparency, objectivity, and public accountability. Sadly, journalism today has become little more than a tool of the Democrat establishment—which has a near-universal backing of the media and, in turn, is able to dominate both the airwaves and the headlines. The devastating result of this is that mainstream media outlets and reporters alike have convinced themselves that these traditional journalistic standards and ethics don't apply when it comes to covering President Trump, his administration, and his supporters, because most believe they are justified in changing the rules to push bias narratives, concoct falsehoods, and manipulate facts—all in their grand effort to derail his presidency and take his supporters down with him.

"Fact-checking" has become another hot-button term in the media world in recent years. Whether it's big tech companies establishing verification teams to censor content on their platforms or major media networks enlisting reporters to scrutinize speeches in real time, fact-checking has undoubtedly changed the way we consume information. As Harlan Hill, a Bernie Sanders supporter turned Republican strategist, put it, "Originally designed to help people sift through the lies and half-truths told by politicians and other public figures, fact-checking has evolved into just another manifestation of the media obsession with denigrating Donald Trump."

As I said in the previous chapter, I have never been crazy about the term "fake news." However, if there is ever a case in which the media deserves the title, it is when they weaponize their so-called fact-checking systems to advance their political agenda. In all too many cases, it has become clear that the media employs this term when they so desperately want to accuse the president and his supporters of lying, but can't find any actual falsehoods in their remarks.

Almost all of the major media outlets and publications in America today have adopted some version of a fact-checking system or reporters who claim to be champions of the truth.

Let's start with ABC and its network's chief White House correspondent Jonathan Karl. He has made it his mission to ask whether White House press secretaries will commit to telling the truth, while overlooking his own journalistic malfeasance. Though he won't mention it, everyone in the media sphere remembers when he put his network to shame after basing an "exclusive" bombshell story about Benghazi on false summaries of emails. As a refresher on that disgraceful incident, according to MSNBC, "Karl told the public he had an exclusive report on internal administration emails, which purportedly showed a top White House official pushing to change Benghazi talking points for political reasons. The report was wrong—it mischaracterized the official's communications; it included fabricated quotes; it told viewers Karl had 'obtained' emails that he had not actually seen; and it effectively got the substance of the story backwards."

Even Kevin Smith, the chair of the Society of Professional Journalists' ethics committee, condemned this "inaccurate reporting," saying, "I don't understand how you can claim to have the emails but then backtrack and say you were quoting from summaries. What was the fact when you initially reported—had the emails or summaries? Were you trumping up the story? Did you know the difference and if you did, why did you misrepresent? In the end, I'd say there is a serious credibility issue with ABC's reporting on this issue."

The reason this matters is that Karl is not only the recipient of numerous awards for his reporting, he holds the esteemed positions of ABC's chief Washington correspondent, the White House Correspondents' Association president, and guest anchors the network's top political show, *This Week with George Stephanopoulos.*

Don't take my word for why this is ludicrous. Here's some of what Media Matters included in a roundup of journalism experts who are hardly impressed with him:

Tim McGuire, a journalism professor at Arizona State University and former president of the American Society of News Editors, said, "If the ethical journalist is dedicated to transparency Mr. Karl seems to have failed that standard." Edward Wasserman, dean of the Graduate School of Journalism at the University of California, Berkeley, and a *Miami Herald* columnist, said his reporting is "extremely sloppy" at best, "highly problematic ethically," and that his "failure to acknowledge and correct is even worse," while Tom Fiedler, dean of the Boston University College of Communication and former *Miami Herald* executive editor, said that at times Karl's reporting suffers from inconsistencies and false descriptions of what he reviews. "This caveat is no small thing," he says, noting how such reporting leaves him "vulnerable to being used for political purposes."

Now consider that Karl's critical book, *Front Row at the Trump Show*, is a bestseller. It's beyond ironic considering that Karl, who had been very critical of my tenure due to our frequent clashes and me calling out his grandstanding in the briefing room, in many ways began the "Acostification" (a term coined by White House reporters to describe reporters who grandstand, named after CNN's Jim Acosta) of the briefing room. The world painfully watched as press briefings transitioned from informative events designed to give the American people answers to pressing questions to circus-like performances from the press, full of divisive questions, political point scoring, and cheap shots against the president.

Karl himself was called out for this by the president in the fall of 2019 for such behavior. After ABC's massive Syria explosion video screwup that conveniently reflected poorly on the president—which I expand on later in the chapter—the president called on Karl at a press briefing on the subject. Karl used the opportunity to smugly ask, "Even after all you have seen—ISIS prisoners freed, all the humanitarian disaster—you don't have any regret for giving Erdogan the green light to invade?" to which the president replied, "When you ask a question like that, it's very deceptive, Jon. It's almost as deceptive as you showing all of the bombings taking place in Syria and it turned out the bombing you showed on television took place in Kentucky." He piled on at another briefing a few days later, telling Karl, "You should get your accounts correct, and you shouldn't be showing buildings blowing up in Kentucky and saying it's Syria, because that really is fake news."

Needless to say, if there is any "Trump show" that Karl is "front row" at, it is because he and his media allies laid the blueprint for it.

All that considered, you can imagine I was surprised to see Karl's critical review of my book *The Briefing*. It was featured in the *Wall Street Journal* after the paper sold the publisher on the fact that Karl was "sympathetic" to my experiences with the press without ever revealing him as the person who would be reviewing it. That was a stretch at best. He seemed to be deeply concerned that my book "deploys an army of metaphors" such as "Energizer Bunny" (what an outrage!) and contains a copyediting mistake over a name, which he corrects by saying "in truth." He acts as if a typo is worthy of a virtuous fact-check, meanwhile turning a blind eye to his deliberate mistakes—some of which sent shock waves through the country. It's a classic example of how fact-checkers on the left don't hold themselves to the same standards they hold everyone else.

Karl's stunts, while certainly shameful, are mere microcosms of a much larger problem with the media's "fact-checking" systems and agenda-driven briefings. If you want to see one of the most disgraceful attempts of "fact-checking" from the media at large, look at the way the press handled President Trump's February 2020 State of the Union address. As Trump was concluding his remarks, Democrat House Speaker Nancy Pelosi started fidgeting with her printed copy of his speech with a disgruntled look on her face. To the viewer, they were wondering what was going on until slowly, clearly as if rehearsed, she started ripping up the pages of her copy of the speech. Asked about her stunt by reporters after the speech, Pelosi called it a "manifesto of mistruths" and said she ripped it because "it was the courteous thing to do considering the alternative." No one cared to ask "What lie specifically, Madame Speaker?" or any substantial follow-up question for that matter. And it was simply reported as fact.

Politico, the outlet that always seems to make sure to fact-check any statement that reflects poorly on Democrats, wrote a 1,466-word article about the incident, titled "The Trump-Pelosi feud spirals out of control," and didn't bother to use a single one of those words to verify the alarming statement made by Pelosi. Instead, they found space to laud her stunt of ripping the speech as "the snub seen around the country." The outlet also found room in their article to point out that Trump "did not once mention the House vote to impeach him in December or the ongoing Senate trial." Seriously? Was he supposed to begin the speech by saying "Good to see you all, no hard feelings for impeaching me? Now onto the state of our nation." Interesting that their reporting now consists of information he did not include, especially when (a) Trump doesn't talk about something they want and (b) there would be no reason or obligation for him to talk about something unfavorable to him during a speech meant to uplift the country. The journalist's role is supposed to be to paint the full picture, which in this case would certainly include notable moments like Pelosi's tantrum, any "elephants in the room" such as impeachment, and most important, factual information to back up any major claims—yes, of course, that would include Pelosi's accusations of "lies." *Politico* chose to conveniently overlook that one.

Politico did, however, make sure to publish an extensive and clearly biased "Live Fact-Check" filled with snarky "fact-check" remarks about the president and others praising Obama. "Unemployment is low right now, but the economic recovery started in earnest under President Barack Obama," they "clarified" in response to this statement by Trump, which doesn't even mention Obama:

"And my fellow citizens, three years ago, we launched the great American comeback. Tonight I stand before you to share the incredible results. Jobs are booming. Incomes are soaring. Poverty is plummeting. Crime is falling. Confidence is surging. And our country is thriving and highly respected again. America's enemies are on the run. America's fortunes are on the rise. America's future is blazing bright. The years of economic decay are over."

Fox News points out that *Politico*'s State of the Union "fact-checking" was just as bad the year prior. When writing about people who cross the border illegally, the outlet was "slammed on social media for declaring that Trump's claim that 'one in three women is sexually assaulted on the long journey north' to America was only partly true—because it's actually 31 percent." *Politico*'s GIF of the fact-check was quickly "ratioed," getting way more negative comments than retweets or likes. Activist Obianuju Ekeocha responded with a woman using a magnifying glass captioned, "Politico fact checkers desperately looking to find the difference between 31% and 1 in 3."

Despite a CBS News poll that showed 97 percent of Republicans and 82 percent of independents approved of Trump's 2020 State of the Union address, the media would have you think it was an abomination. Consider the media analysis from *Politico*'s playbook. It's so misguided and negative. They chose to feature *Guardian* columnist John Harris's summary of the State of the Union address, which read, "IT WAS EVERY REASON why Democrats can hardly stand to be in the same room as the man" and "IT'S TOO HARD TO LIST THE MOMENTS THAT REPULSED DEMOCRATS, but here's a small list of what we saw them sneer at from inside the chamber."

CNN called the State of the Union speech "disturbing, insecure, angry." And let's not forget that CNN chief media correspondent Brian Stelter showered Pelosi with praise after she tore up President Trump's speech, calling the move an "effective" way to steal the spotlight from the president. "Effective"? Seriously? In any other setting, this would be labeled rude. It echoed the network's YouTube video for the 2018 SOTU address, which was titled "Nancy Pelosi's clapback steals Trump's show" and described Pelosi as "the queen of condescending applause." The media celebrated, even gushed over the Democrats' refusal to clap for Trump's successes during both speeches.

Apparently reporting on who clapped and what manner they did it is more important than covering the substance of one of the most important speeches on the planet Earth.

That's not all we can gather from the State of the Union. The media went nuts over Trump awarding the Presidential Medal of Freedom to conservative radio host Rush Limbaugh during his speech. CNN's Jim Acosta said Limbaugh has a "history" of disparaging African-Americans, but neglected to provide any examples when challenged by Rush's producer of thirty years, James Golden, who goes by Bo Snerdley on set and is African-American himself. The *New Yorker* insisted that honoring Limbaugh was "celebrating racial division" and was appalled to see Limbaugh's name alongside the likes of Nelson Mandela, Martin Luther King Jr., Václav Havel,

Rosa Parks, and John Lewis. Likewise, CNN's Maegan Vazquez labeled the radio host "a very different Medal of Freedom" compared to the "elite group" that has received the honor in the past. Missing from their complaints was any mention of Hollywood liberals such as Ellen DeGeneres, Tom Hanks, Oprah Winfrey, or Robert De Niro, who have all received the honor.

To be clear, I don't have any problem with any of these people being presented the award. I've always believed that elections have consequences. President Obama won and had the right to award and acknowledge anyone he wanted. While it's worth noting that in most cases these accomplished people are also left-leaning, it is one of the spoils of victory. It was his right as president. These are the kind of things that happen over the course of elections. That being said, that standard seemed to shift when Trump was elected—hence why the outrage ensued.

Shortly after the State of the Union, after Trump was acquitted from the articles of impeachment in the Senate, CNN published an analysis equating the trial to the Jim Crow South. The headline was, "There's a painful Black History Month lesson in Trump's acquittal" and compared Republicans to white southern mobs. That's not a joke. How offensive that we are now equating a horrible time in our nation's history to Republicans today.

Sometimes the media's fact-checking, or lack thereof, is more subtle.

During the 2016 election, for instance, candidate Trump had been asked about whether or not he would accept the outcome of the vote. When California Democrat and House Intelligence Committee chairman Adam Schiff weighed in about the same subject regarding the 2020 election, by stating, "We cannot trust the ballot box," there was hardly a peep from the media. There is not a shred of evidence that the election in 2016 was tampered with in any way, shape, manner, or form by Russia, so where was the outrage from the media? He was questioning the integrity of our core institution—that should certainly raise some alarm from those in the media. Again in June 2020, another Democrat, this time presumptive presidential nominee Joe Biden, was asked about election results during an interview with comedian Trevor Noah. Biden said his "single greatest fear" is that President Trump will try to steal the election, adding that he was confident the military would have to step in and enforce the results should he win and Trump refuse to leave the White House. Despite this claim having no merits and dangerous implications—crickets from the honorable fact-checkers in the media. The mainstream media had melted down during the 2016 cycle that Trump would not categorically state he had faith in the election outcome. Now, leading Democrats go much further and it's treated as a legitimate concern.

Lawrence O'Donnell, the host of *The Last Word* on MSNBC's prime-time lineup, took it a step further, telling the public that "there will be no one defending [Trump]" on his network. "Because we don't bring on liars," he added during a January 2020 podcast with former senator Al Franken. The implication is that anyone who dares to defend Trump is automatically a liar, and MSNBC will never allow a proper response to attacks on the president. So to all the millions of the Trump voters out there, know that MSNBC thinks you are all liars.

That mindset from a major media network should outrage every American citizen who values a fair and free press. But then again, this is the network that shamelessly threw the sacred journalistic practice of independent verification out the window when it aired an unverified, baseless claim from Iranian state TV about a death toll of thirty U.S. soldiers, which was echoed by NBC News Tehran bureau chief Ali Arouzi when he shared the propaganda video with his national audience. It showed not only a failure to verify dangerous claims, but also a complete lack of respect for families of those deployed. But hey, anything to make President Trump look bad.

Typically, when journalists mess up, which is only human, they apologize and correct the record. This is another sacred rule of journalism. I've worked in politics for years and have a long list of my own typos or errors that I've made. However, the ability to be corrected is a sacred journalistic standard and one that has allowed the industry to maintain the trust of the public for generations. That's not necessarily the case today.

One of the more egregious instances came from none other than ABC in October 2019, when the network issued no on-air corrections for its massive Syria-Kentucky video mix-up after President Trump made the decision to withdraw troops in Syria. Here's why this mattered: The *Washington Examiner* reported that the network's flagship evening news program, *World News Tonight,* "aired footage that anchor Tom Llamas claimed showed the Turkish army bombing Kurdish civilians in northern Syria" but the footage "was actually from a nighttime machine gun demonstration at a gun range in Kentucky." *Good Morning America* aired the same footage the following day, claiming again that it showed the fighting in Syria between the Turks and the Kurds. Though ABC told the *Examiner* in a statement that they took the video down, neither one of the shows issued a correction on-air for what appeared to be a massive, glaring blunder for one of America's biggest and most powerful television networks. The *Examiner* correctly wrote that "the programs responsible for circulating the false information are responsible also for circulating corrections." Indeed, there is never a good reason not to give as much air time to the correction as you did the mistake.

I would be remiss if I didn't include the disgraceful stunt pulled by CNN anchor Don Lemon, who sparked outrage earlier in the year when he along with two of his guests mocked Trump supporters on-air, trading quips in southern accents and pretending to be Trump supporters slamming "elitists with your geography and your maps and your spelling." No apology, just deflection. He claimed that he wasn't mocking Trump's supporters, he was merely laughing at a joke. Wajahat Ali, a *New York Times* and CNN contributor who was featured in the segment, tweeted that his friends were "concerned about my safety" after the president shared the clip. "I refuse to be intimidated and bullied by bad-faith actors who cry fake victimhood, whining about a harmless, silly 30-second clip while endorsing Trump, a cruel vulgarian who debases everyone," he wrote.

The media's response? Move on. Nothing to see here. No apology needed, to which Ivanka Trump responded, "You consistently make fun of half the country and then complain that it is divided," while RNC chairwoman Ronna McDaniel put it this way: "If a Fox News host sneezes wrong, the liberal media makes sure everyone hears about it for days. CNN mocked half the country, no one apologized, and barely a peep from the MSM. Funny how selective the liberal outrage machine is with their outrage, isn't it?" Of course, the left didn't like these small doses of reality.

You would think the media would be especially keen to admit fault and correct their mistakes at a time when public trust in their institution is at an all-time low, but they're not. It goes to show that advancing their agenda is the be-all and end-all.

I find no pleasure in bashing the media. I think it's a national travesty that we as Americans can no longer rely on such a sacred American institution to get our information. However, I do find it incredibly important that we know how to not only identify but also how to push back on bad journalism. My hope is that all of the examples I laid out in this chapter as well as the last serve as a sobering reminder that the media value partisan attacks on President Trump and on freedom-loving Americans more than their responsibility to report the truth.

CHAPTER SIX

★ ★ ★ ★ ★ ★ ★

CORPORATE ACTIVISM

President Trump's economic policies over the past four years are largely responsible for igniting the economic boom that is raising the quality of life and standards of living for Americans of all walks of life.

A Gallup survey released in January 2020 shows just that. Economic confidence is now at the highest point in two decades. Wages rose by 3 percent last year alone—which is about 50 percent faster than average under the Obama administration. Wages for blue-collar workers rose even more rapidly while wages for the lowest 10 percent of Americans grew twice as fast.

As Alfredo Ortiz, president and chief executive of the Job Creators Network, put it in an article for the *Hill*: "Job opportunities are drawing people off the sidelines and into the labor force. Prime age labor force participation has risen by over two million people under Trump. Our economic growth is the fastest in the developed world, and the stock market continues its incredible run, up more than 50 percent since Trump was elected. The smart policies that help small businesses, which create a majority of new jobs, are driving this economic boom. The Trump tax cuts have provided small businesses with a 20 percent tax deduction, allowing them to keep more of their hard earned funds to hire and raise wages. No wonder 80 percent of small business owners say the Trump tax cuts have been good for the economy."

Even during the height of the coronavirus pandemic, confidence in our economy remained remarkably high. Investors trusted Trump's strong economic fundamentals and his ability to get the country back to normal. The May 2020 jobs report, much to the chagrin of the naysayers on the left who promised economic doom and gloom, "gave us the first indication that the post-pandemic rebound would be something special, revealing that employers had created a record-shattering 2.5 million jobs in a single month, beating economists' expectations for a loss of around 9 million jobs," according to former chief executive officer of CKE Restaurants Andy Puzder. He added that 52.6 percent of companies said their businesses are growing, up from 43.1 percent the month before, marking the best score since April 2019 and crushing economists' expectations. "Not wanting to miss out on all the positivity, the stock markets—which are forward-looking—closed up nearly 20 percent for the quarter, their best quarterly percentage increase since 1998."

I can't think of another president who could sustain such incredible economic enthusiasm in the midst of a global crisis. You would think corporations would be forever indebted to him for effectively guiding them through the worrisome time. Well, at least one was.

In July 2020, Goya Foods faced a massive backlash after its CEO, Robert Unanue, praised Trump during an event at the White House, saying, "We're all truly blessed . . . to have a leader like President Trump, who is a builder." Unanue has previously met with President and Mrs. Obama during his Administration but the mere fact he met with Trump was seen as a massive betrayal. During a massive pandemic and time of economic concern, why wouldn't the CEO of a company meet with the president, regardless of which party they belong to? To not meet with President Trump would be the bigger issue.

But as is the case with Hollywood and the media, it's all politics all the time.

"More and more the Radical Left is using Commerce to hurt their 'Enemy,'" President Trump tweeted in response to the backlash the Home Depot faced in July 2019 following news that its cofounder, Bernie Marcus, expressed support for the president and donated to his presidential run.

Calls to boycott the massive retail chain took off on social media after Marcus told the *Atlanta Journal-Constitution* that he plans to support Trump's bid for another term. "While Trump 'sucks' at communication," Marcus said, "the President deserves praise for boosting U.S. jobs, confronting China on trade and taking action against Iranian and North Korean aggression."

Marcus knows better than most that honest, hardworking Americans have suffered at the hands of foreign countries for far too long. With President Trump spearheading a new era in trade that delivers for American businesses of all stripes and gives working Americans a voice in the room, you can't blame him for his enthusiastic support of the president. He was standing up for the Home Depot workforces' interest when supporting the economic renaissance that has brought record gains to the stock markets and brought back the American dream for so many of them.

Never mind that the ninety-year-old cofounder hadn't worked for the Home Depot since 2002, or that he also told the *AJC* in the same interview that he plans to donate around 90 percent of his fortune to veterans with disabilities, children with autism, and funding for medical research; the left went after him and the company anyway. "If you plan on buying a hammer, wood, or ANY home improvement items from Home Depot, you may as well send donations DIRECTLY to Trump's 2020 campaign," read one viral tweet under the hashtag #BoycottHomeDepot by Majid M. Padellan, author of the anti-Trump book *The Liddle' est President*.

President Trump described Marcus as a "truly great, patriotic & charitable man" who is "coming under attack by the Radical Left Democrats with one of their often-used weapons."

"They put out the name of a store, brand, or company and ask their so-called followers not to do business there. They don't care who gets hurt, but also don't understand that two can play that game!" he continued.

He didn't stop there. He urged conservatives to fight back against militant leftists who engage in these intimidation campaigns, saying, "These people are vicious and totally crazed, but remember, there are far more great people ('Deplorables') in this country, than bad. Do to them what they do to you. Fight for Bernie Marcus and Home Depot!"

After decades of watching the right response to the left's unwarranted boycotts with a collective sigh, this was a breath of fresh air. The president was right to call out the left for its corporate bullying tactics, but more important, he was spot-on about the dangerous dynamic that is playing out in corporate culture today. Most people don't realize just how dangerous it is, and that is, in part, because there is a fundamental misunderstanding of the role corporations are supposed to play in our free society and the role they think they ought to play.

There is a widespread belief that corporate America is monolith-ically conservative when, in fact, it leans more leftward today than ever before. Whether corporate titans had an actual sudden change of heart or are just rolling over to the relentless pressure of polit-ical correctness, many have transitioned from valuing capitalism and profit to activism and protests. Corporations have turned from focusing on selling products and services to organizations that pro-mote a set of values, and those values only seem to go one way.

There are times when corporations cave to the left, but there are times when corporations start it.

Enter: Gillette. Last year, the shaving company launched an ad that amassed billions of views in its attempt to tackle "toxic mascu-linity." Men were depicted as violent misogynists and universal idi-ots and implored to "be better." It was nothing more than another strike in the left's war on masculine traits. No one expected to get a progressive gender lesson from their favorite razor company, but Gillette's corporate leaders took it upon themselves to be a part of a political conversation around gender roles. Bad behavior, espe-cially toward women, should not be tolerated, but to try to paint all men with a bad brush is hardly a way to achieve a better outcome.

Perhaps the company leaders who consistently take the cake for woke virtue-signaling are ice cream moguls Ben & Jerry, who introduced a new ice cream flavor, "Pecan Resist," with a tweet stat-ing that the company supports those "who are fighting President Trump's regressive agenda." Their website notes, "There's more to this ice cream than what meets the eye: the derailment of President Trump's MAGA train."

So. Much. Bravery. As if alienating half of the country over ice cream wasn't bad enough, the company took to Instagram and Twitter to call for the defunding of police departments in June

2020. The post depicts a large bowl of ice cream being scooped out by a giant spoon labeled "DEFUND the POLICE"—being redistributed to smaller bowls that represent various welfare programs such as "affordable housing."

As a conservative, I don't care what people who run businesses do in their personal lives or what political opinions they hold. I do find it interesting, however, that businesses have chosen to promote one way of life over another, regardless of whether or not that way of life represents the majority of consumers. When I was growing up, companies were judged by the quality of their product or service, but today it seems like they would rather be judged by the causes they support and policy positions they take.

In an article on Pride Month for *Vox Media*, Senior Culture Reporter Alex Abad-Santos asked, "What exactly are these stores and brands supporting? More importantly, what happens to the money we spend in these stores? Does brand support for LGBTQ issues have any real impact, or is it just, well, branding?" It's certainly a question worth exploring.

"Take, for example, Adidas, which has a special section of its site called the 'pride pack' selling rainbow merchandise to honor Pride Month," he remarked. "But it's also one of the major sponsors for this year's World Cup, which takes place in Russia, a country with anti-LGBTQ laws that make it unsafe for fans and athletes. That contradiction throws into sharp relief the emptiness that can lie at the center of corporate gestures of 'support' for the LGBTQ community.

"Los Angeles Pride selling more tickets than it had space for is just one example," he added. "The rainbow-festooned H&M having a manufacturing plant in China, a country with a history of anti-LGBTQ legislation, is another."

He notes that perhaps the most pertinent example is Gilead sponsoring New York City Pride. Gilead is a pharmaceutical company that makes a pill that reduces the risk of HIV by over 90 percent, but charges thousands of dollars for it, Abad-Santos explains. "Gilead publicly supports LGBTQ rights at one of the biggest LGBTQ celebrations of the year, but in practice, it has not adequately served LGBTQ people who run the highest risk of contracting AIDS, a disease its drug could help prevent."

These examples of blatant hypocrisy beg the question: What is the month-long Pride branding really about? Well, Abad-Santos concludes that "companies who are promoting LGBTQ Pride—and ostensibly cashing in on Pride merchandise or retail—aren't doing much for the LGBTQ community beyond contributing to this vague notion of 'awareness.'"

In addition to looking "woke" on the outside without actually helping the causes they claim to care about, it's safe to assume these companies are somewhat disingenuous.

Not all corporations start with a political agenda like these ones do, but many are willing to instinctively follow the path and do whatever it takes to stay in good graces with the left.

I experienced this firsthand last year during a Pawtucket Red Sox game. The Paw Sox are the triple-A minor-league team for the Red Sox located in Pawtucket, Rhode Island. As I mentioned in the previous chapters, I'm on the board of the Independence Fund, a charity that works with catastrophically wounded veterans. Part of our outreach includes presenting wheelchairs to wounded veterans during events across the country. While in Rhode Island, the Independence Fund teamed up with the Pawtucket Red Sox to give an area veteran who had mobility issues an all-terrain wheelchair and the group asked me to present it at a game in addition to throwing out the first pitch alongside the veteran.

When I arrived with my family, we noticed a group of LBGTQ activists who were there to celebrate Pride Night at the stadium. The Pride group was situated in the outfield and was recognized by the announcer. Then the veteran and I took to the pitcher's mound to throw the first pitch. Everything was good. I represented our cause; they represented theirs. We both coexisted, and everyone seemed happy.

That night, hours after the game had ended, the *Boston Globe* published a story by correspondent Sofia Saric titled, "Sean Spicer throws first pitch at PawSox's Pride Night, and team faces backlash," citing people on Twitter who took offense to the game. It wasn't people who were in attendance at the game who took offense—it wasn't even the LGBTQ Pride group that was there. I kid you not, just a few paragraphs in, the story quoted a tweet that didn't have a single retweet, written by a man who was not at the game, stating, "They paired it with a veterans thing to make it harder to criticize, too, it's gross." This is what journalists do when they want to express their own opinion but can't outright say it. They'll scan social media or pick out a random person from a crowd who shares their view, then report their opinion as hard-hitting journalism in efforts to frame their story however they want. Case in point, the *Globe* journalist took it upon herself to find a handful of random people online who were offended and made them the focal point of the story.

And of course, she found room in her short write-up to claim, "The Trump administration has been heavily criticized for attempting to dismantle LGBTQ rights," despite the fact that I no longer worked in the White House, that no one at the game took issue with my attendance, and not to mention that the Trump administration is the first in history to launch a global campaign to decriminalize homosexuality. Don't bet on the media to tell you the truth about that, though. Even Richard Grenell, who is the former U.S. Ambassador to Germany and is openly gay, insists that Trump's initiatives to help the gay community are "wildly supported by both parties." Don't bet on the media to tell you the truth about that, though.

But I digress. A week later, the Pawtucket Red Sox president Charles Steinberg released an open letter explaining why I had been invited to the game. He wrote: "We did not foresee the confluence of these events, which has wounded many of our friends and fans in the LGBTQ+ community, and the many allies. We are terribly sorry, and we seek to make amends."

"Wounded many of our friends"? It was obvious what was really at play here. The issue was that I worked for President Trump, not that I ever said anything hostile to the LGBTQ community. A veteran who has served our nation had just received a $16,000 wheelchair to support his mobility, yet that received scant coverage.

At this point, the *Boston Globe* now had two veterans in its readership (the one at the PawSox and one a couple of weeks earlier) who received chairs, yet the *Boston Globe* couldn't be less interested in covering their service. Instead, they found the time to cover this nonstory about me and a tiny Twitter microaggression. The *Globe*'s story gained traction, and most media reports about it published after that centered on the "outrage" and the team's apology instead of the deserving American heroes.

Given the context of the whole story, it says a lot about the Pawtucket Red Sox that a week later they caved and issued an apology. What should have been an opportunity for Americans to come together and honor a veteran was quickly turned into a divisive display of corporate activism that ended with cancellation. It is unfortunate that so many companies and organizations choose to back down in situations like this, especially when they know they weren't at fault.

This is how the process typically plays out. A loud minority of leftists will protest something that threatens their agenda. The media, whose personal beliefs are often echoed by the protesters, will cover boycotts and protests as if they're actually news instead of political activism. The corporation that's being protested, afraid of potential backlash, will go into damage control mode and cave to the unpredictable vocal left. The right will respond with a collective eye-roll at best, and the cycle continues.

The left has found tremendous success from this cycle in recent years.

Following the tragic school shooting in Parkland, Florida, in February 2018, the left's agenda quickly escalated from ending school shootings to abolishing the National Rifle Association (NRA) and punishing its members. Gun-control activists organized swaths of boycotts and protests and intimidated dozens of companies into cutting ties with the NRA and anyone affiliated with it.

On February 26, 2018, *USA Today* reported a list of companies that dropped deals with the NRA:

- Enterprise Alamo, Hertz, Avis, Budget, and National all ended discount deals with the NRA within a few weeks.
- Symantec: The cybersecurity company's LifeLock identity theft protection service for businesses and its Norton antivirus software had both offered discounts to NRA members. Those deals are off.

- TrueCar: The online car-buying service is ending its deal for NRA members, who previously saved an average of nearly $3,400 off the retail price of new and used vehicles.
- MetLife: The insurer had offered discounts to NRA members on auto and home policies before axing the deal.
- SimpliSafe: The home security company had offered a special promotion to NRA members, but that ended Friday.
- First National Bank of Omaha: The financial institution cut an NRA-branded Visa credit card.

Let's be clear about this. These were discount and loyalty programs. They had a relationship only because the NRA has a lot of members that they want to tap into. It's basically like being a AAA or AARP member. You get a discount because you belong to a group. These companies are sending a clear message that gun owners are unwelcome customers.

For other retail giants, the consequences of customers exercising their choices are more severe.

On March 22, Citigroup, one of the largest banks in America, tweeted, "Today we announced a new U.S. Commercial Firearms Policy that centers around current firearms sales best practices that will guide those we do business with as a firm," linking to a lengthy post that said it would require all of its clients and business customers to refrain from selling firearms to anyone who hasn't passed a background check or is under the age of twenty-one, and that it would prohibit its customers from selling bump stocks. The *Los Angeles Times* noted on April 10 that the bank announced it "planned to stop lending to manufacturers of assault-style firearms that are sold for non-military use" and that it would stop underwriting securities issued by those gun manufacturers. So essentially, the massive bank banned gun retailers from using their credit card services and alienated a segment of their customer base who did absolutely nothing wrong.

Bank of America followed suit the following month with an assault on its gun-owning customers. The *New York Times* reported that on April 10, the bank announced that it "will stop lending money to gun manufacturers that make military-inspired firearms for civilian use, such as the AR-15-style rifles that have been used in multiple mass shootings."

Interestingly, ABC News' coverage of the boycotts included an article that singled out eight companies that simply hadn't yet announced any action they would be taking against the NRA, writing, "ABC News identified several companies that appeared to have active deals with the NRA but have yet to address the controversy," but most "did not respond to numerous requests for comment." It's not hard to see the implication here: ABC believes these companies ought to respond, so much so that they felt the need to pester them for comment. They're quite literally reporting on things that *didn't* happen in hopes that they do. It is clear, ABC believed those eight companies should have severed ties with the NRA and wanted to make that happen any way they could. In essence, they are creating news.

One of the few companies that did right by them was FedEx. The postal service company put out a statement saying that while they oppose some of the NRA's policy positions, they refuse to change their discount policies because they value their customers for more than just their politics. Imagine that.

These attacks on the NRA seem like child's play compared to the outright assault on some Americans' fundamental rights that we see from some other companies. Following leftist protests and boycotts over the years, for instance, high-profile conservatives have been banned from some of the most prominent financial institutions in America for their beliefs.

In a February 2019 *Wall Street Journal* interview, PayPal CEO Dan Schulman explained who gets booted from the platform and why, noting that it uses the Southern Poverty Law Center—the radical left-wing, anti-Christian organization known for blacklisting conservatives—to help achieve its mission toward "diversity and inclusion." Schulman outlined "the implementation of a political agenda that ultimately restricts ordinary Americans' access to banking services," explained president of the Family Research Council Tony Perkins in a Fox News op-ed.

As a result of this corporate activism, according to *Buzzfeed News*, "PayPal has banned or hobbled the accounts of several prominent people and groups that promote far-right politics. Crowdfunding platforms like GoFundMe, Patreon, and YouCaring have also cut fundraisers for alt-right–associated causes and people."

A corporation will never satiate the mob with simple denunciations of their enemy or endorsements of their positions. They demand total and complete expulsion. In the collective mind of a "cancel culture" mob there is no room for nuance, no room for differing opinions, and no room for compromise.

While I may not agree with what those on the left believe in, we have to remember this is America, a land that extends the same opportunities to all citizens regardless of their status, prestige, or beliefs—as outlandish or crazy as they may be. It's the country that allowed the narcissistic tiger trainer Joe Exotic to run for president in 2016 and again for governor of Oklahoma in 2018, only to become an internet sensation later thanks to Netflix's *Tiger King* series.

The point here is not in any way to defend the offensive comments, beliefs, or actions of anyone but to point out the slippery slope we are sliding down when corporate America starts deciding who to ban.

Whether it's a tiger trainer from Oklahoma or a polished politician from Massachusetts, every citizen has rights enshrined in the Constitution to ensure an equal voice before our government, but what about our corporations? An argument can certainly be made that companies like Google, Facebook, Chase, and PayPal, in many ways, have as much if not more power over our day-to-day lives than the U.S. government. Yet, they are allowed to trample dissenting voices without limit, all at the behest of the most radical among us.

America was founded on the idea that tyranny in any of its forms, be it from a king, corporation, or mob, deserves the unyielding condemnation of a free people. This fundamental American truth has been paid for by the blood of patriots for generations and should not be easily discarded because a few liberal arts majors are mad they saw something on Twitter.

While our forefathers railed against a tyrannical king, they also had the foresight to restrain our own government's power to silence unpopular voices of dissension. However, we have strayed too far from the path our founders set for us. They could have never imagined the power that technology has afforded to many of the corporations weaponized by the left, or how far our government has strayed from its original charge.

Companies like Coinbase, Eventbrite, Mailchimp, Wix, GoFundMe, Uber, and Lyft represent a new dimension of power in American society that can and is being used to tip the scales of political representation. The feckless leadership occupying many of our corporate boardrooms are more concerned with how many retweets they get than upholding the most sacred of American traditions that afforded them the opportunity to sit in that boardroom in the first place.

Another way we see this toxic dynamic play out is with the weaponization of advertisements.

Look no further than Fox News. In March 2018, advertisers for Laura Ingraham's Fox program dropped like flies after she got in a Twitter feud with David Hogg, a survivor of the Parkland Florida school shooting who has become one of the most prominent student voices for gun control. Ingraham, citing an article in the *Daily Wire*, tweeted that David Hogg had complained about university rejections. Hours later, Hogg had called for an advertising boycott, tweeting, "Soooo @IngrahamAngle what are your biggest advertisers . . . Asking for a friend. #BoycottIngramAdverts," he tweeted, then proceeded to post a list of her show's advertisers. That was all it took for companies to obey his demands.

CBS News reported that despite Ingraham apologizing to Hogg, the following fifteen corporations distanced themselves from Ingraham's program days later: Bayer; Ruby Tuesday; Liberty Mutual Insurance; the Atlantis Paradise Island resort; Office Depot; Jenny Craig; Hulu; Nutrish; TripAdvisor; Expedia; Wayfair; Stitch Fix; Nestlé; Johnson & Johnson; Miracle-Ear. Furniture retailer Wayfair said, "The decision of an adult to personally criticize a high school student who has lost his classmates in an unspeakable tragedy is not consistent with our values," while TripAdvisor said, "In our view, these statements focused on a high school student, cross the line of decency."

Those are valid points. I've always believed that kids should be excluded from political punditry. However, it's telling that no major corporations had the same outrage when the left went after Kyle Kashuv, another survivor of the Parkland school shooting who became a nationally prominent gun rights advocate. Fox News reported that because he opposes the majority of his classmates' calls for more restrictive gun laws, "Kashuv said he has received death threats, is bullied at school, has been mistreated by teachers and receives endless criticism on social media—simply for coming out as a conservative." And according to NPR, Harvard University even rescinded his acceptance into the school after discovering that he used racial slurs in texts and Skype conversations when he was sixteen. But adults aren't supposed to criticize kids, right? None of these corporations had a problem with how NBC or CNN treated the Covington Catholics kids, either. It seems that the political affiliation of the kids who are attacked is the only thing that matters.

Tucker Carlson, another Fox News host, faced a similar back-lash last March when progressive media watchdog Media Matters unearthed recordings starting in 2006 of him making inappropriate jokes on shock jock radio program *Bubba the Love Sponge* that many deemed offensive to women. In a statement posted to Twitter, Carlson refused to apologize, saying, "Media Matters caught me saying something naughty on a radio show more than a decade ago. Rather than express the usual ritual contrition, how about this: I'm on television every weeknight live for an hour. If you want to know what I think, you can watch. Anyone who disagrees with my views is welcome to come on and explain why."

It's safe to say the woke left wasn't interested in the opportunity. In a March 11, 2019, article, *Business Insider* reported that at least twenty-seven brands had pulled advertising from *Tucker Carlson Tonight* on Fox News following threats of boycotts over

Carlson's comments. Among the long list of companies were Red Lobster, Samsung, SanDisk, Jaguar, Land Rover, SmileDirectClub, TD Ameritrade, Ancestry.com, and IHOP.

While many conservatives find it cowardly that these companies would pull their advertisements the way they did, it could be argued that they were only looking out for their bottom line. Corporate spin factories might hide behind their fiduciary duty to their shareholders and the fear that advertising on a program with controversial views might turn off customers.

It is hard to imagine a program with more controversial viewpoints than *Real Time with Bill Maher,* yet despite the countless number of comparably outrageous things said by Bill Maher and others on his show, no boycotts have been leveled against Maher. Yes, it's on HBO, which doesn't have ads, but no matter what offensive thing Maher says, there are seldom any calls to cancel him. Beyond that, the left, and some on the right, flock to appear on his show over and over again, seemingly approving of Maher and his prior outrageous statements. When people on the right are deemed to have said something inappropriate, they don't receive nearly the same treatment as Maher. The double standard is palpable.

Caving to the #grabyourwallet campaign—a national boycott aimed at the Trump family and anyone in corporate America who actively supports the president—Burlington Coat Factory, Nordstrom, Macy's, Bed, Bath & Beyond, Neiman Marcus, Marshall's, T.J. Maxx, and Belk have all pulled Ivanka Trump's line from their stores or websites. *USA Today* reported that "the boycott effort targets more than 60 firms affiliated with the Trump family or sell products under the Trump brand name." Just being President Trump's daughter landed Ivanka the ultimate scarlet letter from the left. So much for female empowerment in the workplace. Imagine if the tables were turned and this were Chelsea Clinton instead of Ivanka . . . the left would have undoubtedly gone nuts.

Ironically, it was Chelsea who stepped up to defend Justice Brett Kavanaugh's daughters when the left went after them. She said, "If you can't make your point about Judge Kavanaugh, whatever it may be, without bullying his kids, it's not worth making." This just might have been the first time I ever agreed with Chelsea on something. If you can't advocate for your agenda without bullying someone's kids, in this case a prominent political figure's daughter, perhaps your agenda needs reevaluating.

While it was disappointing to see all of these companies cave to the angry leftist mob, I can't say I was surprised. For years, companies have accepted the left's critique and kowtowed to their demands. It's no coincidence that corporate activism has ramped up following Donald Trump's 2017 presidential inauguration. The corporate boycott wars are at their core a fight against Donald Trump and the American policies he fights for. Businesses large and small are at risk of being run into economic ruin by the left for merely dissenting from their extremist agenda.

The tyranny of woke capitalism is posing a more significant threat by the day. Corporate activism has shifted from promoting political causes to barring groups of Americans from using necessary platforms and services. The implications this has for the future are devastating.

It's not only businesses that are being put at risk—it's also our constitutional rights. If gun manufacturers are being barred from financial platforms and services today, you can bet gun owners will be the target tomorrow. Likewise, if Ivanka Trump is barred from selling shoes in retail stores because of her political affiliations today, you can bet that her consumers will be the target tomorrow.

Our Bill of Rights will be rendered useless if corporate America refuses to allow all Americans to exercise their fundamental rights and freedoms. Whether it's the corporations bullying the people or people bullying the corporations, it's equally as harmful to society. There's nothing patriotic about a free market that favors half of the country and alienates the other half. Our rights are not rights unless we can exercise them. And the left, through corporate America, wants to prevent conservatives from exercising theirs.

It's worth reflecting upon the fact that the left tends to protest, boycott and ban anyone they don't like or anything they disagree with on the right, but rarely do conservatives use the same tactics. Our principles prevent us from stooping to this level, and for the most part, we don't want politics and protests to corrode every sector of society. But it's important to recognize that because we don't express outrage in the same way, the left sees their tactics as effective. It's open season on conservatives, and they will stop at nothing.

Even if *Dancing with the Stars* caved to the boycotts and rescinded my invitation onto the show, the left would have been less than satisfied. ABC would have had to spend the entire season apologizing to the left just to scratch the surface of redemption. The media framed my participation on the show as some sort of rehabilitation tour to atone for my sins of working for the GOP and President Trump.

Chick-fil-A is an unfortunate case in point for how conservatives waste their time when they attempt to appease those who will never accept them. After decades of serving as a beacon of hope for conservatives by refusing to be bullied out of business by the radical left, they caved and cut ties with the Salvation Army and other conservative charities.

Chick-fil-A is one of the last significant chains that observe blue laws—or laws designed to restrict certain commerce activities on Sundays to observe a day of worship or rest. Chick-fil-A has always been closed on Sundays, keeping with the Christian sabbath. Chick-fil-A founder Truett Cathy once explained, "Closing our business on Sunday, the Lord's Day, is our way of honoring God and showing our loyalty to Him."

So aside from their great food that I've personally enjoyed throughout the years, Chick-fil-A stood their ground on this argument for a long time and represented a beacon of hope for conservatives—until now. And the worst part is they never even had to respond this way in the first place. First of all, they did nothing wrong. They weren't donating to hate groups; they were giving money and resources to groups with long-standing commitments to caring for the needy. Second, people go to Chick-fil-A because it has excellent food and outstanding customer service. The company leadership seemed to have forgotten that and tried to cater to the left by bending over backward instead of staying focused on their mission of simply providing exceptional service and food.

Further, no amount of donations to the radical leftist Southern Poverty Law Center or other LGBTQ organizations, which they are giving to now, will be enough to earn forgiveness or acceptance from the left. Take it from the response of the Gay and Lesbian Alliance Against Defamation (GLAAD), an LGBTQ activist group. Immediately after the food chain announced its decision to halt all donations to the Salvation Army, GLAAD demanded the company do more to change its traditional conservative brand. In a statement to CNN, GLAAD director of campaigns Drew Anderson said, "In addition to refraining from financially supporting anti-LGBTQ organizations, Chick-fil-A still lacks policies to ensure safe workplaces for LGBTQ employees and should unequivocally speak out against the anti-LGBTQ reputation that their brand represents."

Compromise is an unachievable goal. The left will never accept them until they are completely driven to the margins of public life. Conservative commentator and *Daily Wire* podcast host Matt Walsh imagines the conversation between the left and its corporate targets going something like this, as outlined on his Twitter account:

Gillette: "Hi here's an ad we made attacking masculinity. Please accept us."
Leftist mob: "You still suck lol."

Boy Scouts: "Dear masters we've literally dismantled our whole organization to please you."
Leftist mob: "Not good enough, bigots."

Dick's: "We're destroying our guns so that you'll love us."
Leftist mob: "You still sell knives, psychos."

NFL: "We're letting our players turn the anthem into a political statement. Be our friend?"
Leftist mob: "Nah."

Chick-fil-A: "We've learned nothing."

Caving to the left is not the answer, as demonstrated by Chick-fil-A, but neither is complacency. We need to follow Trump's lead and go on offense.

★ ★ ★ ★ ★ ★ ★

CHAPTER SEVEN

TECH TYRANTS VS. TRUMP

The emergence of the Big Tech era provided a big opportunity for the right.

Typically, conservatives have felt as though they have the facts on their side when it comes to political issues, and the mainstream media was always a buffer that stood between their ideas and the American public. In other words, the media were the ultimate information gatekeepers.

For decades, this dynamic allowed the left to enjoy a monopoly on the digital world, whether it was news, magazines, or broadcast television. But social media opened the gate and the unintended consequence of that was a massive disruption of the status quo.

Political elections were no exception. I remember hearing the buzz about how the Obama campaign revolutionized digital campaigning. He hired a hundred people to run his digital campaign and even announced his reelection bid on YouTube. He bypassed the media, albeit he arguably didn't need to in order to receive positive coverage, and directly engaged with the world. The Obama White House brags about him being: "the first to have @POTUS on Twitter, the first to go live on Facebook from the Oval Office, the first to answer questions from citizens on YouTube, the first to use a filter on Snapchat."

If Barack Obama's team was a pioneer of social media campaigning, Donald Trump's was the conqueror. Obama shied away from controversial topics, and for the most part, used the online platforms to show a more relatable, humanizing side of him. President Trump took the opposite approach, embracing controversy and digging into hot-button issues. It became, and still is, the main weapon in his arsenal. Obama's posts were polished. Trump's posts were a pipeline into the brain of the president. It came as a surprise to everyone at the time, but it really worked. His authenticity was unmatched. The apoplectic reaction he stirred up from the media has not only exposed the hypocrisy and hysteria of the left-leaning media, but has also bulldozed the path forward for conservatives.

What began in the 2016 election is continuing even more rapidly in the 2020 election. President Trump's senior advisor Brad Parscale's strategy to "flood the zone" with digital messaging constantly reinforces Trump's brand and speaks directly to the people. The way President Trump distills information down in a way that everyone understands energizes the right and presents an inclusive politics that anyone can engage in. I was thrilled, but not entirely surprised when my Twitter blew up after the president weighed in on my joining the *DWTS* cast.

Love him or hate him, Trump undeniably has tremendous success with social media. Since the 2016 election season, Republicans beat the drum about how successful they were collectively on social media, in large part thanks to Trump and his campaign setting new rules. Even the left acknowledges this. In November 2019, the *Guardian* ran an article sounding the alarm about Democrats falling behind Trump in digital campaigning. Michael Slaby, the Obama campaign's chief technology officer in 2008 and chief integration and innovation officer in 2012, writes, "there were some huge, very thoughtful and intelligent efforts on the right" established to "address weaknesses, catch up, do smart things and build data trust." This was a rare moment of honesty. Typically, the left attributes any success of the right in the digital world to some sort of unethical tactics.

Consider what the *Guardian* published several months earlier in a report about Trump's digital successes. A professor of media and communication studies at Ursinus College, Anthony Nadler, warned how the campaign's "ability to micro-target various groups with finely tuned messages pushes campaigns toward anti-democratic behavior." He also compared its use of A/B testing, which Facebook describes as a feature that "lets you change variables, such as your ad creative, audience or placement, to determine which strategy performs best and improve future campaigns," to using a supposedly nefarious tactic of turning Facebook users into "unwitting subjects in what is more or less psychological testing."

A bit dramatic, to say the least. In any other context, this would be considered Campaign Strategy 101. But because it worked in Trump's favor, Nadler describes it this way: "It has a sort of corrupting influence, turning campaigns as a whole toward trying to mobilize people in very niche ways, trying to influence people in a very niche way, and trying to demonize the other side."

The left had no problem with Obama's similar use of social media. The *New York Times* wrote a story "How Obama Tapped into Social Networks' Power" right after his 2008 election. Notice the admiration for Obama's digital savvy in its tone: "Like a lot of Web innovators, the Obama campaign did not invent anything completely new. Instead, by bolting together social networking applications under the banner of a movement, they created an unforeseen force to raise money, organize locally, fight smear campaigns and get out the vote that helped them topple the Clinton machine and then John McCain and the Republicans." Many others in the media applauded Obama as the "social media president." But when Trump and his supporters started to find success online, they took notice and changed their tune entirely.

In March 2020, *The Atlantic* published a lengthy report by McKay Coppins describing "How new technologies and techniques pioneered by dictators will shape the 2020 election," in which they too blasted the Trump campaign's digital strategies. "If candidates once had to shout their campaign promises from a soapbox, micro-targeting allows them to sidle up to millions of voters and whisper personalized messages in their ear," Coppins wrote.

Now here's the irony: he went on to admit that "Parscale didn't invent this practice—Barack Obama's campaign famously used it in 2012, and Clinton's followed suit. But Trump's effort in 2016 was unprecedented, in both its scale and its brazenness," he said.

"What's notable about this effort is not that it aims to expose media bias," he continued, noting that an important shift has taken place in the political media sphere. "Instead of trying to reform the press, or critique its coverage, today's most influential conservatives want to destroy the mainstream media altogether."

So let's unpack that for a moment. When conservatives rightfully criticize the media, it automatically means they want it utterly destroyed. That's a wild assumption at best. Who's to say conservatives don't want to go back to the days of genuine reporting with unbiased reporters that they could rely on to get their news?

The reality is that once the right did well, the left changed the game, and in turn, they had to come up with excuses like this one. And once they were beaten at their own game, it was suddenly considered cheating. Hence the dramatic and outlandish "whispering personalized messages" accusations when the right creates targeted ads.

As we head into the 2020 election, Facebook, Twitter, and other social media platforms that Trump successfully used in the 2016 campaign are changing if not all out banning political ads to deny Trump a second term.

In a January 2019 *New York Times* article, journalist and political consultant Matt Osborne contended that the left has no choice but to employ the very techniques they accuse the right of using. "If you don't do it, you're fighting with one hand tied behind your back," he said. "You have a moral imperative to do this—to do whatever it takes."

A look back at the past few years will show you just that. Through Big Tech, the left has employed every tactic at their disposal to drown out the right.

Dennis Prager, who testified before the Senate Judiciary Committee about Big Tech censorship, explained that his educational website PragerU amasses a billion views a year, the majority of which come from viewers under thirty-five, and has been a long-standing target of the left. "YouTube, which is owned by Google, has at various times placed about 100 of our videos on its restricted list. That means any home, institution or individual using a filter to block pornography and violence cannot see those videos. Nor can any school or library," he said.

"PragerU releases a five-minute video every week. As of this writing, 56 of its 320 videos are on YouTube's restricted list. They include videos such as 'Israel's Legal Founding' (by Harvard law professor Alan Dershowitz); 'Why America Invaded Iraq' (by Churchill biographer Andrew Roberts); 'Why Don't Feminists Fight for Muslim Women?' (by the Somali-American women's rights activist Ayaan Hirsi Ali); 'Are the Police Racist?' (by the Manhattan Institute's Heather Mac Donald); and 'Why Is Modern Art So Bad?' (by artist Robert Florczak)."

It's important to note the reason for the excessive censorship of PragerU and these completely normal and educational topics. Its content is geared toward young people, who are typically shielded from conservative ideas. Where college campuses provide little to no community for the right, leaving conservative students feeling isolated and alone in their beliefs, PragerU offered a small sense of community that allowed young people to belong to.

Demonetization of conservative content is another tactic familiar to many conservative creators. YouTube has demonetized videos from gay conservative talk show host Dave Rubin, feminist and sharia law critic Ayaan Hirsi Ali, Canadian clinical psychologist and professor Jordan Peterson, professional wrestler turned Minnesota governor Jesse Ventura, scholar and critic of contemporary liberalism Christina Hoff Sommers, and conservative podcast host Steven Crowder. It's no coincidence that they all lean right of center.

Typically, the tactics are not as obvious. The left came out with "shadow bans" in hopes that they wouldn't always have to explain their outright discrimination of conservatives. Former Twitter software engineer Abhinav Vadrevu explained to Project Veritas the intent behind Twitter's shadow bans: "The idea of a shadow ban is that you ban someone but they don't know they've been banned, because they keep posting but no one sees their content. So they just think that no one is engaging with their content, when in reality, no one is seeing it. But at the end of the day, no one else interacts. . . . No one else sees what you're doing. So, all that data is just thrown away. It's risky though, because people will figure that out."

He was right. People have started to figure it out, though, given the nature of the bans, it's likely we'll never know the extent to which we are being censored. Twitter, Facebook, Reddit, and Pinterest have all reportedly used this method to keep followers of conservative accounts from seeing their content in their feed, but you can bet that those are only the ones that got caught. Essentially, because social media is in many ways the new public square, shadow bans amount to nothing less than an assault on free speech.

For all the talk of election integrity that comes out of Big Tech, you would be shocked to find they themselves are some of the biggest culprits of election tampering.

A recent Project Veritas exposé into Google revealed that Google's "Head of Responsible Innovation," Jen Gennai, believed Google would prevent "the next Trump situation" and that the company uses artificial intelligence to reduce people's ability to discover right-leaning content over left-leaning content in the name of "fairness." Additionally, a member of Google's "transparency-and-ethics" group suggested it be made harder to find content from Ben Shapiro, PragerU, and Jordan Peterson because they are "nazis." For what it's worth, both Shapiro and Prager are Jewish. The mental gymnastics required to draw that conclusion is astonishing.

As Robert Epstein, a senior research psychologist at the American Institute for Behavioral Research and Technology, has uncovered, "Google's search algorithm can easily shift the voting preferences of undecided voters by 20 percent or more—up to 80 percent in some demographic groups—with virtually no one knowing they are being manipulated." He also claims that Google's algorithms "are manipulating people every minute of every day," and that the tech giant has the ability to flip more than 25 percent of elections worldwide.

Platforms like Spotify have suspended political advertising in 2020 altogether. I can't help but think these decisions would not have been made if online political ads worked in the left's favor. Other platforms allow political advertising but rest assured they have their hands all over it. For instance, Big Tech has been known to weaponize ads of Republican candidates at the critical junctures of election campaigns. Breitbart reported that "Facebook decided not to approve one of the ads by the pro-life group Susan B. Anthony List within one week of the contentious 2018 midterm elections, which raises the question of social media companies' undue influence in American electoral politics. The Susan B. Anthony List ad chastised Tennessee Senate Democrat candidate Phil Bredesen for his pro-choice views, while also promoting Tennessee Republican Marsha Blackburn as a 'pro-life champion.'"

When the tech giants can't directly influence an election, they'll try to influence the conversation around a political topic. According to the *Wall Street Journal,* Google engineers openly discussed manipulating search results to help shape the narrative around President Trump's travel ban on travel to and from terror-prone countries in January 2017, writing, "Google employees discussed ways they might be able to tweak the company's search-related functions to show users how to contribute to pro-immigration organizations and contact lawmakers and government agencies." The email chain reviewed by the *Wall Street*

Journal suggests "employees considered ways to harness the company's vast influence on the internet in response to the travel ban," and one internal email states: "I know this would require a full-on sprint to make happen, but I think this is the sort of super timely and imperative information that we need as we know that this country and Google, would not exist without immigration." Talk about corporate activism.

Together, Google and Facebook control the majority of all online advertising, which in turn makes up a good chunk of all advertising in America. There is no practical alternative. It is impossible to run an effective political campaign today without advertising and engaging on the world's most popular internet platforms. The type of interference in campaign activity that Google, Facebook, Twitter, and the other tech giants are engaged in now represents an existential threat to our democratic system. In the same way that Republicans successfully embraced talk radio to do an end run around the media, these social media platforms allowed Trump to bypass the media and speak directly with voters. Recognizing the success of Trump, these platforms have now doubled down on shutting down ways that they can be used by Trump again.

What's more, if that interference occurred on any of the more traditional advertising platforms, such as broadcast television or radio, it would undoubtedly be illegal. The Federal Communications Act provides for fines, and even the revocation of broadcast licenses, for refusing to carry the campaign ads of candidates.

How is it, then, that Alphabet—Google's parent company—and Facebook, megacorporations with a combined market cap of $1.44 *trillion*, are allowed leeway to pick election winners and

losers in ways that would cost a tiny AM radio station in Dubuque
its broadcasting license?

In short, it's because our laws and our understanding of the
role tech companies play in our lives and political processes have
not caught up to the era of the tech giants. But beyond that, it's
because our society has allowed them to. For the most part, we
haven't been paying attention to who's in charge. Thankfully, various conservative journalists and outlets have stepped up in recent
years to shed light on unexpected key players and decision makers
working behind the scenes to censor conservatives.

In the infancy of the internet, Congress passed a law, section
230 of the Communications Decency Act, that shields the social
media platforms from liability. Legally, they are considered platforms, not publishers, and unlike a newspaper that defames a person, they can't be sued.

In an exposé for conservative media outlet PJ Media, for
instance, Tyler O'Neil wrote that in October 2018, the Southern
Poverty Law Center (SPLC) led a coalition of five groups funded by
leftist billionaire George Soros in launching a "Change the Terms"
campaign. The purpose was to pressure Big Tech companies to
"reduce hateful activities on their platforms." It sounds like a
worthwhile initiative—that is, until you unpack what's actually
behind the SPLC. If there's one thing you can count on the SPLC
for, it is to smear anything or anyone they don't like. That's not
an exaggeration. The multimillion-dollar political smear machine
hides under the guise of a human rights organization and
operates with one goal in mind: paint any opposition to the far
left as morally depraved and therefore unworthy of participating
in public life.

Such was the case for Dr. Carol Swain, an African-American author and former political science and law professor at Vanderbilt University, who was smeared in several newspapers, including her hometown paper, the *Tennessean*, as a white supremacist sympathizer by then–SPLC national spokesman Mark Potok. The context for the attack was a review Dr. Swain gave for a film titled *A Conversation About Race*, which she endorsed for classroom use because it, in her words, "offered a perspective on race rarely encountered on university campuses." In an article for the *Wall Street Journal*, Dr. Swain described the SPLC's retaliation as "vicious and effective," recalling her humiliation and shock when she found out her photo was plastered on the front page of several newspapers across the country with the words "Carol Swain is an apologist for white supremacists."

It's beyond astonishing that someone as accomplished and respected as Dr. Swain could be smeared in this way, and even more absurd considering she is a black woman accused of being a white supremacist.

The great neurosurgeon and secretary of housing and urban development Ben Carson earned a spot on SPLC's list of "extremists" for holding traditional views on marriage and the family. Think about that for a moment. An African-American, world-renowned medical hero and former presidential candidate who grew up in poverty on the streets of Detroit, raised by a loving mother who couldn't read herself, but made him write weekly book reports to keep him out of gangs, was defamed by a so-called civil rights group. His story should have been the embodiment of what the SPLC claims to champion, but because he held conservative views, he earned nothing other than a target on his back. So unless you ascribe to the same progressive political agenda as the SPLC, they consider you on "hatewatch."

During their time as senior fellows at the Family Research Council, a Christian public policy ministry in Washington, DC, Ken Blackwell, and Bob Morrison wrote about their experience being placed on SPLC's "Hate Map," which they say made them a target for a man who "entered our office with a backpack full of Chick-fil-A sandwiches (day old), a pistol, and dozens of bullets. He was prepared to shoot us all because, as he confessed, SPLC's Hate Map told him where he might find us." Thankfully, he was stopped by a guard who took a bullet while barring the gunman from entering.

Other groups and individuals targeted by the SPLC don't typically have the platform or resources that the FRC does to garner public support or fight back. Many of them face career obstacles and permanent reputational damage—and that's exactly the point.

In April 2019, the American Family Association and the Family Research Council combined their resources to purchase a full-page ad in the *Wall Street Journal* that called on PayPal, Spotify, YouTube, Amazon, CNN, and MSNBC by name to terminate their relationships with the SPLC. The ad called the SPLC a "hate-for-cash machine" that has "expanded its definition of 'hate' to non-violent conservative, Christian, and parent organizations who opposed the SPLC's political agenda.

"Those who use SPLC as their authority on hate and extremism should stop immediately," it demanded. "A bad tree cannot produce good fruit. Will corporations and media outlets continue to align themselves with an organization that its own employees say is racist, bigoted, and rife with sexual misconduct and discrimination? If so, their partnership can only produce rotten fruit."

A month later, Breitbart reported the following: "PayPal CEO Dan Schulman admitted that his company worked with the SPLC to identify, and to blacklist, conservatives. Google has also worked with the SPLC to flag content on its platforms, as has Facebook. Giant corporations like Apple, and Hollywood celebrities like George Clooney, have continued to pour donations into the SPLC's coffers: the embattled organization reportedly enjoys a massive half-billion-dollar endowment."

The tech and media giants can no longer claim ignorance of the truth about the SPLC. If a full-page ad in one of the most influential publications in the world, along with numerous public defamation lawsuits, isn't enough to get their attention, the words of SPLC's former spokesman and senior fellow Mark Potok should be. "I want to say plainly that our aim in life is to destroy these groups, completely destroy them," he said of the groups they target.

All of this considered, it should be unimaginable for the SPLC to be granted any authority over online speech.

In his book, *The Manipulators*, Peter Hasson writes that the SPLC-led "Change the Terms" campaign aims to "pressure all major technology service providers into setting speech codes that govern what their clients say both on and off their platforms. The coalition demands that each company agree to implement a specific set of policies already drafted by the activists."

It gets worse. "The activists' targets aren't limited to Facebook, Google, and Twitter but also include credit card companies and crowdfunding sites," he adds. "Once a company caves to the pressure and agrees to adopt the left-wing contract, it has essentially deputized the SPLC to decide who can stay on its platform or use its services and who must leave." We've already started to see this successfully implemented. The SPLC confirmed the Daily Caller's report that they are policing YouTube's content as part of its "Trusted Flaggers" program.

In February 2020, *Axios* reported that Google would be giving the left-wing media outlet The Young Turks (TYT) a six-figure payment for them to launch a YouTube course to teach users how to do local journalism. The investment is "part of YouTube's $25 million commitment to news efforts, which is part of the $300 million Google News Initiative that was announced in 2018," according to *Axios*, which, notably, called TYT "a logical fit for this type of investment."

The Young Turks is a far-left media outlet run by Cenk Uygur, who has a lengthy history of being anything but an objective journalist and at times an Armenian genocide denier. He has come under fire in the past for advocating for disturbing and crude comments. Some of those remarks, including one suggesting "the genes of women are flawed," according to the *Huffington Post*, were bad enough to get him fired from the left-wing political action committee Justice Democrats. Even former Democratic presidential candidate Bernie Sanders was forced to (begrudgingly) retract his endorsement of Uygur's congressional campaign in 2019 due to the commentator's abhorrent remarks about Jews and women.

His nephew and prominent Young Turks contributor Hasan Piker isn't much better. While President Trump was honoring ISIS victim Kayla Mueller during his February 2020 State of the Union address, Piker thought it was a good idea to live-stream himself mocking her for sexual trauma. It wasn't out of character. In 2019, he applauded the "brave f*cking soldier" who injured former Navy SEAL and Republican Texas representative Dan Crenshaw and said during a podcast that the United States deserved 9/11.

In a statement to the *Washington Free Beacon*, Executive Director of the Armenian National Committee of America Aram Hamparian said, "A talk show founded by an Armenian Genocide denier, named after Armenian Genocide perpetrators, is a poor platform for teaching responsible journalism." You think?

It's not just how they censor the right. Big Tech also protects the left. In August 2019, a man approached CNN's Chris Cuomo and called him "Fredo," a reference to the younger, dumber brother in the Godfather movies. Cuomo responded by saying that Fredo was the equivalent of the n-word to Italians and said "you're going to have a problem," to which that man replied, "what are you going to do about it?" Cuomo replied "I'll f*cking ruin your sh*t. I'll f*cking throw you down these stairs." The entire episode was caught on video, so what happened next? YouTube took it down. "YouTube has removed the original viral 'fredo' video from the channel 'THAT'S THE POINT with Brandon' for violating their 'harassment and bullying' policy,' reported PJ Media.

In July 2018, Twitter created a task force of academics to fight partisan echo chambers, incivility, and intolerance. I don't know what's worse—the fact that the academics hired are vehemently anti-Trump or Twitter's nerve to select peacemakers from the field known for being the biggest culprits of bias and intolerance. They should be the last people on earth to draw any type of free speech boundaries.

You don't have to read between the lines to see the bias. Senior Twitter manager Ian Brown called for the jailing of President Trump and Dan Scavino. "All I want for Christmas is for @DanScavino and @realDonaldTrump to go to jail next year. #MAGA," he wrote. In January 2019, he wrote, "Can somebody impeach this mother------ before it's too late?"

The examples of anti-conservative statements from employees of Big Tech are plentiful. But what really matters is what they do with those biases. Consider what Donald Trump Jr wrote in his book *Triggered* in regard to the fight against Big Tech monopolies:

> Considering how the deck is stacked, what my father, and I to a lesser extent, have accomplished on Twitter is remarkable. Evan Williams, another co-founder of the social media giant, recently called my dad a "genius" and a "master of the platform." He's right; he is. But just imagine how powerful our Twitter accounts would be if the playing field were level. And level for everyone, including you.
>
> Think about it. If they can minimize the president of the United States, or at least try, what can they do to you? Recently, an expert on the subject estimated that somewhere between 2.5 million and 10 million voters have been swayed to Hillary by Big Tech's tactics during the election. There goes the popular vote! Make no mistake. They did it before, and they're going to do it again. As long as the outrage machine is still operating, it's never going to stop.

The 2020 election is just months away, and it certainly hasn't stopped. If anything, it has ramped up like never before.

Case in point: in May 2020, Fox News reported that Twitter slapped a warning label on one of President Trump's tweets for the first time, cautioning readers that despite the president's claims, "fact-checkers" say there is "no evidence" that expanded, nationwide mail-in voting would increase fraud risks—and that "experts say mail-in ballots are very rarely linked to voter fraud."

Within minutes, President Trump accused Twitter of "interfering in the 2020 Presidential Election . . . based on fact-checking by Fake News CNN and the Amazon Washington Post." The president added that the platform "is completely stifling FREE SPEECH" and vowed: "I, as President, will not allow it to happen!"

Twitter's new warning label was issued even though a Twitter spokesperson acknowledged to Fox News that Trump's tweet had not broken any of the platform's rules, and even though several experts have called mail-in balloting an invitation to widespread fraud, including a commission that was co-chaired by former president Jimmy Carter.

Just a few weeks later, in the wake of the George Floyd protests, Snapchat announced it would no longer show President Trump's account on its "Discover" feature, which highlights popular and newsworthy topics and regularly spotlights the president's account.

"We are not currently promoting the President's content on Snapchat's Discover platform. We will not amplify voices who incite racial violence and injustice by giving them free promotion on Discover," Rachel Racusen, a spokeswoman for Snapchat's parent company, told the left-wing entertainment blog The Wrap in a statement.

Trump's reelection campaign immediately responded with a statement by then campaign manager Brad Parscale, saying "Snapchat is trying to rig the 2020 election, illegally, using their corporate funding to promote Joe Biden and suppress President Trump.

"Radical Snapchat CEO Evan Spiegel would rather promote extreme left riot videos and encourage their users to destroy America than share the positive words of unity, justice, and law and order from our President," Parscale said. "If you're a conservative, they do not want to hear from you, they do not want you to vote."

Again in July, after protesters attempted to topple a statue near the White House and establish an "autonomous zone" free of any law enforcement, imitating the notorious one in Seattle, President Trump rightfully stepped in, tweeting, "There will never be an 'Autonomous Zone' in Washington, D.C., as long as I'm your President. If they try they will be met with serious force!" The Twitter warriors quickly took action, blocking users from liking or engaging with it. They issued a statement claiming the tweet was "glorifying violence." Think about the weight of those words for a moment. Supporting American sovereignty and law and order was just deemed an act of violence. Can you imagine a country where these tech tyrants dictated law?

If Senator Kamala Harris was in charge she made it clear that she would ban Trump's ability to communicate verbally altogether, telling CNN's Anderson Cooper that his Twitter platform "should probably be taken from him." Seemingly unbothered by the outrageous suggestion, Cooper only drew attention to the question of whether or not Trump supporters might see it as a negative thing. How in the world did this elected official take an oath to defend the Constitution, let alone run for the president of the free world?

With Biden beholden to the radical leftists in his party, it wasn't long before he adopted a similar sentiment. In a June 29, 2020, letter, Biden's campaign manager, Jen O'Malley Dillon, desperately urged Facebook to censor Trump's Facebook page and take specific action to curb what he and his campaign can broadcast on the platform.

At the heart of Big Tech censorship is nothing less than an effort to take away the First Amendment rights of conservatives and Trump supporters. When President Trump stands up to them, he's really standing up for you.

For these companies to abandon their principles and commitments—squashing any last bit of confidence that the American people once had in their ability to operate fairly—tells you everything you need to know about how much is at stake this election. They are throwing all of their eggs in the anti-Trump basket without any concern for how many users, revenue streams, or business opportunities they leave behind. And this will only ramp up as the 2020 election gets closer.

There is no doubt Big Tech is increasingly putting their thumbs on the scale of political discourse in this country, and we must reexamine the way we respond. We can take a page right out of President Trump's playbook. This looks like speaking up and holding Big Tech's feet to the fire. Nothing is going to change until conservatives unite in our frustration and speak up.

The first step is staying informed. The Media Research Center recently launched its TechWatch initiative, which can be found at Newsbusters.org/techwatch, "to defend conservative speech online and expose efforts by top tech companies and their employees to silence conservative voices with Orwellian speech controls." You can use this as a resource to stay up-to-date on the latest in Big Tech censorship. Keep an eye on what's going on legislatively, and support the elected officials who are trying to do something about the online war against Trump. Senator Josh Hawley is a great example. He recently introduced a proposal that would give Americans the ability to sue major tech companies if they are engaging in selective censorship of political speech.

Second, but no less important, don't use censorship as an excuse to give up. It's all the more reason to find ways to circumvent

Big Tech with our ideas and messages. I have the privilege of being able to do this on my daily Newsmax show, *Spicer & Co,* where I'm able to communicate with my audience without fear of being censored, but I realize not everyone has that unique opportunity. However, most of us do have smartphones, which is all that you need to send an email, start a podcast, send a text, call a representative, or launch an app. Likewise, most of us have legs and knuckles, which means we can knock on doors, vote in elections, and donate to causes we believe in.

Yes, we are at a disadvantage, but we can rest assured that we have a fighter on our side who is laying out a blueprint for us to fearlessly fight back.

CHAPTER EIGHT

GRADE SCHOOLS AS BATTLEGROUNDS: ABCS AND ZER AND ZES

It's long been said that children are an indicator of where a country is headed. With socialism on the rise in America, we must look to our youngest citizens to find out how we got here and what we can do to change the dangerous trajectory we are on.

I'd be remiss if I didn't quote the great Ronald Reagan when he warned that "freedom is never more than one generation away from extinction." Reagan probably never imagined his warning would become a reality so soon. Thankfully, President Trump shares in his belief and sees his warning as the imminent threat that it is.

During his Fourth of July speech at Mount Rushmore, which was praised by many on the right as his single greatest speech, President Trump told an enthusiastic crowd under a moonlit sky that "our nation is witnessing a merciless campaign to wipe out our history, defame our heroes, erase our values and indoctrinate our children," adding that "our children are taught in school to hate their own country."

The media quickly fact-checked this statement as false in their seemingly coordinated reports that dubbed the speech as "dark" and "divisive," but as you'll see in this chapter, it couldn't be more true.

Does America's history include some dark and shameful chapters? Of course—and they ought to be taught in every classroom. But does that mean American ideals should be smeared and demonized in the malleable young minds of children, who then grow up to hate the very country that has given more freedom and prosperity to more people around the world than any other? Of course not. While we haven't always lived up to the ideals enshrined in the Constitution and the Bill of Rights, they remain the standard of freedom and prosperity for the rest of the world to look up to.

What happens at the elementary level often goes unnoticed, especially when compared to the never-ending news supply of college campuses chaos. This imbalance causes us to miss the root of the problem, which is that left-leaning and progressive ideas start long before college.

Having kids of my own made me realize just how easy it is to influence developing minds. They will believe almost anything a trusted adult tells them.

I can remember when elementary schools were centered around the fundamental skills of reading, writing, and arithmetic, or "the Three R's." Today, it's more likely the R's children will learn are "racism, refugees, and right-wing bigotry." That's no exaggeration. In many ways, the left is redefining what "school" is, and they are creating their own alphabet to do it.

A IS FOR ACTIVISM

Activism in normal American life might conjure up images of the March for Life, the Women's March, or your local GOP's Super Saturday. These activities are all anchored in the founding American principle that free people have the right to assemble and petition their government. While these activities are rooted in American tradition, they are also voluntary and, at least in theory, never favored by the government. We would be up in arms if the Trump administration gave federal workers a day off to attend a Trump rally, but don't bat an eye when a radical left-wing school board handpicks the "activism" they deem appropriate for our children.

Cloaked in the ideas of civic engagement, the left has been waging a campaign in schools all across America. The latest—and often most visible—trend of leftist activism in schools is encouraging students to partake in protests, and bending the rules to be able to use precious classroom time to do so.

Right in my backyard of Northern Virginia, Fairfax County Public Schools are now allowing students excused absences for participating in political protests. The Fairfax County District School Board member who introduced the policy said, "I think we're setting the stage for the rest of the nation with this. It's a dawning of a new day in student activism, and school systems everywhere are going to have to be responsive to it." Is this really why kids are in school?

A few months earlier, New York City public schools allowed excused absences for students protesting climate change. "We applaud our students when they raise their voices in a safe and respectful manner on issues that matter to them," the New York City Public Schools' Twitter account noted. "Young people around the world are joining the #ClimateStrike this week—showing that student action will lead us forward." What happened to applauding them for good grades?

Three days after that, Portland, Oregon, public schools announced they too will allow students to cut class to participate in the Global Climate Strike.

"All high school and middle school students who leave school on Sept. 20 for the Global Climate Strike will be given an excused absence if they pre-arrange the absence with their teacher(s) and notify staff when they leave," it stated.

But it goes beyond merely allowing it. The statement went on to actively encourage teachers to use the curriculum to coincide with the event, stating, "We are also encouraging middle and high school educators to use these tools for climate literacy education in their lessons next week to help students think critically about the science and sociology behind this important topic.

"K–5 aged and Elementary School Students: We encourage Pre-Kindergarten to fifth-grade educators to participate in developmentally appropriate 'Climate Change Awareness' learning-based activities within the school Friday," it continued. "This can include an array of educational activities on this important topic like: school-wide assemblies, film screenings, relevant readings and lessons."

K–5 students should be learning their multiplication tables, not how to recite talking points about a complex political issue. My point here has nothing to do with the issue, in this case climate change, rather it is first, whether this is the role for public schools and second, the notion that taxpayer-funded bureaucrats should be the ones in charge of choosing which issues are worth using school time to support. I'm all for a better environment but that's not the point. Taxpayer-funded schools and educators should not be deciding which issues and causes are deemed worthy of a day out of school.

In March, four parents of Portland Public Schools students sued the district for using public resources to promote outside interest groups and the "personal political preferences" of the school board and its teachers. The lawsuit alleges the parents' and students' civil rights were violated when the district coerced students into participating in anti-gun activity and took part in a national school walkout to protest gun violence on March 14, 2018.

"The district organized and promoted partisan, anti-gun positions on a massive scale, with close coordination between the School Board, the Superintendent, the Portland Association of Teachers, outside anti-gun groups and even local anti-gun politicians," according to James Buchal, the attorney and Multnomah County Republican Party chairman who filed the suit on the parents' behalf. "Highly misleading propaganda, coupled with emotional manipulation of 50,000 Portland schoolchildren, allowed PPS [Portland Public Schools] to create political theater designed to manipulate public opinion and pressure elected officials to ban guns."

The parents in the case were understandably disturbed by their public school system imposing a view on their children without their consent. Some equated the school's actions to "mobilizing Portland schoolchildren for political purposes," and they are exactly right. Political protests are usually adult actions that exclude children who lack the skill set necessary to make up their minds on complex issues. Whether or not you agree with the protests at hand is not the point. The point is that children should be taught about issues as they grow older, learning to make their own decisions. And even at a young age, if they want to learn about these issues it should be their parents, not a government-run, taxpayer-funded school that facilitates that discussion.

The Portland parents' lawsuit sheds light on another major issue when it comes to this type of school-sponsored activism.

"The 2018 demonstrations were not isolated instances, but part of a pattern that has also seen publicly-reported demonstrations at PPS (Portland Public Schools) on several prior occasions, including large scale demonstrations arising out of the election of President Donald Trump. The 2018 demonstrations are part of a larger pattern of political misuse of public resources mobilizing students to advance political positions, which has included efforts related to such national issues as 'climate change,' 'net neutrality,' and illegal immigration, as well as local issues like school bond measures," the lawsuit states.

Of course, the examples listed are all pet issues of the left. Seldom, if ever, are student protests associated with conservative causes. That is because schools foster what students care about and more important, what they learn. The protests are almost always one-sided because the teachers and district board members are almost always one-sided.

So it only makes sense that Portland Public Schools would go on to allow students to cut class for climate change just months after they were served a lawsuit for similar actions.

If you are reading this and saying to yourself, "I agree with the causes so it's no big deal," ask yourself this: If conservatives took control of your school board and wanted kids to attend pro-life rallies, would you feel the same?

Here's the bottom line: By granting excused absences for protests, schools are sending a message that activism takes priority over classroom learning. Each minute wasted on protesting the left's current pet issue is a minute that could have been used to teach students critical skills that are needed to succeed. Our children need the skills to compete with countries like China that seek to become the world's dominant economy.

On March 19, 2019, the day before a large-scale school climate strike, the *Guardian* published a column by progressive youth organizer David Reed titled "If children don't join the climate strike, their schools are underachieving." The subtitle is just as bad. "Activism is more important than grades. Any responsible teacher should be encouraging their pupils to walk out," it reads. I've had many great teachers who have had an impact on my life, but what I remember about them and what I loved about them is what I learned from them, not the causes they believed in.

Reed starts his piece by posing the question, "For what does excellence in education look like if it's not pupils being engaged enough on issues such as climate change to do something about them?

"Rather than calling schoolchildren truants when they show up for society in a way that puts the rest of us to shame—we should be using the strikes as a measure of school performance." He suggests that "any secondary school that doesn't have pupils informed enough to join the protests is underachieving.

"Perhaps that sounds like irresponsible, progressive nonsense," he says—and he would be exactly right. Protesting has no place in any sort of academic progress measurement for children. If a parent or guardian wants to take their child to an event, rally, or protest that favors a particular cause, that is their right. It is not the right of English or math teachers to advance their personal beliefs on students.

In an October 2017 column for the *Washington Post*, educator and former Reuters national security editor Valerie Strauss says, "When we think about the role of student action in schools, consider that merely allowing protest is not enough." She suggests we push schools even further to advance things like social justice and tackle systems of power. "We can change the future if we start now," she concluded.

Here's the key: "We can change the future."

There it is; their goal is to use this period in children's lives to advance a progressive agenda. For the left, it is not merely enough to give the next generation of Americans the tools to forge a successful future; they must ensure that the future is the one they deem worthy.

Strauss's aspirations are not only widespread among teachers and administrators; they are also embedded in the curriculum. In the summer of 2019, K–8 schools in eight states across the country adopted the curriculum designed by Pollyanna, a nonprofit corporation with a mission to "advance systemic change" by working with academic institutions to achieve their "diversity, equity and inclusion goals." Their political objectives are far from subtle, but that didn't stop American schools from adopting them.

The grade-three teaching material designed by Pollyanna has been adopted in some elementary schools in Virginia, North Carolina, California, New Jersey, New York, Rhode Island, Missouri, and Illinois, according to the website Townhall. The material falls under a unit titled "Stories of Activism—How One Voice Can Change a Community (and Bridge the World)," and teaches students how they can be "agents of communal, social, political, and environmental change."

The Pollyanna grade-six material falls under a unit that describes a U.S. society that's "plagued with violence and efforts of dehumanization" and states that "existence is resistance."

Kids should be on the playground, not on the front lines of the left's political battles. But so long as the left needs them to achieve victory, they will continue to use them as their fighters.

Of course, it's a good thing that children today are passionate about the world they live in. Protesters of any age can be a powerful tool and a force for good. The danger arises when kids are told what to protest instead of learning the critical thinking skills needed to understand why or what they should protest and care about.

I IS FOR INDOCTRINATION

According to a report by the National Assessment of Educational Progress (NAEP), the teaching of U.S. history to American students lags behind all other subject matters. The latest NAEP survey finds that proficiency levels for fourth-, eighth-, and twelfth-grade students are in the 20th, 18th, and 12th percentile, respectively. It's no coincidence that young proponents of radical leftist policies are rising at the same time history literacy is declining. This reminds me of the old axiom "you study history so you don't repeat it." Well, if these kids are never studying history in the first place, how can they even begin to grasp this? The less they know about history, the more they flirt with the likes of socialism and march for things they don't understand.

That explains why activism is only the second phase of the left's plan for children. They first need to groom the developing minds—and they don't waste any time doing so.

STEP 1: SMEAR AMERICA

I remember a time when being anti-American would get you socially ousted, if not fired from your job. Americans were proud of their country and unified in their values. Today, many young people proudly wear the socialist or communist label and openly bash America. The left has been sowing the seeds of anti-Americanism in the minds of schoolchildren for decades, but only now are we seeing the full fruit of their labor.

Instead of teaching an accurate and unbiased story of America, many schools paint America and its values as things that students need to rebel against.

Lee Francis, a history teacher at Massey Hill Classical High School in North Carolina, demonstrated this perfectly. His students learned about the First Amendment's tenets of free speech by watching him stomp on an American flag at the front of the classroom. According to a Daily Caller report, a student's Facebook post narrated the incident, explaining that the history teacher "asked students if they had a lighter (they said no, they aren't even allowed in school), then when there was no lighter he asked for scissors. When there were no scissors he took the flag and stomped all over it. He is saying this was teaching First Amendment rights." So, ideally, he would have preferred a lighter or scissors, but he had to resort to crumpling and stomping. Classy. It makes you wonder, why does he have to choose such a polarized example to talk about free speech? Is this the best way to demonstrate the rights afforded to us under the First Amendment?

In another obvious display of contempt for America, an elementary school in New Jersey banned students from saying "God bless America" following the Pledge of Allegiance—a tradition that was started by kindergarten teachers at the school in 2001 to honor 9/11 first responders. They did not make it optional; they banned it. Why?

More recently, Sabold Elementary School in Springfield, Pennsylvania, put the same patriotic tradition to an abrupt halt after the Freedom from Religion Foundation filed a complaint and demanded the school immediately cease the practice of reciting "God bless America" on the loudspeaker. According to the complaint, "When a public school regularly proclaims, 'God bless America,' it sends a message to its students that the school is endorsing and compelling belief in God."

Phrases like "God bless America" and "One nation under God" have transcended all generations of Americans on both sides of the political aisle and are protected by the U.S. Constitution—on or off school property. Public school students often don't realize that they possess a wide range of free-expression rights under the Constitution. They are free to express their ideas—even if they are political or controversial—write articles, assemble in groups, criticize their school or its teachers, and even petition their school administrators on issues—both inside and outside of school grounds. In the seminal student speech case *Tinker v. Des Moines Independent Community School District,* the U.S. Supreme Court said that students "do not shed their constitutional rights to freedom of speech and expression at the schoolhouse gate" and the Court has stood firm in that belief time and time again.

While these stories made headlines, most of the left's work in this area is more subtle and discreet. A tremendous amount of time and effort is put into discrediting America's founding and Founders within the curriculum.

From an early age, students learn of an America that is unjust and oppressive, that wealth and capitalism are evil, and that socialism and social justice are the ultimate cures. Their teachers focus primarily on the flaws of our Founders and America's mistakes while ignoring all the good things about America. Are we perfect? No. Did we make mistakes? Yes. But are we still the greatest country in the world? Yes.

Columbus Day, which has been renamed to "Indigenous Peoples Day" at many schools, is now an annual opportunity to remind students of America's "evil" founding. According to a survey published in May 2020 by the University of Phoenix, less than half of Americans know the basic meaning behind Memorial Day, while a full 50 percent had also never heard of the term "gold star family," which refers to a family who has lost a loved one in military service.

Stop and think about that. Almost one million Americans have died in service to this nation and our freedom, and we have watered down the day to recognize them to a day for car sales and barbecues. It's crazy to think that half of young Americans can recite all sorts of left-wing buzz words and phrases but don't know what a gold star family member is.

On September 17, 2019, Real Clear Investigations published an exposé detailing the ways in which "woke history" is making alarming inroads in U.S. schools. The term "woke" would be defined by the left as perceived awareness of issues. Those with common sense who are familiar with the term know it to be a word used by leftists to virtue-signal and characterize themselves as enlightened and intellectually superior about political issues while conservatives are still sound asleep. The exposé sounds the alarm about how "kids are receiving classroom instruction in how race, class, gender, sexuality and citizenship status are tools of oppression, power and privilege"—all of which fall under the "woke" vocabulary. "They are taught about colonialism, state violence, racism, intergenerational trauma, heteropatriarchy and the common thread that links them: 'whiteness.' Students are then graded on how well they apply these concepts in writing assignments, performances and community organizing projects," it prefaces. The piece went on to highlight dozens of deeply concerning examples of the modern-day anti-American curriculum in K–12 schools.

Will Swaim, president of the California Policy Center, is quoted in the piece saying the curriculum is coming "dangerously close to turning the American exceptionalism on its head. Yes, we're exceptional—exceptionally evil. It is remindful of re-education camps in Vietnam or China. It is indoctrination rather than education."

If there's one thing you can count on California for, it's to lead the way in destroying institutions with leftist lunacy, which is why I wasn't surprised to read Real Clear Investigations' long list of outrageous examples of the curriculum in the Golden State's schools.

"Students at schools in Anaheim, San Jose, Oakland, and San Francisco are taught how to write a manifesto to school administrators listing 'demands' for reforms," he writes. "Some conduct a grand jury investigation to determine who was responsible for the genocide of the state's Native Americans. And one class holds a mock trial to determine which party is most responsible for the deaths of millions of native Tainos: Christopher Columbus, the soldiers, the king and queen of Spain, or the entire European system of colonialism."

You'd think I'm joking with the next one. A Charter High School in Lawndale, California, assigns students to write "breakup letters with a form of oppression." Among the so-called forms of oppression students can write to are Eurocentric curriculum, toxic masculinity, heteronormativity, and the Dakota Access Pipeline. Grades are measured by how much the letters "persuade their audience of the dehumanizing and damaging effects of their chosen topic."

Talk about a bad breakup. "It's not you, the Dakota Pipeline, it's me."

Such anti-American sentiment is not confined to the schools of California. It is embedded into the curriculum across the country—and Pollyanna, the nonprofit driving youth curriculums, plays a vital role.

Part of this curriculum includes material for grade-five students. This unit description states "unfortunately, a dominant narrative for immigration often presents the false image of a melting pot, without analyzing the structures of power that dictated either the exclusion or inclusion of various groups of people, and how such treatment simultaneously impacted the idea of what an 'American'—or more accurately, a resident or citizen of the U.S.—should 'look like' and be." According to the grade-seven unit description, students learn about their "implicit bias" and will be able to dispel myths such as "'biodeterminism."

There is also the Youth Equity Stewardship, or YES! Program in many K–12 schools. Topics include social justice, "lenses of diversity," and "equality to equity to borderless." That last one references Nican Tlaca, a term used by proponents of a borderless society in which indigenous peoples rule.

Considering what young students are taught in school, it only stands to reason that when they grow up they won't believe that America is something worth fighting for.

It wasn't long ago that many on the left had screeched hysterically that we were on the brink of World War III. Thankfully, their predictions were wildly miscalculated but it certainly got me thinking . . . What if we were approaching a major war? Many in the leftist media practically sided with Iran and half of the country was more sympathetic to an Iranian terrorist than our own leader. You have to ask what our military will look like in the coming generations.

Eric Metaxas, a first-generation American and author of *If You Can Keep It: The Forgotten Promise of American Liberty*, describes the ultimate danger of the rising anti-American generation. "Patriotism means that despite our differences, we can nonetheless all agree on something larger, something that transcends us as individuals," he says. "It means we can celebrate what is good and heroic and true in our culture and nation; it means we understand that we are all in this together and need to make it work; it means we understand that when we petulantly cease to love our country, we saw off the very limb on which we all sit."

Unfortunately, students today learn the opposite. The antipathy toward American patriotism that is cultivated in the classroom could undoubtedly have devastating consequences.

STEP 2: DISCREDIT PARENTS

Perhaps the most nefarious tactic the left uses on children is manipulating them into doubting what they grew up learning at home or in church. Many teachers are indirectly telling kids that their parents and pastors—or any other figures of moral authority in their lives—are wrong.

"Of course, the experts in school know more about social studies than mommy and daddy, who work in different fields," a child would understandably presume. After all, the doctor knows more about medicine than their parents. A lawyer knows more about the law than their parents. So, of course, the history teacher knows more about history than their parents! And while teachers probably do know more about their assigned subject than the average parent, they are not responsible in the way they are presenting their knowledge that is skewed by their own worldview.

This innocence of children blinds them to the manipulation of their teachers, who undoubtedly exploit their naïveté. Leftist teachers slowly position themselves as the final authority by targeting the things in the Bible and in the Constitution that contradict their leftist worldview and threaten their authority in a child's eyes.

During a public school talent show in New York City, the Manhattan PTA president dressed as a woman to perform an erotic dance routine in front of kids as young as five years old. The performance included pelvic gyrations and G-string flashes, according to the New York *Daily News*.

The curriculum that is being mandated, as well as the performances and activities being presented in these schools, is not only incompatible with many people's religious beliefs, but it is also confusing to children, who lack the cognitive development needed to grapple with such delicate and complex concepts.

One of the left's great victories surrounding young people in the past few years was successfully turning the Boy Scouts of America into Scouts of America. By opening its membership up to girls, the Boy Scouts caved to political correctness and destroyed one of the last institutions for male fellowship at a time when young boys needed it most. I was a Cub Scout and a Boy Scout. It gave me a sense of belonging, friendship, and purpose. I learned camaraderie and core values without the distraction of girls. Being able to hang out with guys and go camping was a great bonding experience. We followed the Boy Scout Oath and Law and through it learned not only how to camp, start a fire, and survive the outdoors, but we also learned values and respect. We learned certain skills the same way girls learned a set of skills and values in the Girl Scouts. During the formative years, there is value in groups of boys and groups of girls organizing separately. It doesn't mean they have to, but it's nice to have outlets where they can.

If someone doesn't ascribe to the Boy Scouts values, then they simply shouldn't join.

The Boy Scouts represented a traditional holdout in the left's territory. In the Scout Oath we pledged to keep ourselves physically strong, mentally awake, and morally straight and the Scout Law instructed us to be courteous, kind, obedient, and reverent.

The right has already ceded academia, youth sports, and even the Boy Scouts to the left, and now we're slowly ceding our right to parent and protect our children in accordance with our values. We are undoubtedly at a critical cultural moment in which our children's future is at stake.

If there has ever been a time to take action, it is now.

When I was a kid, parents could trust the school system to focus on academics. School was for learning and the home was for playing and instilling values. And for the most part, they were separate. That is no longer the case. The good news is parents don't have to render themselves powerless as the left indoctrinates their kids, and resorting to homeschooling or private school is certainly not the only option.

To fight back, you first have to know what you're fighting. This is not a battle to get the school curriculum to favor your side of the political aisle. It's about stopping the left from undermining your role as a parent and instilling in your kids their twisted values.

Second, we have to be willing to get our heads, hearts, and souls in the game.

There is more political consensus against the left's child lunacy than many on the right realize—and we must use that. There are two interconnected ways of winning a culture war. Legally: launching an uncompromising, all-or-nothing attack in the political arena. And culturally: inspiring ordinary people to care and to fight. Traditionally, the left has been better at both than the right has, but there are occasional exceptions we can learn from.

Earlier this year, parents in Battle Ground, Washington, showed the power of successfully fighting the left culturally. The public school district was about to implement Planned Parenthood's pro-abortion, pornographic "comprehensive sex education curriculum" known as FLASH, but an unprecedented school board district vote rejected it.

This was thanks to the efforts of concerned parents who mobilized local groups and churches to protest and raise awareness of the curriculum. Thousands of people ended up turning out and through protest, prayer, and meaningful dialogue with officials and community members, they were able to influence the vote.

Planned Parenthood was furious, but parents reclaimed their right to have a say in their child's education. This is something that is very important to President Trump, who is giving power back to families through school choice, allowing parents to make decisions about the best schools to send their children to without being tied simply to their zip code. This frees children from underserved schools and parents from schools they disagree with.

And finally, the classroom is a battleground but so is your kitchen table and your car. Parents often underestimate the influence they can have just by talking to their kids. I firmly believe the most effective way to protect kids from indoctrination is to talk to them—even more so than taking legal action or protesting. Your kids spend about eight hours in school every day and closer to five or six awake at home; if you are not taking the time to instill values in your kids, you can be sure someone else is.

CHAPTER NINE

★ ★ ★ ★ ★ ★ ★

INSTITUTIONS OF HIGHER INDOCTRINATION

While the left would have you think young Americans are a lost cause for Republicans, President Trump sees that there is a unique opportunity to win them over.

Last summer, Zogby released a largely underreported poll that revealed nearly half of Gen Z voters (ages 18–24), approve of President Trump. He "scored well with younger Millennial voters aged 18–29 (51% approve/46% disapprove) and Generation Z voters aged 18–24 (49% approve/51% disapprove)." Millennial voters, they say, who have been harsh critics of Trump and his presidency are now split on the prospects for the U.S. economy under his presidency.

Perhaps it was an outlier—but even still, there is a strong case to be made for younger generations swinging right.

Generally, these individuals tend to be tech-savvy, discerning, open-minded, pragmatic, and individualistic. Having spent their entire lives channeling their ideas and experiences online, they value free expression and may be less inclined to support the censorship they see from the liberal mob. We're already starting to see pushback on the "cancel culture" that has plagued our society over the past few years.

If the left wasn't so busy brainwashing them on college campuses, they would likely recognize that President Trump is delivering on the things they care about: future job prospects and opportunities, free speech, economic stability, safe communities, justice in our prison system, improving income inequality, and progress for minority communities.

Unfortunately, that isn't the case. The conservative surrendering of higher education to the left only makes us that much more responsible to follow President Trump's lead and fight on all fronts—no matter how entrenched they may be. And believe me, when it comes to the educational front, restoring conservatism is no easy task.

It's no secret that college campuses are bastions of liberalism. Most Americans have probably seen viral video clips of leftist students screeching at events, burning flags, defacing statues, vandalizing campus property, socking conservative students in the face, or joining in on their professors scolding a Trump supporter. The past few years were marked with campus hysteria, violent protests, and student-led lawsuits—all of which played out on a national platform and led us to the point of President Trump stepping in and signing an executive order to uphold the tenets of free speech on college campuses.

I thought that was the worst of it, until visiting these notorious college campuses for myself. Each campus that I was invited to speak on revealed something new about the tactics used to keep conservative views off-campus.

In 2019, I was invited to Northeastern Illinois University to participate in a discussion with former Democratic National Committee chair Donna Brazile. To say I wasn't greeted with a warm welcome is an understatement. Multiple NEIU students and faculty members penned an open letter to the university president, demanding that she cancel my appearance at the school. Apparently, my mere presence was "an insult to all NEIU students and employees who are members of groups targeted with violence and vitriol by the Trump administration. . . . It would be an affront to humanity to host Spicer at NEIU. We urge you to withdraw the invitation immediately."

There's a lot to unpack there. "Targeted by violence"? You can disagree with policies. That's what makes our country great. But to claim they are being targeted by violence is insane. There is a new phenomenon whereby if someone on the left does not like the views of someone else, they don't feel "safe" anymore. Seriously. I have heard this over and over that my mere presence on a college campus makes students feel unsafe.

The letter prompted protests before and during the event and included an audience member storming the stage shouting "shut it down," among other far worse chants and expletives. While I had been on several college campuses where people had chanted and screamed, this was the first time I had participated in an event where an individual rushed the stage. Thankfully, security immediately subdued the student and escorted him out of the facility.

More often than not, it's the professors, administrators, and others in positions of authority on campus who lead the charge against open dialogue and free thought. When chants from protesters started to drown out the discussion, the moderator pathetically said it was "a sign of health . . . where people can be yelling in protest, and at the same time we have the ability to have a robust but civil conversation." But doesn't his comment seem contradictory? How can you have a civil conversation while someone is yelling over me? That is literally contradictory to the definition of a civil conversation. And it's actually rude to the people who are there to listen. We keep allowing the lowest common denominator to rule. If one person is offended or wants to yell, we all must sit back and take it.

Having a robust discussion and being able to hear both sides of a debate is what college is supposed to be about. Students must be able to take the information presented to them and grow as a person through this type of discourse. Shouting down one side sounds exactly the opposite of what a "liberal arts education" is supposed to be about. It's not inclusive. It's actually being exclusive to anyone who doesn't share a particular set of values.

After the event concluded, it became clear to me the real reason campus leftists were so adamant and determined in their efforts to prevent it from happening. Despite their best efforts to frame the discussion as an unconscionable act of violence and dissuade students from attending, the event was sold out, and the room was packed. There was an obvious interest among the student body. What faculty and administrators don't understand is that there is, in fact, a yearning for students to hear both sides and learn more, and their attempts to curtail such events only grows that hunger. But time and time again, they ignore that reality, and in turn, we see one side that dominates the conversation and yells down the other.

When the College Republicans group at the University of California, Berkeley, through a grant covered by Young America's Foundation, invited me to their campus for an event, they were given a small room that could accommodate only a fractional number of the students who reserved tickets. Many who were in line were not able to enter.

The *Daily Californian*, the student-run campus newspaper, wrote that despite the fact that nearly 800 students signed up to attend my talk, only a fraction made it into the medium-sized room, adding that "when Sean Spicer walked up to the lectern in front of a crowded Evans Hall lecture room he was met with a round of applause that took him aback." I remember telling the crowd "that was not the introduction I was expecting, but I appreciate it." Receiving that applause showed that despite the administration's best efforts to derail the event, many students wanted to have a conversation and were hungry for opposing views.

Interestingly, I began the event by walking onstage and saying to everyone there that clearly there was a lot of interest in the event tonight, and I wanted to make a simple proposition: if they would let me talk, I would stay there as long as I was able to answer every one of their questions. If we agreed up front that we would all show each other a level of respect, then everybody would have the opportunity to speak their mind no matter what it was. And that's exactly how it played out. I waited until everyone had their questions answered. If it can happen on campus at Berkeley, it can happen anywhere.

I have to admit I was really nervous about speaking at Berkeley. Let's just say the track record of conservatives speaking on campus was not reassuring. Previous speakers had been met with fires and threats of violence. I had learned to judge a venue by the amount of security that had been assigned to me. Prior to the event, campus police shared their emergency plan with me. While I was thankful that they had thought through these plans, it was hardly reassuring.

As concerned as I was about getting onstage at Berkeley, I soon realized that more than anything else, many of these students either wanted to have their voices heard or ask a question that would further their understanding of viewpoints they were not normally exposed to.

More than protesting and yelling, this is a matter of treating each other with respect. You can disagree with each other's point of view, but where the left gets it wrong is that they don't want people on the right to even be able to express their point of view. I don't mind listening to the other side. In fact, I want to hear their point of view. But all I ask is simply to respect the other person in the same way and give everyone the equal opportunity to speak.

Every time I'm with a student group on campus, I'll ask how many conservative speakers they've had, and most of the time, I'm either the first or one of a handful. Part of the college experience is being thrust into a diverse environment where, for the first time, students learn to live with people of various backgrounds and beliefs. But colleges today don't allow them that experience.

If it wasn't for the funding of the Young America's Foundation, which graciously funded all of my campus speeches, and the Leadership Institute, an educational organization that offers grants to student groups to host conservative speakers, most conservative student clubs wouldn't have the resources to invite a speaker. No wonder why many college students graduate without being exposed to conservative ideas from a conservative perspective.

A recent study by the National Association of Scholars found that liberal professors outnumber their conservative counterparts nearly 9 to 1 at the highest *U.S. News*–ranked private and public colleges. At many schools, the gap is much larger. At UC Berkeley, for instance, conservative professors are outnumbered 28.4 to 1 and at the University of Massachusetts Amherst, the ratio is an astonishing 92 to 0.

Liberal commencement speakers also outnumbered conservatives by a wide margin. The Young America's Foundation's 2018 Commencement Speakers Survey found that among the country's top 100 universities, only three hosted a conservative-leaning speaker—one less than the results from the same study in 2017. In 2016, that number was 12. It won't be long before it's down to zero.

This wouldn't be as problematic if the commencement speeches were used to inspire all students regardless of their background, beliefs, or future career paths. But that's not the case, at least not anymore. Today, the speeches are used as a final effort to indoctrinate. When I was in college, commencement speakers gave inspiring final charges to students before embarking on the real world. It was an opportunity for schools to impart one final lesson on graduates.

In the rare instances that someone linked to a Republican or conservative actually is invited, protest usually ensues. This past June, Wichita State University Tech canceled an invitation to Ivanka Trump to be part of a lineup of commencement speakers following the protests that were sparked after the killing of George Floyd by a Minneapolis police officer.

According to a story in the *New York Times*, officials at the university canceled her invitation, which, by the way, was virtual because of the coronavirus, based on how President Trump had responded to George Floyd's killing. "In light of the social justice issues brought forth by George Floyd's death, I understand and take responsibility that the timing of the announcement was insensitive," Sheree Utash, the school's president, wrote in a statement on Thursday, the same day Ms. Trump's speech was announced.

"For this, I'm sorry that was never the intent, and I want you to know I have heard you, and we are responding."

Ivanka declared that she was a victim of cancel culture and released the video of her address online anyway. She wrote on Twitter, "Our nation's campuses should be bastions of free speech. Cancel culture and viewpoint discrimination are antithetical to academia. Listening to one another is important now more than ever!"

That is exactly what creates the attitude among students to boycott speakers and opinions contrary to their own.

When Vice President Mike Pence was invited to address Notre Dame's graduating glass in May 2017 students were beside themselves. They were likely never taught how to handle a conservative speaker on campus—so naturally, they disgraced their school by staging a walkout during the speech. According to CNN's coverage of the event, 146 people were involved, and videos showed students "standing as Pence took the podium, then walking out of the ceremony and gathering outside Notre Dame Stadium, where they held a short alternative 'graduation ceremony.'"

Ironically, Pence told the assembled graduates that Notre Dame was a "vanguard of freedom of expression and the free exchange of ideas."

In each of these examples, you have to wonder what the protesters—and sometimes even administrators and faculty—are actually afraid of. That the students might actually learn something? If they can't handle someone of another political party at a commencement speech, how are they going to succeed in life, let alone handle basic interactions with people of different ideological backgrounds in the workplace?

Congressman Dan Crenshaw seeks to answer this question in his book, writing, "The latest threat to our American story is outrage culture, identity politics and the victimhood ideology that it elevates. The threat is born of small beginnings, as big threats so often are. It starts with toxic personal narratives wrapped in the cheap cloth of victimhood, always looking to an external culprit to blame for real or perceived injustices. At first, this blame is assigned to an individual—your unfair boss, your neglectful parent, a teacher who refused to see your potential, or just perpetual bad luck. But this isn't enough for the outrage enthusiast. There must be more culprits. More oppressors to be blamed for your misfortune. These individual culprits become group oppressors, thus expanding the category of oppressors from mere individuals to entire groups of people. The narrative becomes group-on-group oppression as a way to explain any and all misfortune or unhappiness that might occur."

Throughout the year, college administrators and professors force their ideology onto students using a wide variety of tactics, including speech codes, language guides, and the refusal of recognition, funding, and event space for conservative groups.

One of the most egregious forms of censorship used on college campuses today is the "heckler's veto." The Foundation for Individual Rights in Education (FIRE), known as the free-speech watchdog, says the term comes from when a heckler—one seeking to silence a speaker—"vetoes" a speech by severely and substantially disrupting it so that it cannot continue. When a college cancels an event due to the disturbance (or even due to the potential for such a disturbance), the college grants a heckler's veto to that individual. The term also encompasses situations when a college punishes students or professors for the potential or actual reaction to their expression, such as when it imposes large security fees on student groups for hosting a controversial speaker or revokes a professor's network access due to complaints about the professor's online speech.

Such was the case at Portland State University when a cowbell-clad protester shut down a conservative speaker's event as campus police stood idly by. According to a March 12, 2019, Campus Reform report, the school stood by the protester and contended he was within his rights to engage in "disruption."

It's not uncommon for faculty and administrators to partake in the heckler's veto themselves.

At one of the speeches I gave at the University of Pennsylvania on March 27, 2019, I asked the faculty representative what the procedure would be if my speech was protested or interrupted. They explained to me that the first time it occurred, the protester would be allowed to finish their rant. On the second time, they would be asked to stop, and on the third time, they would be reminded of the rules. Only upon the fourth time would they be asked to leave. I looked in bewilderment about why it was going to take four warnings, and they explained to me that they wanted to recognize the students' rights. I thought to myself, since when does an individual have the right to disrupt a room full of hundreds of people so their rights can be preserved while the rights of everyone else in the room who wanted to listen to the discussion were not acknowledged? The school's first priority was clearly to allow the students, not the guest speaker, to express themselves even if it meant disrupting the event for everyone else in attendance.

That's when I realized how bad the problem really was. The fact that disruptive audience members are given three opportunities before being addressed by faculty or being held accountable revealed that the incentive is to disrupt, not to be respectful.

Thanks to these speech-suppressing policies, students quickly learn that all they have to do to sideline speakers they don't like is simply declare their views offensive and threaten to riot. A September 2017 Brookings Institution report revealed that 51 percent of students feel that this tactic is acceptable, while 19 percent believe violence is an acceptable tactic to shut down offensive speech. Think about that for a minute. A fifth of students think violence is okay to shut down free speech. College campuses are supposed to be the places of tolerance and inclusion, yet today they are increasingly fostering incivility and even violence. It is outrageous that so many students have adopted this mindset, but putting all of the blame on them is misplaced. They learn from the best, oftentimes their trusted professors, that speech is violence and violence is speech. You have to wonder what lesson this teaches to young people entering the real world.

For one, such a mentality sets students up for failure both in the workplace and in the real world. College is about academics, but it's also about learning the life skills needed to socialize, work, and otherwise interact with people of all backgrounds and beliefs. It's a place for students to learn to accept that things won't always be pleasant and realize their personal discomfort is not a reason to punish others. Instead, they learn that their feelings take precedence over other people's rights and that some people's feelings are more important than others.

Jonathan Haidt, a social psychologist and the author of *The Coddling of the American Mind*, remarked on how the hypersensitivity of today's college graduates translates into the workplace: "Leaders in the business world see problems like hypersensitivity and the constant conflict over small things. Bright hires go running to HR, every time there's a conflict, and then, they won't show up at the meeting with the person who supposedly offended them."

Stress and conflict are basically guaranteed in the workplace. Just look at the grueling survival-of-the-fittest environment on Wall Street. This should be deeply concerning to parents who invest thousands of dollars into their child's education.

Students need to learn that bad things happen, that inappropriate things happen, and that people make awful mistakes. Our goal should be to root them out and punish bad people but not to think the world is going to stop every time that happens.

When Young America's Foundation hosted Ben Shapiro at the University of Connecticut in March 2018, the school not only restricted public access but provided counseling to students who may have felt offended by his conservative views.

Coddling students over political events is almost always one-sided on college campuses, as demonstrated by absurd claims of "trauma" and "fear" over conservative speakers and student groups, the numerous instances of childish coping activities such as the University of California, Irvine's "group cry" over Trump's election, and Barnard College's event to mourn Hillary's loss with "feminist coloring pages." I'd be remiss not to mention when Evergreen State College's provost told professors to take students' feelings into account when grading, or when Santa Monica College spent $60,000 to turn their computer lab into a "safe space."

The list goes on and on but rarely is this hypersensitivity applied when it comes to conservatives. Professors and administrators not only turn a blind eye to violence and other attacks aimed at conservatives; some even encourage and participate in them. A professor at Orange Coast College in California made headlines after calling Trump's election an "act of terrorism" in

2016 and was later awarded "Faculty of the Year" by her colleagues. Likewise, a California State University Fullerton lecturer was reinstated in 2017 after he was fired for physically assaulting a conservative student during a politically charged protest on campus. That's not a typo. He was reinstated after assaulting a student.

According to an August 2017 report from *Inside Higher Ed*, professors at Purdue University and Stanford University assembled a "Campus Antifa Network" to serve as a "big tent" for the notoriously violent Antifa group, which has been designated as a terrorist group by the FBI. Of course, that designation means very little to those who have a complete disregard for the FBI and other law enforcement officials.

Last fall, the University of Pennsylvania, a self-proclaimed sanctuary campus, shut down an event featuring former Immigration and Customs Enforcement director Tom Homan after more than five hundred students and alumni, along with dozens more from Brown University, Cornell University, Columbia University, the Massachusetts Institute of Technology, and Harvard University, signed a petition and demanded a permanent ban on all invitations to current and former ICE or U.S. Customs and Border Patrol officials. So let's be clear, the agencies that enforce the county's duly passed laws are somehow supposed to be branded as evil for doing the job that they, by law, are tasked with doing.

Local campus police officers are often the ones who bear the brunt of the left's disdain for law enforcement. Last April, a petition that circulated at Yale University demanded that campus police officers disarm themselves and make donations to Black Lives Matter. Ironically, these same students attend a university named after slave trader Elihu Yale, and in the words of the chair of Yale's William F. Buckley Jr. Program, Robert Kimball, in his 2016 *Wall*

Street Journal op-ed, Yale was "deeply involved in the slave trade." But don't expect any of those students to toss their diplomas.

Brooklyn College was so disgusted by the mere presence of police that it asked its campus officers to use bathrooms out of sight from the student body to avoid offending anybody. I wonder what these same people would do if they found themselves as a victim of a crime. Who are they going to call when they're in trouble? Police officers aren't perfect, but they're the ones to consistently put themselves in harm's way to protect even those who disrespect and disparage them like this.

When intolerant leftists on campus can't get their way through event roadblocks, speech codes and language guides are often weaponized to silence conservative ideas. The Foundation for Individual Rights in Education (FIRE) reports that nearly one in three American colleges currently have at least one policy that "clearly and substantially restricts freedom of speech."

For Amherst College, the stifling free-speech policy was reflected in a forty-page "Common Language Guide" issued to students. Note how the guide defines these terms:

> CAPITALISM: "An economic and political system in which a country's trade and industry are controlled by private owners for profit, rather than by the state. This system leads to exploitative labor practices, which affect marginalized groups disproportionately."

> REVERSE OPPRESSION: "There is no such thing as reverse oppression. Oppression is predicated upon access to institutional power. Marginalized communities do not have access to institutional power. For example, women

can be as prejudiced as men, but women cannot be 'just as sexist as men,' because they do not hold political, economic, and institutional power."

TOXIC MASCULINITY: "Masculinity as defined by violence, sexual acts, status, aggression, and the oppression of others. Toxic Masculinity hurts everyone, including cisgender men. It is characterized with rigid gender roles and expectations that are often violently enforced. Men are unable to express or feel emotion, and the fear of being deemed in proximity to being gay or a woman is a constant threat."

One that stands out to me is capitalism, otherwise known as the backbone of the American dream. Absent from the list is any mention of socialism or communism, which are the embodiment of the "exploitative labor practices" the guide mentions to disparage capitalism.

Make no mistake, language guides are meant to silence conservative thought, and failure to abide by them often comes with real consequences. A student at the Indiana University of Pennsylvania, for instance, was recently barred from a religion class for saying that the official view of biologists is that there are only two genders.

This wasn't an isolated incident. Students across the country put their reputation, academic standing, and even their safety on the line to defend their conservative views on campus.

ANTI-AMERICANISM 2.0

A few years ago, Harvard University announced that Chelsea Manning and myself would be added to the list of new visiting

fellows at the Institute of Politics at Harvard. Manning is a former U.S. military intelligence analyst convicted of treason, but it
was I who received a majority of the protests by leftist on campus. Here's the interesting thing: beyond the fact that Chelsea was
convicted of treason she has no background in politics. What did
the Institute of Politics think Chelsea was offering the students?
She served in the army at a rather low level and then was charged
with twenty-two counts and convicted under the Espionage Act
of passing out classified information. After serving seven years in
prison, her sentence was commuted by President Obama. Aside
from being able to explain what it felt like to have her sentence
commuted by the president, there was no other political experience. As a side note, it's worth noting that Wikipedia describes her
as a whistleblower and activist. So if you are convicted of espionage
it's totally cool as long as the left embraces why you did it. Got it.

As a side note, it is worth nothing that the Institutes of Politics,
or IOPs as they are called, at every major university, Harvard,
Cornell, Georgetown, the University of Chicago, are all run by
Democrats.

Upon examination of the anti-American sentiment fostered at
elite institutions like Harvard, you wouldn't have expected anything else. And if you thought the anti-Americanism in grade
schools was bad, brace yourself for what colleges and universities
teach. The indoctrination ramps up as students are empowered to
invite speakers and explore other ideas.

On almost every college campus, revisionist history of some
sort is taught in place of U.S. history. According to a 2016 report
from the American Council of Trustees and Alumni (ACTA),
U.S. History is not a staple course for history majors at most top

universities, with less than one-third of *U.S. News & World Report*'s top 25 liberal arts colleges, top 25 national universities, and top 25 public institutions requiring U.S. history as a requirement for history majors. That is off-the-charts absurd.

"Many institutions instead specify that history majors must take classes in areas outside of the United States," ACTA notes. "History majors at Williams College have the option of taking 'Soccer and History in Latin America: Make the Beautiful Game,' and students at Swarthmore may enroll in 'Modern Addiction: Cigarette Smoking in the 20th Century' in order to fulfill history major requirements." Additionally, "'Hip-Hop, Politics, and Youth Culture in America' and 'Mad Men and Mad Women' are classes that fulfill the American history requirement at University of Connecticut and Middlebury College, respectively, instead of courses that cover subjects such as the Revolutionary War or the Emancipation Proclamation."

It's no wonder so many of today's youth are going around demanding the demolition of historical statues and monuments that they know nothing about. These are the same passionate young people who spent four years at colleges and universities that specialize in disparaging capitalism and praising socialism. In January 2016, *Market Watch* reported *The Communist Manifesto* is among the three most frequently assigned readings at American universities, and Karl Marx is the most studied economist. So it's safe to assume they are not only historically illiterate, they are straight-up spoon-fed Marxist propaganda.

It doesn't take much digging to find blatant examples of this. Just start by browsing course catalogs at any given college or university. At the University of Massachusetts, for instance, students are offered a "Resistance Studies Initiative" course that teaches them all ways in which they can resist the evils of capitalism and its "exploitative practices."

A "teach-in" event at California State University declares that America was "built on a racist capitalist system" that was "meant to weaken the minority," while an exam in an introductory political science course at San Diego Miramar College equates capitalism to a "process of exploitation" and claims that awful sweatshop conditions are an inherent part of the process. This past year, Colorado State University listed "America" and "American" as offensive words "to avoid." Read that again and let that set in. The words that represent the freest and most prosperous country in the world, not to mention the very place we reside in and enjoy the privilege to teach and receive an education, are too offensive to utter at an academic institution.

Just days after Trump's inauguration, students at Brown University vandalized a veterans memorial, ripping American flags to shreds. Campus Reform reports that one student who helped organize the memorial, Nicky Strada, took to Facebook to express outrage at the fact that classmates had disrespected America's war heroes and the country's flag, writing, "Today was a sad day. Hundreds of flags were set up on the main green of Brown University by 2 veterans in honor of Veterans Day tomorrow, and when I got out of class, people had snapped them, ripped them, and threw them aside."

Equally disturbing, a professor at Broward College thought it was a good idea to use an American flag as a doormat for a campus "art display," according to another Campus Reform report in January 2019. The cut-up, bleached flag was designed specifically to have visitors unknowingly step on it. A Broward College student and disabled Marine Corps veteran, Jess Karcher, wrote: "People are stepping on the flag as they enter most of whom don't realize it's an American flag. The artist had a camera set up, taking pictures of people stepping on it as part of her artwork. I find this extremely disrespectful and kick in the gut as a veteran. I have lost many friends whose caskets were draped with that same flag."

At Boston University, Alexandria Ocasio-Cortez's alma mater, just three out of the forty-nine guest speakers invited to campus last year leaned conservative in their ideology. Further, the school proudly hosted a panel based on the premise that America and Israel are "fascist states." It's no wonder she peddles the insane lunacy she does through the halls of Congress. It could easily be presumed that she was never even exposed to American's founding ideals, considering she spent four years learning that America is evil and that socialism is the answer to all of its problems.

Colleges reflect this sentiment of fundamentally transforming the America we know and love, while studies reflect the multifaceted shift in American values as a result. A recent *Wall Street Journal*/NBC survey revealed a drastic 20-point drop in the number of young Americans today versus two decades ago who name patriotism, religion, and having children as important values.

This is, in part, a direct result of today's college curriculum, which is designed to transform, not to teach, as well as campus resources that are used to indoctrinate, not educate.

Anti-Trumpism on college campuses is unlike anything we've ever seen. For starters, nearly 50 percent of college students say their professors rant against President Trump during class, according to a recent poll by College Fix. A professor at the University of California, Riverside, declared that "all" Trump supporters are "white nationalist terror supporters." A George Washington

University psychiatrist compared Trump's rallies to Adolf Hitler's, while a Minot State University professor hung posters on her office door comparing Trump to a KKK member, Hitler, Mussolini, and Stalin. Meanwhile, an Ohio State University professor was caught on tape using class time to go on a fifteen-minute rant against the "racist" Trump.

The curriculum is just as alarming. Following Trump's election, Columbia University offered a course on "persistent racism" of "Trumpism." The University of Maryland, Baltimore County, spent an entire week promoting "resistance" to the Trump agenda. Harvard University and UC Berkeley hosted an online anti-Trump "Resistance School."

You'll never have to wonder why college students are liberal again. Just look at what they're exposed to.

A drastic change in higher education came with the federal government's Obama-era takeover of student loans, which allows students to receive expensive degrees that have questionable value at best. The *Wall Street Journal* reported in August 2019 that college students are leaving campus drowning in an average of over $39,900 in student loan debt, and 15 percent of graduate students alone carry more federal student loan debt than their annual income. They should be seriously considering whether or not they'll get a return on their investment. The handling of student loans is all the more reason to reject the radical Democrat's "college for all" proposal.

Perhaps one of the most obvious displays of recklessness in higher education is the astronomical spending on absurd classes and useless programs such as Duke University's nine-week Men's Project to destabilize "toxic masculine privilege." Campus Reform reports that "[o]ver the course of the nine-week program, men will participate in weekly discussion groups conducted through an 'intersectional feminist lens,' with the hope of helping male students learn an 'intersectional understanding of masculinity' and creating 'spaces to destabilize masculine privilege.'" If we are going to compete with the likes of China in the coming years, we need to graduate students ready to take on the challenges of this century. This will not cut it.

Speaking of China, the Education Department recently opened an investigation into Harvard and Yale after the schools tried to hide the fact that they received $6.5 billion in foreign funding from countries such as China and Saudi Arabia. A month before, Harvard's chemistry department chairman was arrested for lying about receiving millions of dollars from China as part of the country's long-term plot to catapult itself to the forefront of scientific development. It's incredibly revealing that these schools incessantly bash America while secretly taking money from countries known to be hostile to the United States. They beat the drum about America being a bad word, yet they enable China's nefarious tactics. Let's not kid ourselves here. China has an agenda. Its leaders are trying to seep into all sectors of society, and college administrators and professors are allowing it to happen right under their noses. Remember that study about American values declining among young people? Now you see why.

Students need to graduate ready to compete with China, not admire it.

TRUMP'S COMMITMENT

"He took a hard punch in the face for all of us!"

These were the words of President Trump in March 2019 during a fiery speech at the Conservative Political Action Conference

(CPAC), the largest and most influential gathering of conservatives in the world. He was speaking about conservative youth activist Hayden Williams, who was socked in the face by a left-wing activist at the University of California, Berkeley just days before while helping conservative groups recruit new members on behalf of the Leadership Institute.

"I turned on my television the other day, and I saw somebody that was violently punched in the face . . . and I said that's disgusting," Trump said. He then urged Williams to sue the attacker, the university, and even the state, joking that Hayden is "going to be a very wealthy young man."

The crowd erupted with chants of "U.S.A., U.S.A," to which Trump responded by announcing that he will sign an executive order that would require colleges and universities to support free speech in exchange for federal research dollars. "If they want our dollars, and we give it to them by the billions, they've got to allow people like Hayden and many other great young people and old people to speak," Trump said. "If they don't, it will be costly."

Williams still had a black eye when the president proceeded to unexpectedly call him up onstage and hand him the microphone to speak briefly.

"There are so many conservative students across the country that are facing discrimination and harassment and worse if they dare to speak up on campus so I'm glad that we could bring this to the forefront, and I'd just like to say if these socialist progressives had their way they would put our Constitution through the paper shredder in a heartbeat so it's as important now than ever to work at Leadership Institute and Campus Reform exposing these liberal abuses to the public," Williams said.

"These students do it because they have a love of our nation and freedom and, frankly, a love for you, Mr. President."

A few weeks later, on March 21, 2019, Trump made good on his pledge and signed into law a monumental executive order designed to protect free speech on college campuses.

"Under the guise of speech codes, safe spaces, and trigger warnings, these universities have tried to restrict free thought, impose total conformity and shut down the voices of great young Americans like those here today," he said at the East Room in the White House, while surrounded by conservative student activists who had been targets of left-wing censorship. As he did with Williams at CPAC, the president invited several students onstage just before signing it, giving them a platform to tell their stories.

One of those students was Kaitlyn Mullen, a conservative student activist who made headlines after being the subject of a faculty-led harassment stunt at the University of Nebraska. *Business Insider* reported that Mullen had been recruiting members and displaying materials on behalf of Turning Point USA, a conservative group founded by Charlie Kirk, in 2017 when she found herself on the receiving end of a loud, disruptive protest from Courtney Lawton—a graduate student at the University of Nebraska. A video of Lawton shouting, "Becky the neo-fascist, right here. Wants to destroy public schools, public universities. Hates DACA kids," went viral, setting in motion a series of events rising all the way to the state legislature, where conservative senators demanded the graduate student be fired from her teaching position at the university. Mullen told Campus Reform that "at least three professors circled the table while carrying signs and yelling things like 'f**k Charlie Kirk' and 'TPUSA Naziz,'" adding that she "didn't even engage, but I kept tabling as I wasn't going to let them silence me," but conceded that after a while, "I got overwhelmed and scared and started to cry," at which point the professors "screamed [that] I was crying for attention."

Do you see how problematic this is? The professors, who I assume are there to teach, are attacking a student who has a different point of view. Why would any student have a dissenting point of view after seeing this?

Trump introduced Mullen, saying, "Kaitlyn was approached by staff and a graduate instructor and was berated and cursed at," and gave her the podium to tell her story.

Next, he gave the floor to Ellen Wittman, a junior at Miami University in Ohio and the school's chapter president of the pro-life group Students for Life. "Ellen planned an annual event to display small wooden crosses representing the lives of the unborn," President Trump said, adding that "school officials informed Ellen that she would be required to post signs all over campus providing a 'trigger warning' to other students regarding her display."

And finally, he invited Northeast Wisconsin Technical College student Polly Olsen, who was blocked from handing out valentines with biblical phrases on her campus in February 2018, to tell her story onstage. She used the opportunity to talk about how her late mother taught her about the First Amendment, remarking, "Freedom of speech is near and dear to my heart. My mother told me while she was homeschooling me that I would have to know what my First Amendment rights were because someday they would be violated, and I would have to stand up for them." She held up a small red valentine in the shape of a heart as she spoke, explaining that she was carrying on her mother's legacy by giving out the valentines.

"College officials stopped her and told her that she would be restricted to a so-called 'free speech zone' because some people might find her cards offensive," President Trump said. "I don't. I love that card. In fact, Polly, give me some. I'll send them around to my friends."

Interestingly, the mainstream media was reluctant to include any of these students' stories in their write-ups of the event. The *New York Times*, for instance, published a recap of the signing titled "Trump Signs Executive Order Protecting Free Speech on College Campuses," but failed to even mention any of the students who spoke, who were arguably the highlight, if not the focal point of the event. Instead, they wrote that "the order raises questions about the role of government in regulating speech" and found college liberals like Emily Chamlee-Wright, the president of the Institute for Humane Studies at George Mason University, to weigh in about the "bloated bureaucracies in government agencies and on college campuses" that "Trump's executive order would create."

Perhaps they felt personally attacked when Trump said, "Today, we are delivering a clear message to the professors and power structures trying to suppress dissent and keep young Americans—and all Americans, not just young Americans like Ellen and Kaitlyn and Polly—from challenging rigid, far-left ideology. People who are confident in their beliefs do not censor others—we don't want to censor others—they welcome free, fair, and open debate. And that's what we're demanding."

Trump described the executive order as a "historic action to defend American students and American values that have been under siege."

The order directed the Office of Management and Budget, in coordination with twelve agencies that make federal grants, to ensure colleges and universities are protecting the First Amendment rights of their students and promoting free inquiry and debate, or risk losing billions of federal taxpayer dollars. It's important to note that compliance with the First Amendment protections already applied to public institutions, but they were largely disregarded for years with little to no accountability.

The order also called for more transparency in higher education. Private universities, which are known to have more flexibility in dictating speech, would be required to commit to their own institutional rules. "Private universities should be held to their own policies on free speech," Trump declared. "So, from now on, federal agencies will also use their grant-making authority to promote transparency for students at private schools. These colleges should not be able to promise free speech in theory, and then impose restrictive speech codes in practice, which is what many of them do."

Further, Trump directed the Education Department to "propose a plan that will require colleges and universities to have skin in the game by sharing a portion of the financial risk of the student loan debt," which would ensure students have the vital information about the financial risk and career outcomes associated with student loans.

Trump knows that fighting for American ideals means taking the fight directly to the classroom. And that's exactly what he did and what he continues to do.

Back in June 2017, Trump took action to champion trade schools and apprenticeships to help prepare students to compete in a global economy. He wanted to give young workers an alternative to the "crushing debt" associated with four-year college degrees, and did so by launching an initiative to expand vocational training programs and apprenticeships to equip young Americans for the "jobs of the future." It was accompanied by executive orders that loosened federal restrictions on such programs and paved the way for better partnerships between college students and businesses. Each of these initiatives was met with overwhelming bipartisan support, and while they were essential first steps, there is more that can be done. We must go on offense. We can't expect younger generations of Americans to embrace capitalism and patriotism if they are learning the exact opposite in schools.

We can follow Trump's lead by standing up for ourselves and for marginalized college students. He tells conservatives to not lie down and be passive, but rather to fight back and go on offense. Before Williams walked off the CPAC stage, Trump told him to "sue the college, the university, and maybe sue the state."

Since then, conservative students have increasingly been paving the way for victory by taking legal action against colleges. Several months after the order was signed into law, Young America's Foundation won a $66,000 free speech lawsuit against the University of Florida. The students joined the ranks of many other student groups from across the country who took on their schools and successfully held them accountable, including the College Republicans at UC Berkeley who recently won a $70,000 lawsuit over bias and roadblocks in bringing conservatives speakers to campus.

Sites like Campus Reform and the College Fix have emerged, opening the public's eyes to what's actually being taught on campuses. Read them. Pay attention to them. Demand accountability from the radical activists masquerading as educators.

In recent years, conservative youth organizations have been on the rise in schools and on college campuses. Charlie Kirk, the founder of TPUSA, was just a teenager when he started a massive, grassroots youth-based movement on college campuses across the country. What President Trump did was empower them. He, along with his top administration officials and campaign staffers, started attending their events and gave them credibility.

Again in December 2019, President Trump addressed a Turning Point USA summit, this time in West Palm Beach, Florida. "Every young person in this room has a vital role to play in the never-ending mission of defending the America we love," he said.

"The future of our nation depends on the courage and devotion of its young people. It depends on all of you. Conservatives and patriots cannot and must not surrender our cherished institutions and culture to the radical, America-hating left. We must have the heart, which we have, and the tenacity, which we have, to preserve them, protect them, and reclaim them. Our nation badly needs more young people like those here tonight to study up, work hard, and then go into government, go into journalism, go into media, go into teaching, and, yes, go into academia, and retake these institutions, rebuild our culture, and take back our country."

If that's not an encouragement for students who have long felt ostracized, like they didn't have a place in the hostile world of left-wing academia, I don't know what is.

★ ★ ★ ★ ★ ★ ★

CHAPTER TEN

JOURNALISM SCHOOL TO SOCIAL JUSTICE WARRIOR: A REVOLVING DOOR

The journalism student doesn't fall far from the legacy media tree.

To understand the mindset of today's journalists you have to look at the journalism schools they went to. They learn the fundamentals of journalism through a warped far-left perspective, which is then reinforced in the newsroom.

"Today, too many journalists aren't interested in doing the work, they just want the rewards," writes Derek Hunter in his book *Outrage, Inc.* "For a journalist or pundit to achieve some level of fame, all he or she has to do is get on TV. And the bar for entry for that has been lowered to the point that you'd need a shovel to get under it. . . . Add in the immediacy of the Internet age—report the story first, check the facts later—and you have a profession where verification is for suckers. Twitter followers, Facebook fans, page views and TV hits are the hard currency of journalism."

This became apparent to me through my interactions with younger journalists who arrived onto the political scene over the past decade. I watched them enter the newsroom wide-eyed and eager to change the world—which sounds like a good thing—until you remember that it's not their job to change the world at all.

Much of the curriculum in today's most prestigious journalism schools reflects a shift from teaching students how to report on the world as it is to teaching them how to report on the world as they think it should be.

The University of Arizona's journalism school states: "It doesn't matter the medium—we teach you how to gather information, analyze it, boil it down, and then communicate it effectively, accurately, quickly and ethically—all to make the world a better place. That is journalism."

I get the first part, but did you catch the end of that statement? Make the world a better place? Since when is that the role of reporters? If anything, making the world a better place is a role reserved for doctors, politicians, philanthropists, and the like—not reporters. Reporting is supposed to be all about the facts, conveying to the public the who, what, where, and why, and letting them make up their minds about what they believe based on the facts that are presented to them. Clearly, the role of journalism has crossed over into activism and determining what a "better place" is.

What I believe to be a better place includes a country with a much more limited role of government, while many liberals would believe a better place would include a much more expanded role of government. And this is where the root of the problem lies. A better place is defined by those who hold the power, and in the case of journalism school, that power is wielded at the podium. When journalism professors teach that the role of journalists is to make the world a better place, if they happen to come from a liberal background, then their students are inherently taught to advance a liberal agenda.

This mission statement from the University of Arizona's journalism school is not unlike those of many mainstream media corporations. Both institutions foster the idea that journalism is more about getting people to believe in a "better place" than getting them to believe the truth, pleasant or not.

Campus Reform also reported that the public university hired radical leftist professor Noam Chomsky to teach a course titled "What is Politics?" from 2017 to 2020. The course description states that it will explore "issues in contemporary political analysis, human values and political goals, how governments differ and why they change, and how nations differ from one another."

Here's why this is problematic. The announcement from the school described Chomsky as a "world-renowned linguist" and one of the most "cited scholars in modern history," conveniently leaving out his long list of concerning views, which would undoubtedly be woven into his teachings on human values and political affairs. This is the guy who told the BBC during an interview in November 2017, just months before he was hired by the University of Arizona, that the Republican Party is the most dangerous organization in "human history." He echoed his same sentiment in a May 2018 speech at St. Olaf College, a liberal arts college in Minnesota, where he declared that Republicans and Christians are intent on "destroying organized human life."

Back in May 2006 on the Lebanon-based television station Al Manar TV, Chomsky argued that "Hezbollah's insistence on keeping its arms is justified" and claimed that Hezbollah leader "Nasrallah has a reasoned argument and persuasive argument that [the arms] should be in the hands of Hezbollah as a deterrent to potential aggression." A month later, Hezbollah used these arms that Chomsky supported to launch an attack on Israel, Camera. org first reported. Just imagine how he would cover similar topics to classrooms full of developing minds.

So here we have Arizona students learning that journalism is about making the world a better place, while getting a heavy dose of Chomsky's radical geopolitical beliefs. It's not hard to see why so many young people leave college as leftists.

North Carolina A&T State University is no exception. Its journalism school states: "As a [Journalism and Mass Communication] major, you will be able to acquire an education that will make two critical differences in your life. First, it will prepare you to satisfy your interests, advance your causes, and express your passions. In this way, it will help you make good progress toward realizing yourself. Second, it will prepare you to serve your organizations, communities, nation, and world. In this way, it will help you make the kind of difference that moves humanity forward. . . . . You will be ready to make the world a better place for yourself and others."

Again . . . "A better place"? It is no longer about providing people with the facts but instead leading them to their own personal value system. If a person is taught early on that the right is bad, then guess what? They're going to grow up thinking that the right is bad. Likewise, if that same person is taught early on that the left is good, guess what? That person will grow up thinking that the left is good. Suddenly, this whole "better place" becomes very clear.

In January 2019, New York University's Arthur L. Carter Journalism Institute hired one of its alumni, Lauren Duca, to teach a course called "The Feminist Journalist." Duca, a former *Teen Vogue* columnist, first gained notoriety from an interview with Fox News's Tucker Carlson, in which she defended the following remark she made on Twitter about Ivanka Trump: "Ivanka Trump is poised to become the most powerful woman in the world. Don't let her off the hook because she looks like she smells good." This was in response to a story breaking about a leftist passenger who was removed from a JetBlue flight after he berated and screamed at Ivanka in front of her young children.

The course description refers to the "ongoing American dumpster fire," claiming that there is "only one side to journalism, and it is motivated by building a truer, more equitable democracy." The course also "renders feminist journalism a moral necessity" and suggests that "we cannot build to social justice without adequate representation of intersectional perspectives." No, it's not you— this is hard to follow for anyone outside of the progressive academia bubble.

In the fall of that same year, the journalism school introduced a course called "Reporting on the Far Right." The course description outlined a plan to identify and track far-right movements and uncover the identities of white supremacist propagandists with the aid of guest reporters.

Perhaps the most egregious display of bias in student journalism can be found at the Columbia University School of Journalism, one of the most influential institutions in its field and home to the Pulitzer Prize.

In a special report on Columbia University's pervasive leftist bias and its influence on the journalism world, the Media Research Center noted that in March 2013, Columbia "saw a change of leadership when Steve Coll, former president of the liberal, George

Soros-funded New America Foundation, was named the new president of Columbia University's Journalism School." In the press release for his appointment at the school, Coll, who was formerly the managing editor at the *Washington Post* as well as head of the New America Foundation, a progressive public policy organization that has received $4.2 million from left-wing donor George Soros since 2000, spoke of his big plans for the institution. "The Journalism School has a chance across the next decade to extend its leadership as an institution with worldwide influence," he said. And boy was he right.

Since he made that statement, the influence of the Columbia University School of Journalism on society has been substantial, to say the least. It has fostered its long-standing reputation of breeding generations of journalists who go on to work for the most influential media outlets and broadcast networks in the country. MRC notes that alumni have gone on to work in positions at the *New York Times*, Bloomberg, ABC News, NBC News, CBS News, CNN, the *Los Angeles Times*, the *Washington Post,* and *USA Today*. Alumni have also worked at a number of left-wing outlets including *Mother Jones*, the *Huffington Post*, NPR, and *The Nation*—the same operations their former professors staff.

The Media Research Center found that there was a "significant left-wing bias prevalent at the school—a bias that then migrates with its graduates to permeate the daily operations of news organizations across the United States." Below are some of the alarming details highlighted in their report:

> **68 Percent of the Professors Work for Liberal Outlets:** *The faculty list of the Columbia University School of Journalism reads like a Who's Who of liberal organizations. Of the 40*

full-time members of the faculty, 27 work at left-wing news outlets and organizations including the Huffington Post, Slate, Mother Jones, Salon, The Nation, *and Greenpeace. Adjunct faculty work at Al Jazeera, Alternet, the Daily Beast,* Salon, *and* The Nation.

More than \$9.7 Million in Soros Funding: *Columbia University has received \$9,708,486 from liberal billionaire George Soros's Open Society Foundations.*

The report goes on to highlight other professors on the staff who operate under Coll's leadership. "Todd Gitlin, a professor and chair of the journalism Ph.D. program, was one of the founders and first presidents of the radical left-wing group Students for a Democratic Society," it says. "Lately, Gitlin has been an outspoken supporter of the 'amazingly intense,' 'sweet tempered' Occupy movement. He is also listed on the journalism school's site as a 'faculty expert' on both ethics and American politics.

"Victor Navasky, head of the prestigious *Columbia Journalism Review,* came to the school from *The Nation,*" it continued. "Navasky worked as editor of the hard-left magazine, where he still serves as Publisher Emeritus. Professor Betsy West was fired from CBS for her involvement in 'Rathergate.' She now teaches 'Video Storytelling' at Columbia."

Further, president of Columbia University Lee Bollinger has repeatedly advocated for massive government funding of journalism. Back in July 2010, he wrote a column for the *Wall Street Journal* titled, "Journalism Needs Government Help," in which he argued that "trusting the market alone to provide all the news coverage we need would mean venturing into the unknown—a risky proposition with a vital public institution hanging in the balance." What I find "risky" is entrusting the state to dictate what is newsworthy in a country that is designed to allow private citizens to speak truth to power.

This school alone should concern any American who cares about a free and fair press. Liberal journalism schools like the Columbia School of Journalism do not exist in a vacuum. They are integral parts of a much larger liberal institution.

Journalists are a product of what journalism schools teach them, and unfortunately, it's not much. If you put left-leaning direction in one way, you're going to get left-leaning values to come out the other way. Professors bombard their journalism students with nonstop left-wing rhetoric and rely primarily on left-leaning source material and examples. Somehow we are still surprised that they end up with progressive outcomes, but we shouldn't be. Consider the following:

The student newspaper of Northwestern University, the *Daily Northwestern*, made headlines in December 2019 after its editors issued a groveling, nine-paragraph apology over its decision to simply cover a campus speech that was deemed offensive to some students on campus. The event was hosted by the College Republicans club and featured former attorney general Jeff Sessions.

Everything about the event made it newsworthy—it was arguably a gold mine for a journalist. Protesters rushed the room and climbed through open windows, attempting to shout down one of the most high-profile speakers the school had ever hosted. The *Daily Northwestern* did exactly what they should have done in such a situation. They sent a reporter and a photographer to cover the talk and the student protesters, and after the event was disrupted, they tweeted photos of the protesters and contacted them for comments by phone using the university's directory.

Below is part of the actual statement issued by the paper's editorial board. It offers a rare window into the mind of today's youngest journalists and tomorrow's mainstream news reporters.

Last week, The Daily was not the paper that Northwestern students deserve.

On Nov. 5, former Attorney General Jeff Sessions spoke on campus at a Northwestern University College Republicans event. The Daily sent a reporter to cover that talk and another to cover the students protesting his invitation to campus, along with a photographer. We recognize that we contributed to the harm students experienced, and we wanted to apologize for and address the mistakes that we made that night—along with how we plan to move forward. One area of our reporting that harmed many students was our photo coverage of the event. Some protesters found photos posted to reporters' Twitter accounts retraumatizing and invasive. Those photos have since been taken down. On one hand, as the paper of record for Northwestern, we want to ensure students, administrators and alumni understand the gravity of the events that took place Tuesday night. However, we decided to prioritize the trust and safety of students who were photographed. We feel that covering traumatic events requires a different response than many other stories. While our goal is to document history and spread information, nothing is more important than ensuring that our fellow students feel safe—and in situations like this, that they are benefitting from our coverage rather than being actively harmed by it. We failed to do that last week, and we could not be more sorry.

So let's get this straight. They "contributed to the harm students experienced, and we wanted to apologize for and address the mistakes that we made" despite having no explanation whatsoever for how covering the event undermined anyone's safety or well-being. What? Isn't what they did the very definition of journalism? Covering an event based on who was there and what occurred. Think about the lesson that these young journalists learned, which is that telling the truth and reporting a story accurately doesn't pay off. The second they capitulated set the example for their professional career going forward. If posting a photo of the event "harmed" students, then these students will have a rude awakening in the real world.

The cringeworthy notion that "nothing is more important than ensuring that our fellow students feel safe" is astonishing.

"Safe" . . . ? This is unbelievable. By this standard of omitting newsworthy stories that happen to make some people uncomfortable, we wouldn't report about crime, war, incurable medical situations, and so much more. What's next?

What I found most concerning was the future implications for the paper. The editors announced that they will "work to balance the need for information and the potential harm our news coverage may cause," adding that they met as a staff "to discuss where their reporting and empathy fell short," and are actively reexamining how they'll "address similar situations in the future and how to best move forward."

If the editors are to be believed, the *Daily Northwestern* will entirely abandon journalistic principles for the sake of sensitivity. The smallest bit of controversy surrounding a topic or event would be enough to bar student journalists from covering it.

It's embarrassing and a travesty that such a sentiment was expressed at one of the best-regarded journalism schools in the country, but this was not an isolated incident. If this is one of the best, can you imagine the worst? Just to be clear, the harm only goes one way. If a right-leaning student was harmed (wait, I guess that's impossible if they are conservative) by some left-wing speaker, I'm certain the paper would be encouraged to overlook it and write favorably about the speaker.

Equally as concerning, a front-page column in Washington University's student newspaper published on February 6, 2019, was titled "It's OK that conservatives don't feel welcome." It was written by a student staff writer, Sean Lundergan, following President Trump's 2019 State of the Union address, to "reflect on the young members of the ideological movement that created him."

"Conservative ideas do not deserve equal consideration to that afforded liberal and left ideas, because conservative ideas are not equal to liberal and left ideas," the staff writer declared. "There is no legitimate argument for supporting Donald Trump and his allies, at least not one that holds up in any academic community worth its salt." Talk about open-mindedness.

During the summer of 2016, after the Republican convention, the *Washington Post* ran a front-page Style section article about me being "the outsider's insider." It detailed how through my role at the RNC, I (the Washington insider) was assisting candidate Trump (the outsider) with communications and messaging. My alma mater, Connecticut College, posted the story on their

Facebook page without comment, other than citing it was about one of their 1993 graduates. You would have thought the school gave me tenure as a professor. The outrage that ensued was absurd. One student took to the comments to express how he felt unsafe on campus as a result of the post. So, a post on a Facebook page made him feel unsafe on campus. I almost feel for the guy. I hope he never goes out alone at night in the city.

Earlier in the year, Act on a Dream, a student-led organization at Harvard College that advocates for progressive immigration policies, held a rally at the school calling for the abolition of Immigration, Customs, & Enforcement (ICE) and repeatedly chanted "Abolish ICE." In their reporting of the article, staff members for the *Harvard Crimson*, the student-led paper at Harvard, contacted ICE for a request for comment on the protest. This standard journalistic practice was enough to ignite intense backlash from leftists on campus.

In a petition to the paper, the Harvard student government and seventeen other student groups called for a boycott until the paper bowed to their ludicrous demands, which included:

1. Apologize for the harm they inflicted on the undocumented community.
2. Critically engage with and change their policies that require calling ICE for comment.
3. Declare their commitment to protecting undocumented students on campus.

Evidently, these students believe that the *Crimson* "has a responsibility to prioritize the safety of the student body they are reporting on" and "must reexamine and interrogate policies that place students under threat."

As a reminder, these government workers are doing their jobs to enforce the laws that were passed and now are being demonized by them.

"Responsible journalism includes being conscious about the impact caused by their actions as a news organization," they wrote. Again, it's all about having an impact, not necessarily the facts.

Of course, reporting on controversial events and reaching out for comment are standard journalistic practices, but that's not the case for today's rising journalists. When considering what they are being taught, you can't attribute their mistakes to naïveté or inexperience—they were just copying the professionals.

Consider the NPR and the *Washington Post*'s Stone and Holt Weeks's fellowship, which teaches aspiring journalists about the role of journalism in "making the world a better place." The fellows, according to the application, will learn "from the very best at both institutions" that a major aim of journalism is "to comfort the afflicted and afflict the comfortable."

Interestingly, what's absent from all the talk of sensitivity and comforting the afflicted in journalism is any regard for conservatives students, who are arguably the most marginalized and disparaged group on college campuses today.

Students are incessantly told to be sensitive to others but there's a complete disregard for students who hold conservative views. Leftist views go unchallenged while conservative views are almost always portrayed in a negative light. Campus publications and journalism courses across the country give us just a small glimpse into that reality.

The question we should all be asking of journalism institutions when reflecting upon this is: What ever happened to letting readers decide? The left has realized over the years that the more facts people have, the less likely they are to side with their view. They are no longer able to do that because they are afraid the facts won't win readers over. Ironically, with all the talk of truth and accuracy these days, it's amazing how much is left out by reporters. They can leave certain facts out if they don't match up with their desired outcome—and that's a scary state of journalism, from the classroom to the national newsroom.

It can be demoralizing to think about taking on the left's monopoly on the entire journalism world. But the good news is we don't have to do it on our own.

The next generation of journalists are currently learning the journalism ropes during the Trump era, which means they're getting a constant, much-needed reminder of their proper role in society.

From the early days of the Trump administration, both myself as press secretary and Trump as the president have ensured that conservative journalists and talk show hosts have all had a voice at the White House. I routinely used Skype to bring in outside local TV and print reporters from the briefing room and made it a point to call on them during briefings. I often took the time to meet with some of them afterward. I credentialed any reporter from a bona fide news organization, from documentary film crews and radio hosts to bloggers, columnists, historians, academics, and independent journalists to attend White House briefings. Like President Trump, my intent was not to judge based on some arbitrary or ideological bar but to be as open as possible in order to provide access to the widest group of news outlets—and to provide the public as much information and range as they sought. Isn't that what a free press is all about?

President Trump has spent time with several right-leaning outlets to ensure that the mainstream media does not have a monopoly of what we read, see, and hear.

On March 20, 2020, I returned to the White House briefing room for the coronavirus task force briefing—this time, on the other side of the podium on behalf of my daily show on Newsmax TV. I asked the president two straightforward questions, designed to give answers to Americans on two pressing issues. I had planned to cover the topics on my episode that evening—a perfectly reasonable situation.

Nevertheless, outrage from some members of the media ensued. NBC White House correspondent Kelly O'Donnell declared that it was "simply not appropriate" for me to be there. As I wrote in a column for the *Hill*, while I disagree with her assessment, I give her credit for being one of the only reporters to put her name on the record regarding her criticism. Hiding behind anonymity, a columnist at one website wrote that I "shouldn't be allowed anywhere near a White House briefing room again." Ironically, the same outlet published a story the same day based on my question about stock dumps—the question that no other reporter asked.

This idea that they get to decide what is "appropriate" and who should be allowed in the briefing room tells you all you need to know. These legacy and left-leaning media outlets and correspondents want to have a monopoly on how and what is reported. When I was growing up we had four networks, ABC, NBC, CBS, and PBS. All the TV news funneled through them. If it did not air in the morning or at night it was like it did not happen. The internet, right-leaning sites, and networks and social media have challenged their monopolistic stranglehold.

President Trump's press office, at least during my tenure, allowed for greater media access, while many in the media actually fought for less. They bemoan the interaction and access to right-leaning media. It's worth asking why that is.

Further, the president is unapologetically bringing the flaws and biases within today's journalism practices to the forefront. His constant demand for honest reporting and free speech is making journalism students less susceptible to indoctrination.

The New York University course, "Reporting on the Far Right," that I mentioned earlier was recently canceled after just two students signed up for it. My speculation is that they are seeing the "fake news" war play out on a national stage and don't want to take part in it.

Further, more and more conservative students are circumventing their school's left-wing student newspapers and starting publications of their own. The Leadership Institute's Student Publications Workshop has provided students with the tools needed to set up and run conservative publications such as the *Dartmouth Review, Cornell Review,* and *Lone Conservative.*

The left's long-standing domination over the student journalism world is starting to dwindle. Last May, the far-left student publication at Rutgers University, the *Daily Targum,* lost its access to over half a million dollars after students voted to cut its funding for the first time in 150 years.

While conservative student publications are on the rise, many journalism schools are facing enrollment declines. Mizzou University, home to 98 percent of faculty who donate to Democrats and ground zero for a litany of left-wing campus protests—including one that involved a professor assaulting a conservative journalism student—was forced to close dorms and reported a 31 percent enrollment drop in their School of Journalism.

The types of mainstream publications that echo the radical bias taught in journalism schools are also suffering. Many investors are rethinking their decisions to invest in outlets that push ideology and outrage content. Some are pulling out entirely.

Last year, for instance, Disney announced that its over $400 million investment into Vice Media was essentially worthless after disclosing a $353 million loss on the media giant. This came shortly after VICE, the left-wing media company that was once valued at $5.7 billion, laid off dozens of staff members and canceled several of its affiliated brands.

A year prior, Mic Network, another far-left digital platform that was once worth more than $60 million, sold to Bustle Digital Group for an embarrassing $5 million, while Mashable, once valued at $250 million, sold for less than $50 million. Gawker, the left-wing website that went bankrupt in 2016, was in many ways the parent of woke media clickbait websites. Bustle Digital Group had big plans to relaunch it, but announced last year that it was calling it off.

Altogether, 2019 was a sobering year for many left-wing media groups. *Business Insider* reports that at least 7,800 media employees lost their jobs during the year. Among them were 150 Verizon media employees who worked for Yahoo, AOL, and the *Huffington Post*. Vice Media cut 265 jobs, Bustle cut 35, NBC cut 82, the *Washington Post* cut 20, and CNN laid off 100. BuzzFeed continued its long list of cuts from the previous year by laying off 220 additional employees.

It's easy to see how the modern-day college experience translates into the newsroom. Left-wing journalists pursue outrage campaign clickbait instead of truth, and they are paying the price with their failing careers.

President Trump summed this dynamic up perfectly on Twitter last year. "Fake News and bad journalism have caused a big downturn," he wrote in response to the increasing media layoffs. "Sadly, many others will follow. The people want the Truth!"

Instead of cozying up to the liberal media like so many in his position have before him, President Trump is willing to call them out and hold them accountable.

The significance of Trump's presidency goes far beyond holding the media accountable. Unless we stay the course and fight back alongside the president, the revolving door between journalism schools and radical left-wing warriors will continue for generations to come. It's not far-fetched to think that our country will be nearly unrecognizable in the coming years if we fail to do so.

Whether it be in journalism schools, elementary schools, college campuses, Hollywood, corporations, or the mainstream media, President Trump is facing the left head-on. More important, he is giving Americans a reason to fight back and a blueprint to win. Because of his leadership, we are reminded that our beliefs and convictions are worth fighting for, and that ceding more ground to the left is not an option.

You don't have to like him, and you certainly don't have to approve of all his tactics, but you can no longer deny that this upcoming election presents us with a battle for the soul of this great nation. I know which side I'll be on.

ACKNOWLEDGMENTS

To my family—my wife Rebecca, who is the best editor, sounding board, marketer and promoter, my amazing children Rigby and Will, my mom Kathy, brother Ryan, sister Shannon, Emma, Harry, Bo, Josefine, my mother-in-law Sally Miller, the Grossmans, the Connollys, the Martels, and the Marvins.

Katie Armstrong, who has kept me on track for the past year and is the backbone of my business operations.

Gabi Salas.

The entire cast and crew involved with *Dancing with the Stars* for making my experience truly once in a lifetime, but especially:

My partner Lindsay Arnold Cusick, Jenna Johnson for stepping in and all of the professional dancers: Alan Bernstein, Brandon Armstrong, Sasha Farber, Emma Slater, Pasha Pashkov, Cheryl Burke, Peta Murgatroyd, Valentin Chmerkovskiy, Gleb Savchenko, Witney Carson, Keo Motsepe, and Daniella Karagach.

My fellow cast members whom I had the pleasure of getting to know: Mary Wilson, Ray Lewis, Lamar Odom, Sailor Brinkley-Cook, Karamo Brown, Kate Flannery, James Van Der Beek, Lauren Alaina, Ally Brooke, Kel Mitchell, and Hannah Brown.

The producers and execs who made this possible and worked tirelessly to make it look great: Deena Katz, Valoree Papsidera, Andrew Llineras, Eric Biermann, Stephanie Waters, Mike Roth, Michelle DeBillis, Adam Reia, Grant Greeley, and Erin Andrews.

The team that made show days and being on set the best it could be: Erika Archibeck, Sherill Harris, Kimi Messina, Donna Bard, Dave Williams and Big Mike Ingram, Dr. Gina Minchella, Julie Nostrom, and Zena Shteysel Green.

The PR team members who were true professionals: Caly Johnson, Melanie Fitzpatrick, and Mitch Messinger.

The social media team: Marlynda Do, Taylor Montemarano, and Aimee Raquel.

The podcast and BBC team: Kym Johnson, Fabrizia Mauro, and Lisa Ledterman.

The wardrobe department, who made sure everything was taken care of and looked great (with the exception of the green ruffled number from week one): Steven Lee, Mr. Garo, Art Conn, and Eric Van Wagoner.

The amazing band: Ray Chew, Travis Garland, and Felicia Barton.

The veterans and their families and caregivers who came to support me at the show tapings: Jason, Melody, Madison, Macey, and Mia Butler, Jasmine and Brandon Dodson, Fawn and Stephen Robinson, Stephanie and Michael Trost, Twyla and Andrew Williams, Marcus Dwayne and Briarly Suzanne Wilson, Yolany Guzmán, Kara Mitchell, Michael Kreiner and Maureen Giborees-Kreiner, Janine Morales, Nicole Heffel, Maria Guirado, Damon and Keri Eversole, and Ashley Moorehead as well as the teams at the Independence Fund and the Yellow Ribbon Fund.

My friends who came to the shows to support me: Reince and Sally Preibus, Amy, Kelley, Sosie, and Sage Connolly, Holly Grossman, John Sankovich, Jeff Snyder, Carey Coles Pitts, Meera and Emily Pattinson, the Baio Family, Lauren and Janet Hernandez, Amy and John Steward, Katie and Cynthia Hrkman, Patrick and Marie Adamson, Bridget and Matthew Faraci, Mike Flint and Cheri O'Laverty Flint, Christopher Nigg, Cassie Majestic, Deirdre, Caroline, and Catelin Carnes, Carolyn and Elizabeth Svorinic, Tim and Kristina Burger, Sarah, Dallas, and Emma Lawrence, Shaily Federman, Elizabeth Manressa, Susie Wollard, Jason, Patty, and Jackson Roe, Blayne Fertitta, Heidi Collins, Susan Leingang, Jennifer and Sarah Jean Carver, Abigail Hall and Alexandra Clark of Poplitics, Sheena Tahilramani.

Some of the social media influencers who came out to shows and I had the pleasure of meeting: Michael Gruen, Jason Wilhelm, Mav and Cash Parker, and Parker Pannell.

The entire staff at the SLS hotel, my home base in LA, for making my stays at the SLS Beverly Hills so seamless, but especially Zachary Serrano, Patrice Desvarieux, Corey Ganivet, Natalie Doss, and Michael Coons.

Everyone who took the time to vote for me week after week, especially those who were so helpful in my weekly "campaign" including: Donald Trump Jr., Kimberly Guilfoyle, Sara Carter, Scott and Renee Baio, Jesse Watters, Governor Mike Huckabee, Sarah Sanders, Dan Scavino, Stephanie Grisham, John and Anne Fredericks, Matt Boyle and Brietbart radio, Larry O'Connor, Dean Cain, Kristy Swanson, Patriots Hall of Famer Matt Light, MyPillow CEO Mike Lindell, country music star John Rich, Dan Bongino, Pete Hegseth, Arthur Schwartz, Jeff Snyder, Elizabeth

Manresa, John Sankovich, Holly Grossman, Mark Larson, Jason Miller, Boris Epshteyn, Comfortably Smug, Paul Bedard, Charlie Kirk, Bill White, Lee Zeldin, Brian Eure, Heidi Collins, Tommy Hicks, Kellyanne Conway, Tammy Bruce, David Brody, Jack Posobiec, Katie Pavlich, Erin Perrine, Kayleigh McEnany, Lisa Boothe, Jessica Ditto, Howie Carr, Hugh Hewitt, John Cardillo, Rudy Giuliani, Seb Gorka, Katrina Pierson, Michael Cernovich, Gina Loudon, Lara and Eric Trump, Ronna McDaniel, Ninio Fetalvo, Carolina Hurley, Marc Lotter, Cara Mason, Jerry and Becki Falwell, Cassie Smedile, Andy Surabian, Tammy Bruce, and Reince and Sally Preibus

A special thank-you to President Trump for his continued support.

Hannah Blair for her help researching, writing, and editing.

The team at point1, Greg Capelli, Jimmy Keady, Ben Marchi, and Evan Stewart.

Linda McMahon, Brian O. Walsh, Kelly Sadler, Cora Mandy, Mallory Fields, John Britten, Kayla Gowdy, Isaac Piller, Grayson Stribling, and everyone at America First Super PAC.

My attorney, David Limbaugh, who has done an amazing job assisting with my post–White House career.

The team at Hachette led by Kate Hartson.

The staff of the Army Navy Country Club for always making sure we had a place to practice, especially Patrick King, Andrew Welch, Rebecca Pipkins, and Drew Loszynski.

All of the great studios that graciously hosted us on the road and at home: Chris Collins Dance Studio in Alexandria, Virginia, Ballet Nova in Falls Church, Virginia, Ballet Florida and Fred Astaire Dance Studio in West Palm Beach, Florida, Newport

Academy of Ballet in Newport, Rhode Island, Little Dance Studio in Erie, Pennsylvania, Omni Salsa Dance Studio in Houston, Texas.

My shipmates and fellow service members at USTRANSCOM, USTRANSCOM Public Affairs, the Joint Transportation Reserve Unit, the Navy element and NOSC St. Louis.

The team at Newsmax for getting *Spicer & Co* on the air and working hard to discuss some of these issues every day—Chris Ruddy, Elliot Jacobson, Stephanie Cassidy, David Wasser, Lyndsay Keith, Louis Charlip, Anna Laudiero, Nardos Mesmar, Kristen Hildebrand, Diego Ciborro, David Smolar, Jake Pollack, Emerald Robinson, and Jordan Clifford.

NOTES

CHAPTER 2: AN OUTISDER: *DANCING WITH THE STARS*

Page 26: **Don't Let Sean Spicer Tap-Dance Out of Infamy on 'Dancing'** 21 Aug. 2019, https://www.nytimes.com/2019/08/21/arts/television/dancing-with-the-stars-sean-spicer.html.

27: **Sean Spicer's 'Dancing with the Stars' controversy, explained** 19 Sep. 2019, https://www.vox.com/2019/9/19/20870373/sean-spicer-dancing-with-the-stars-controversy.

27: **Sean Spicer's Spice Girls spectacle on 'DWTS' is not okay—CNN.** https://lite.cnn.com/en/article/h_f06a6d7e25f04c93f3e8f7cdc086f521.

34: **What Does 'Dancing with the Stars' Host Tom Bergeron Think** 21 Aug. 2019, https://www.cheatsheet.com/entertainment/dancing-with-the-stars-tom-bergeron-sean-spicer.html/.

37: **Sean Spicer on 'Dancing With the Stars' Backlash: 'I Expect It . . .'** 17 Sep. 2019, https://www.hollywoodreporter.com/live-feed/sean-spicer-dancing-stars-backlash-i-expect-it-1240253.

38: **Karamo Brown Explains the Intense Death Threats His Son** 26 Sep. 2019, https://www.etonline.com/karamo-brown-explains-the-intense-death-threats-his-son-received-after-dwts-sean-spicer-backlash.

38: **Karamo Brown Continues to Support Sean Spicer | *Time*.** 29 Oct. 2019, https://time.com/5713442/karamo-brown-sean-spicer-dwts-friends/.

39: **Sean Spicer Breaks Down Crying After 'Dancing . . .—TMZ.com.** 17 Sep. 2019, https://www.tmz.com/2019/09/17/sean-spicer-breaks-down-crying-dancing-with-the-stars/.

47: **Who Let Sean Spicer Play Woody from 'Toy Story'?—*Vanity Fair*.** 15 Oct. 2019, https://www.vanityfair.com/hollywood/2019/10/dancing-with-the-stars-sean-spicer-woody-toy-story.

48: **Sean Spicer Goes Full Woody From 'Toy Story' in Bizarre** 15 Oct. 2019, https://www.thedailybeast.com/sean-spicer-goes-full-woody-from-toy-story-in-bizarre-dancing-with-the-stars-performance.

48: **No, Sean Spicer Really Can't Dance—The New York Times.** 4 Nov. 2019, https://www.nytimes.com/2019/11/04/arts/dance/sean-spicer-dancing-with-the-stars.html.

56: **'Dancing With the Stars' Premiere: TV Ratings Monday, Sept. 16.** 17 Sep. 2019, https://www.hollywoodreporter.com/live-feed/dancing-stars-premiere-tv-ratings-monday-sept-16-2019-1239954.

57: **Why Sean Spicer survives on 'Dancing with the Stars': Rules** 11 Nov. 2019, https://www.usatoday.com/story/entertainment/tv/2019/11/11/why-sean-spicer-survives-dancing-stars-rules-explained/2515869001/.

62: **CNN's Brian Stelter hammered for covering Sean Spicer's** 12 Nov. 2019, https://www.foxnews.com/media/cnn-brian-stelter-sean-spicer-dancing-with-the-stars-abc-jeffrey-epstein.

64: **Sean Spicer eliminated from ABC's 'Dancing with the Stars'** 12 Nov. 2019, https://www.cnn.com/2019/11/12/media/sean-spicer-dancing-with-the-stars/index.html.

64: **Dancing with the Stars Season 28 (2019) Odds & Props: Ray** 23 Aug. 2019, https://www.sportsbettingdime.com/news/entertainment-props/dancing-with-the-stars-season-28-2019-odds-props/.

CHAPTER 3: LIGHTS, CAMERA, ACTIVISM

70: **Sean Spicer Hands Kimmel a Rare Ratings Win . . .—The Wrap.** https://www.thewrap.com/sean-spicer-jimmy-kimmel-live-ratings/.

71: **PragerU Thanks TBS's Samantha Bee for 'Full Frontal' Assault** https://www.cnsnews.com/blog/craig-bannister/prageru-thanks-tbss-samantha-bee-full-frontal-assault-over-35000-raised-and.

71: **Samantha Bee Plans Tweaks to 'Full Frontal'—Variety.** https://variety.com/2018/tv/news/samantha-bee-full-frontal-changes-late-night-1202905677/.

72: **Samantha Bee Talks 'Full Frontal'—Yahoo News Canada.** https://ca.news.yahoo.com/samantha-bee-talks-full-frontal-194233744.html.

73: **Jimmy Kimmel: Late-night hosts are liberal 'because it . . .'** https://www.washingtontimes.com/news/2018/feb/5/jimmy-kimmel-late-night-hosts-are-liberal-because-/.

73: **Jimmy Kimmel speaks his mind—CBS News.** https://www.cbsnews.com/news/jimmy-kimmel-speaks-his-mind/.

74: **Sean Spicer's cameo at the Emmys was yucky—The** https://www.
washingtonpost.com/news/the-fix/wp/2017/09/18/sean-spicers-very-yucky-
cameo-at-the-emmys/.

75: **HUGE Fake Scammer Exposed and Don't Ever Do What** http://
cyberspaceandtime.com/DkJqlo4VIJc.video+related.

77: **Fox's Greg Gutfeld pulls in more viewers than Bill Maher and** https://www.
washingtonexaminer.com/news/foxs-the-greg-gutfeld-show-pulls-in-more-
viewers-than-some-networks-late-night-shows.

78: **Tim Allen Comedy 'Last Man Standing' Canceled by ABC After** https://
deadline.com/2017/05/last-man-standing-canceled-by-abc-after-6-
seasons-1202089263/.

78: **'The Conners' without Roseanne beaten by everything, drops in** https://
www.stormfront.org/forum/t1262029-2/.

79: **Ellen DeGeneres defends friendship with George W. Bush** https://www.
businessinsider.com/ellen-degeneres-defends-friendship-with-george-w-
bush-football-game-2019-10.

80: **Emmys host Michael Che says the only white people who thank.** https://
www.foxnews.com/entertainment/emmys-host-michael-che-says-the-
only-white-people-who-thank-jesus-at-award-shows-are-republicans-ex-
crackheads.

81: **Faith-Based Movie 'Overcomer' Earns $8.2 Million in Opening** https://
getuperica.com/123889/overcomer-movie-opening-weekend/.

82: **Hollywood tries to speak for us but really, they just don't get it** https://www.
foxnews.com/opinion/hollywood-tries-to-speak-for-us-but-really-they-just-
dont-get-it.

83: **The War of the Woke: Hollywood Turns on its Viewers | The** https://
spectator.org/the-war-of-the-woke-hollywood-turns-on-its-viewers/.

84: *New York Times*—**Book List Bias |** *National Review.* https://www.
nationalreview.com/2018/04/new-york-times-bestseller-list-biased-book-
news/.

85: **Alec Baldwin Pleads Guilty in Fight Over Parking Spot—The** https://www.
nytimes.com/2019/01/23/nyregion/alec-baldwin-pleads-guilty-harassment.
html.

86: **American Airlines Fights Back After Alec Baldwin's Twitter** http://abcnews.
go.com/blogs/entertainment/2011/12/alec-baldwin-what-happened-on-
american-airlines-flight.

86: **Comedian Bill Maher has a long history of fat shaming—Insider.** https://
www.insider.com/bill-maher-calls-for-return-of-fat-shaming-2019-9.

86: **Bill Maher accused of making fried chicken joke to . . .—Fox News.** https://www.foxnews.com/entertainment/bill-maher-accused-of-making-fried-chicken-joke-to-black-republican-congressman.

87: **Bill Maher criticized for booking Milo Yiannopoulos as guest** https://www.cbsnews.com/news/bill-maher-criticized-for-booking-milo-yiannopoulos-as-guest/.

87: **Five reasons why liberals should boycott Bill Maher—New** https://www.nydailynews.com/opinion/reasons-liberals-boycott-bill-maher-article-1.2981756.

89: **Moguls and starlets: 100 years of Hollywood's corrosive** https://www.theguardian.com/film/2017/oct/19/moguls-and-starlets-100-years-of-hollywoods-corrosive-systemic-sexism.

89: **Showtime Snubs Melania From New "First Ladies' Series."** https://trendingpolitics.com/showtime-snubs-melania-from-new-first-ladies-series/.

90: **L. Brent Bozell & Tim Graham: Hollywood Never Apologizes** https://patriotpost.us/opinion/51959-hollywood-never-apologizes-for-ultraviolence-2017-10-20.

91: **A Handmaid's Tale of Protest—The New York Times.** https://www.nytimes.com/2017/06/30/us/handmaids-protests-abortion.html.

92: **'First Man': Neil Armstrong film fails to fly flag for US patriotism.** https://www.telegraph.co.uk/films/2018/08/29/first-man-neil-armstrong-film-fails-fly-flag-us-patriotism/.

93: **Leftist Netflix-Obama connection shows why you should** https://www.lifesitenews.com/opinion/leftist-netflix-obama-connection-shows-why-you-should-cancel-your-subscription.

94: **'Euphoria,' HBO's raw teen sex junkies are all shock, no value.** https://nypost.com/2019/06/15/euphoria-hbos-raw-teen-sex-junkies-are-all-shock-no-value/.

95: **15 Stars Who Imagined Violence Against Donald Trump, From** https://www.thewrap.com/hollywood-stars-donald-trump-violent-death-kathy-griffin-snoop-dogg/.

95: **Editorial: Stop this sick fantasy before it becomes reality** https://www.theledger.com/opinion/20181103/editorial-stop-this-sick-fantasy-before-it-becomes-reality.

96: **Barron Trump Thought Kathy Griffin's Beheaded Trump Image** https://www.tmz.com/2017/05/31/barron-trump-thought-donald-beheaded-image-real/.

96: **Madonna: 'Blowing up White House' taken out of context—CNN.** https://www.cnn.com/2017/01/23/entertainment/madonna-white-house/index.html.

97: **Cruz slams Jim Carrey's 'vicious, angry' painting of . . . – The Hill.** https://thehill.com/blogs/in-the-know/in-the-know/444589-cruz-slams-jim-carreys-vicious-angry-painting-of-alabama.

99: **'The Chosen' $10M crowdfunded show out now . . .—Fox News.** https://www.foxnews.com/entertainment/the-chosen-jesus-show-crowdfunded.

99: **How a Crowdfunded Christian TV Series Could Change** https://thefederalist.com/2020/02/17/how-a-crowdfunded-christian-tv-series-could-change-the-entertainment-industry/.

CHAPTER 4: THE RISE AND FALL OF LEGACY MEDIA

102: **CNN's Brian Stelter lampooned after saying 'journalists . . .'** 18 Dec. 2019, https://www.foxnews.com/media/cnns-brian-stelter-lampooned-journalists-shouldnt-advocate-for-impeachment-outcome.

103: **CNN's Brian Stelter Accuses 'Right-wing Smear Machine' of** https://www.newsweek.com/cnns-brian-stelter-accuses-right-wing-smear-machine-spreading-lies-about-1135374.

106: **CNN Analyst Joe Lockhart Admits He Fabricated** https://www.dailywire.com/news/cnn-analyst-joe-lockhart-admits-he-fabricated-conversation-between-gop-senators.

106: **'Democracy Dies in Darkness': Washington Post Hides** https://www.dailywire.com/news/democracy-dies-darkness-washington-post-hides-ryan-saavedra.

108: **After 100 days, the media are still embarrassing themselves** https://www.washingtonpost.com/lifestyle/style/after-100-days-the-media-are-still-embarrassing-themselves-covering-trump-just-not-as-much/2017/04/27/8de913fe-2a86-11e7-be51-b3fc6ff7faee_story.html.

109: **Liberal media smears against Liberty University show dire need.** https://www.washingtontimes.com/news/2020/apr/28/liberal-media-smears-against-liberty-university-sh/.

109: **The New York Times Is About to Face a Reckoning for Its Lies.** https://townhall.com/columnists/harmeetdhillon/2020/02/28/the-new-york-times-is-about-to-face-a-reckoning-for-its-lies-n2562162.

109: **The Real Trump-Russia Quid Pro Quo—The New** https://www.nytimes.com/2019/03/27/opinion/mueller-trump-russia-quid-pro-quo.html.

111: **Opinion | Study: 91 percent of recent network Trump coverage** https://www.washingtonpost.com/blogs/erik-wemple/wp/2017/09/12/study-91-percent-of-recent-network-trump-coverage-has-been-negative/.

111: **How we evaluated Americans' trust in 30 news sources | Pew** https://www.pewresearch.org/fact-tank/2020/01/24/qa-how-pew-research-center-evaluated-americans-trust-in-30-news-sources/.

CHAPTER 5: ADVOCATE NEWSROOMS AND THEIR TEAM RULES

117: **Jimmy Kimmel offers lame apology for using blackface—Los** https://www.latimes.com/entertainment-arts/story/2020-06-24/jimmy-kimmel-blackface-apology-comedy.

118: **What Ever Happened to Joy Reid's Alleged Hackers?** https://www.mediaite.com/opinion/whatever-ever-happened-to-joy-reids-alleged-hackers-and-that-fbi-investigation/.

122: **Liberal 'View' hosts blast #MeToo 'witch hunt' and . . .—Fox News.** https://www.foxnews.com/entertainment/the-view-al-franken-me-too-witch-hunt.

123: **CNN, MSNBC ignore Matt Lauer rape allegations, NBC** https://www.foxnews.com/media/msnbc-cnn-matt-lauer-rape-nbc-harvey-weinstein.

124: **'Jaw-dropping hypocrisy': CNN's Stelter gets reality-checked** https://www.bizpacreview.com/2019/03/07/jaw-dropping-hypocrisy-cnns-stelter-gets-reality-checked-when-he-accuses-fox-of-dehumanizing-democrats-730545.

128: **ABC, CBS Uninterested in Van Attack Against Trump Supporters.** https://www.newsbusters.org/blogs/nb/nicholas-fondacaro/2020/02/09/abc-cbs-uninterested-van-attack-against-trump-supporters.

129: **Dan Gainor: Virginia gun rights rally incredibly peaceful** https://www.foxnews.com/opinion/virginia-gun-rights-rally-peaceful-media-dan-gainor.

130: **Bloomberg's sexist remarks fostered company culture that** https://abcnews.go.com/Politics/bloombergs-sexist-remarks-fostered-company-culture-degraded-women/story?id=67744180.

130: **Bloomberg on Releasing NDA Agreements and . . .—YouTube** https://www.youtube.com/watch?v=mN0odmrDqxk.

133: **As Trump's Poll Numbers Rise, Media Begin Censoring Press** https://thefederalist.com/2020/03/26/as-trumps-poll-numbers-rise-media-begin-censoring-press-conferences/.

133: **Trump's dangerous coronavirus briefings: Why the media must** https://www.washingtonpost.com/lifestyle/media/the-media-must-stop-live-broadcasting-trumps-dangerous-destructive-coronavirus-briefings/2020/03/21/b8a2a440-6b7c-11ea-9923-57073adce27c_story.html.

134: **CNN skips revived WH briefings after yearlong . . .—Fox News.** https://www.foxnews.com/media/cnn-skips-revived-white-house-briefings-after-yearlong-complaints.

134: **David Limbaugh: Kayleigh McEnany gets vitriol . . .—Fox News.** https://www.foxnews.com/opinion/kayleigh-mcenany-liberal-media-david-limbaugh.

138: **Trump Fights Back | The American Spectator.** https://spectator.org/trump-fights-back/.

140: **CNN Report Describes a Baby Who Survives an Abortion as** https://dailycaller.com/2020/02/25/cnn-baby-abortion-fetus-that-was-born/.

141: **L. Brent Bozell and Tim Graham,** *Unmasked: Big Media's War Against Trump* (Humanix Books, 2019).

141: **SF Board of Supervisors sanitizes language of criminal justice** https://www.sfchronicle.com/bayarea/philmatier/article/SF-Board-of-Supervisors-sanitizes-language-of-14292255.php.

144: **Donald Trump Jr.** *Triggered: How the Left Thrives on Hate and Wants to Silence Us* (Hachette Book Group, 2019).

146: **Mark R. Levin,** *Unfreedom of the Press* (Simon & Schuster, 2019), https://www.goodreads.com/book/show/44595959-unfreedom-of-the-press.

146: **Mike Huckabee Commentary: Coverage of Tragic Attacks** https://tennesseestar.com/2019/08/07/mike-huckabee-commentary-coverage-of-tragic-attacks-proves-the-mainstream-media-are-not-objective-reporters-they-are-democrat-party-press-releases/.

147: **CNN Headline Rewritten Within the Hour—Editing Out** https://dailycaller.com/2020/04/09/cnn-edits-headline-cut-criticism-senate-democrats/.

147: **CNN's obsession with Trump's ice cream intake . . .—Fox News.** https://www.foxnews.com/media/cnns-trump-ice-cream-lampooned-report-dessert.

148: **New York Times Ripped for Soleimani Obituary Post in** https://www.dailywire.com/news/new-york-times-ripped-for-soleimani-obituary-post-in-comparison-to-brutal-obit-for-sexist-football-coach.

148: **NBC News on Twitter: 'Watch live coverage as Gen. Qassem . . .'** https://twitter.com/nbcnews/status/1214737261931180038.

150: **CNBC criticized for referring to Soleimani killing as . . .—Fox News.** https://www.foxnews.com/media/cnbc-qassem-solemani.

151: **Jason Meister: To Smear Trump, New York Times Pivots from** https://www.foxnews.com/opinion/new-york-times-trump-russiagate-hoax-racism-jason-meister.

152: **IWF Details How Mainstream Media Ignores, Demeans** https://www.aim.org/aim-column/iwf-details-how-mainstream-media-ignores-demeans-conservative-women/.

155: **White House task force on coronavirus another example of** https://www.cnn.com/2020/01/30/politics/donald-trump-coronavirus-diversity-obama/index.html.

156: **ABC's Karl expresses 'regret' over false Benghazi report** http://www.msnbc.com/rachel-maddow-show/abcs-karl-expresses-regret-over-false.

156: **Media Observers on ABC's Jonathan Karl Benghazi Talking** https://www.mediamatters.org/abc/media-observers-abcs-jonathan-karl-benghazi-talking-points-story-sloppy-and-inaccurate.

157: **Trump rips ABC News reporter over network's Syria . . .**—Politico. https://www.politico.com/news/2019/10/16/trump-abc-syria-reporter-048688.

158: **'The Briefing' Review: Speaking for Himself—WSJ** https://www.wsj.com/articles/the-briefing-review-speaking-for-himself-1532404860.

159: **The Trump-Pelosi feud spirals out of control—POLITICO** https://www.politico.com/news/2020/02/05/trump-pelosi-sotu-feud-110800.

159: **Trump State of the Union 2020: Live fact-check & transcript** https://www.politico.com/interactives/2020/trump-state-of-the-union-2020-live-fact-check-transcript-2-4-20/.

161: **Bizarre State of the Union 'fact checks' fall flat, as media** https://www.foxnews.com/politics/bizarre-sotu-fact-check-trump.

161: **Pencil Neck Hijacks Senate: We Can't Trust the Ballot Box** https://www.rushlimbaugh.com/daily/2020/01/22/pencil-neck-we-cant-trust-the-ballot-box/.

162: **Lawrence O'Donnell: MSNBC better than CNN because 'we . . .'** https://www.washingtonexaminer.com/news/lawrence-odonnell-difference-between-msnbc-and-cnn-is-we-dont-bring-on-liars-to-defend-trump.

162: **MSNBC parrots US casualties number provided by Iranian** https://www.washingtonexaminer.com/opinion/msnbc-parrots-us-casualties-number-provided-by-iranian-government.

163: **ABC issued no on-air corrections for its massive Syria** https://www.washingtonexaminer.com/opinion/abc-issued-no-on-air-corrections-for-its-massive-syria-kentucky-mix-up.

CHAPTER 6: CORPORATE ACTIVISM

166: **The state of small business is strong** | The Hill. 3 Feb. 2020, https://thehill.com/opinion/finance/481205-the-state-of-small-business-is-strong.

167: **Andy Puzder: Signs of a 'V'-shaped recovery—a welcome** https://fox40jackson.com/headlines/andy-puzder-signs-of-a-v-shaped-recovery-a-welcome-bounce-back-in-economy/.

168: **Atlanta billionaire plans to give almost all of it away** AJC.com. https://www.ajc.com/news/local/atlanta-billionaire-plans-give-almost-all-away/gHi8FZhfwh4dFmaXCQksKK/.

170: **Emily Gralak Thesi—Cardinal Scholar—Ball State University.** 6 Dec. 2019, https://cardinalscholar.bsu.edu/bitstream/handle/123456789/202084/2019GralakEmily-combined.pdf?sequence=1&isAllowed=y.

170: **Top Rebellious Flavors | Ben & Jerry's.** 2 July 2020, https://www.benjerry.com/home/whats-new/2019/07/rebellious-flavors.

172: **LGBTQ Pride Month: How Brands Turned Pride Month . . .—Vox.** 25 June 2018, https://www.vox.com/2018/6/25/17476850/pride-month-lgbtq-corporate-explained.

173: **Sean Spicer throws first pitch at PawSox's Pride Night, and** 20 July 2019, https://www.bostonglobe.com/metro/rhode-island/2019/07/19/sean-spicer-throws-first-pitch-pawsox-pride-night-sparks-controversy/8TvgWkxR10pprcVHp0KHEP/story.html.

174: **Trump administration dismantles LGBT-friendly policies—Politico.** 19 Feb. 2018, https://www.politico.com/story/2018/02/19/trump-lgbt-rights-discrimination-353774.

175: **PawSox Issue Apology About Including Sean . . .—GoLocalProv.** https://www.golocalprov.com/news/pawsox-issue-apology-about-including-sean-spicer-and-chick-fil-a-on-pride-n.

177: **NRA fallout: Companies cut ties after Parkland, Fla., school** 26 Feb. 2018, https://www.usatoday.com/story/money/2018/02/26/nra-companies-parkland-school-shooting/372271002/.

177: **Bank of America to Stop Financing Makers of Military-Style Guns.** 10 April 2018, https://www.nytimes.com/2018/04/10/business/bank-of-america-guns.html.

178: **NRA losing corporate ties amid calls for boycott in wake of** 27 Feb. 2018, https://abcnews.go.com/Politics/nra-losing-corporate-ties-amid-calls-boycott-wake/story?id=53400451.

178: **Consumers Beware: PayPal has weaponized financial system** 6 March 2019, https://www.foxnews.com/opinion/paypal-has-politically-weaponized-the-financial-system-by-aligning-with-hard-left.

180: **PayPal, GoFundMe, and Patreon Banned a Bunch of People** 2 Aug. 2017, https://www.buzzfeednews.com/article/blakemontgomery/the-alt-right-has-a-payment-processor-problem.

180: **Laura Ingraham advertisers: 15 drop Fox News show as host** 2 April 2018, https://www.cbsnews.com/news/laura-ingraham-advertisers-drop-show-she-goes-on-vacation/.

181: https://www.foxnews.com/politics/parkland-shooting-survivor-kyle-kashuv-emerges-as-conservative-role-model-second-amendment-champion.

181: **Harvard Rescinds Offer to Parkland Survivor Kyle . . .—NPR.** 18 June 2019, https://www.npr.org/2019/06/18/733809263/harvard-rescinds-offer-to-parkland-survivor-after-discovery-of-racist-comments.

181: **At least 27 advertisers have stopped advertising on Tucker** 11 March 2019, https://www.businessinsider.in/at-least-27-advertisers-have-stopped-advertising-on-tucker-carlsons-fox-news-show-in-recent-months-after-the-hosts-controversial-comments-heres-the-list-/articleshow/68363708.cms.

182: **Burlington Coat Factory faces storm over Ivanka—Courier-Post.** 13 Feb. 2017, https://www.courierpostonline.com/story/news/local/south-jersey/2017/02/13/ivanka-trump-burlington-coat/97862136/.

CHAPTER 7: TECH TYRANTS VS. TRUMP

187: **The Digital Transition: How the Presidential Transition Works** 31 Oct. 2016, https://obamawhitehouse.archives.gov/blog/2016/10/31/digital-transition-how-presidential-transition-works-social-media-age.

188: **Democrats have fallen behind Trump in digital campaigning** 2 Nov. 2019, https://www.theguardian.com/us-news/2019/nov/02/democrats-trump-2020-digital-social-media-campaign.

189: **'Way ahead of the field': inside Trump's unprecedented social** 3 July 2019, https://www.theguardian.com/us-news/2019/jul/02/way-ahead-of-the-field-inside-the-trump-campaigns-unprecedented-social-media-campaign.

189: **How Obama Tapped into Social Networks' Power—The New** 9 Nov. 2008, https://www.nytimes.com/2008/11/10/business/media/10carr.html.

190: **The 2020 Election Will Be a War of Disinformation—The Atlantic.** 10 Feb. 2020, https://www.theatlantic.com/magazine/archive/2020/03/the-2020-disinformation-war/605530/.

191: **Democrats Faked Online Push to Outlaw Alcohol in Alabama** 7 Jan. 2019, https://www.nytimes.com/2019/01/07/us/politics/alabama-senate-facebook-roy-moore.html.

191: **Don't Let Google Get Away with Censorship—WSJ.** 6 Aug. 2019, https://www.wsj.com/articles/dont-let-google-get-away-with-censorship-11565132175.

192: **Twitter Censorship: What Is Shadow Banning?—Breitbart.** 11 Jan. 2018, https://www.breitbart.com/tech/2018/01/11/twitter-censorship-what-is-shadow-banning/.

193: **Insider Blows Whistle & Exec Reveals Google Plan to Prevent** https://www.projectveritas.com/video/insider-blows-whistle-exec-reveals-google-plan-to-prevent-trump-situation-in-2020-on-hidden-cam/.

193: **Google and Big Tech bias hurts democracy, not just** 13 Sep. 2018, https://www.usatoday.com/story/opinion/2018/09/13/google-big-tech-bias-hurts-democracy-not-just-conservatives-column/1265020002/.

194: **Spotify will stop running political ads in 2020—CNN—CNN.com.** 27 Dec. 2019, https://www.cnn.com/2019/12/27/media/spotify-political-ads/index.html.

194: **Facebook Apologizes, Restores Censored Ad for Marsha** 1 Nov. 2018, https://www.breitbart.com/politics/2018/11/01/exclusive-facebook-apologizes-restores-previously-censored-susan-b-anthony-list-ad-promoting-marsha-blackburn/.

194: **Google Workers Discussed Tweaking Search Function to** 20 Sep. 2018, https://www.wsj.com/articles/google-workers-discussed-tweaking-search-function-to-counter-travel-ban-1537488472.

195: **The Digital Duopoly Still Reigns the Ad World, According to a** 22 March 2019, https://www.adweek.com/programmatic/the-digital-duopoly-still-reigns-the-ad-world-according-to-a-new-report/.

195: **47 CFR § 73.1944—Reasonable access. | CFR | US Law | LII** https://www.law.cornell.edu/cfr/text/47/73.1944.

196: **COMMUNICATIONS DECENCY ACT, 47 U.S.C. §230,** http://www.columbia.edu/~mr2651/ecommerce3/2nd/statutes/CommunicationsDecencyAct.pdf.

196: **SPLC Leads Soros-Funded Groups in 'Orwellian . . .'—PJ Media.** https://pjmedia.com/news-and-politics/tyler-o-neil/2018/10/29/splc-leads-soros-funded-groups-in-orwellian-attempt-to-ban-hate-speech-on-social-media-n61795.

197: **What It's Like to Be Smeared by the Southern Poverty Law** 11 Sep. 2017, https://www.wsj.com/articles/what-its-like-to-be-smeared-by-the-southern-poverty-law-center-1505171221.

197: **Ben Carson placed on Southern Poverty Law Center's** https://www.washingtontimes.com/news/2015/feb/8/ben-carson-placed-on-southern-poverty-law-centers-/, July 2020.

198: **SPLC: Sliming Ben Carson Smearing Pro Life Christians,** 13 Feb. 2015, https://www.christianpost.com/news/splc-sliming-ben-carson-smearing-pro-life-christians.html.

198: **Hypocrisy about hate—SPLC Exposed.** 19 April 2019, http://splcexposed.com/wp-content/uploads/2019/04/19_WSJ_SPLC_ad_white.pdf.

199: **Southern Poverty Law Center Faces Racism, Corruption** 28 March 2019, https://www.breitbart.com/politics/2019/03/28/southern-poverty-law-center-faces-racism-corruption-sexual-harassment-claims/.

199: **Southern Poverty Law Center: 'Our Aim in Life Is to Destroy** 1 Sep. 2017, https://pjmedia.com/news-and-politics/tyler-o-neil/2017/09/01/southern-poverty-law-center-our-aim-in-life-is-to-destroy-these-groups-completely-n53297.

199: Peter Hasson, *The Manipulators: Facebook, Google, Twitter, and Big Tech's War on Conservatives* (Regency, 2020), 315–16.

199: SPLC Confirms They're Helping Police Videos on YouTube 1 March 2018, https://dailycaller.com/2018/03/01/splc-youtube-google-trusted-flaggers/.

200: YouTube to fund launch of The Young Turks local news 11 Feb. 2020, https://www.axios.com/youtube-young-turks-local-news-academy-05829e4b-e3f6-4aa1-8f15-d1ac13b60ccd.html.

200: Bernie Sanders Endorses 'Young Turks' Host Who Called For 12 Dec. 2019, https://dailycaller.com/2019/12/12/bernie-sanders-endorses-cenk-uygur/.

200: Progressive Group Ousts Cenk Uygur Over Past Sexist Writing Marans, D. 2017, 23 Dec. 2017, https://www.huffpost.com/entry/justice-democrats-ousts-cenk-uygur_n_5a3eb4d1e4b025f99e178181?guccounter=1

200: Bernie Sanders Retracts Endorsement of Cenk Uygur After 13 Dec. 2019, https://www.nytimes.com/2019/12/13/us/politics/bernie-sanders-cenk-uygur.html.

200: Young Turks Contributor Hasan Piker Mocks ISIS Victim Kayla 5 Feb. 2020, https://dailycaller.com/2020/02/05/young-turks-contributor-hasan-piker-mocks-kayla-mueller/.

201: Google Provides Six-Figure Sum to Liberal Outlet with History 11 Feb. 2020, https://freebeacon.com/issues/google-provides-six-figure-sum-to-liberal-outlet-with-history-of-genocide-denial/.

201: YouTube Removes Cuomo 'Fredo' Video, Restores It After https://pjmedia.com/news-and-politics/tyler-o-neil/2019/08/13/youtube-removes-cuomo-fredo-threat-video-restores-it-after-trump-jr-tweet-n68033.

201: Twitter brings in anti-Trump academics to combat . . .—Fox News. 31 July 2018, https://www.foxnews.com/tech/twitter-brings-in-anti-trump-academics-to-combat-intolerance.

201: Twitter exec: 'Jail,' 'impeachment' for Trump, calls social media 15 July 2019, https://www.washingtonexaminer.com/washington-secrets/twitter-exec-jail-impeachment-for-trump-calls-social-media-chief-racist-d.

202: Donald Trump Jr., *Triggered: How the Left Thrives on Hate and Wants to Silence Us* (Center Street, 2019).

203: Twitter puts warning label on a Trump tweet on mail-in ballots 26 May 2020, https://www.foxnews.com/politics/twitter-applies-warning-label-to-trump-tweet-warning-of-mail-in-ballot-fraud-risk.

203: Snapchat Stops Promoting Trump's Account for . . .—The Wrap. 3 June 2020, https://www.thewrap.com/snap-stops-promoting-trump/.

203: **Trump campaign statement on Snapchat | Donald J. Trump for** 3 June 2020, https://www.donaldjtrump.com/media/trump-campaign-statement-on-snapchat/.

204: **Twitter Flags Trump for Warning Activists Not to Build an** 23 June 2020, https://dailycaller.com/2020/06/23/twitter-flags-trump-autonomous-zone/.

204: **Kamala Harris calls for suspension of Trump's Twitter account** 1 Oct. 2019, https://www.foxnews.com/politics/kamala-harris-suspend-trump-twitter-account.

204: **'Suppress the vote or incite violence': Biden urges Facebook** 1 July 2020, https://www.washingtonexaminer.com/news/suppress-the-vote-or-incite-violence-biden-urges-facebook-to-censor-trumps-page.

205: **Techwatch | Newsbusters.** https://www.newsbusters.org/techwatch.

CHAPTER 8: GRADE SCHOOLS AS BATTLEGROUNDS: ABCS AND ZER AND ZES

209: **Virginia School District to Give Students One Day Off . . .—NPR** 27 Dec. 2019, https://www.npr.org/2019/12/27/791889392/fairfax-va-schools-to-give-students-one-day-off-per-year-for-civic-engagement.

209: **NYC Public Schools on Twitter: 'We applaud our students . . .'** 12 Sep. 2019, https://twitter.com/nycschools/status/1172206230200344576.

210: **District News—Detail Page—Portland Public Schools.** 16 Sep. 2019, https://www.pps.net/site/default.aspx?PageType=3&DomainID=4&ModuleInstanceID=1492&PageModuleInstanceID=1594&ViewID=ad4d6d9d-7046-48e7-a548-a6a23a68d076&RenderLoc=0&FlexDataID=149-065&PageID=1&IsMoreExpandedView=True.

212: **Federal Defendants' Answer—NationBuilder.** 13 March 2019, https://assets.nationbuilder.com/multnomahgop/pages/4043/attachments/original/1552493168/PPS_complaint_%283-13-19_final%29.pdf?1552493168.

213: **If children don't join the climate strike, their schools are** 14 March 2019, https://www.theguardian.com/commentisfree/2019/mar/14/children-climate-strike-schools-activism-pupils.

213: **Educator: Schools shouldn't merely allow students to protest** 19 Oct. 2017, https://www.washingtonpost.com/news/answer-sheet/wp/2017/10/19/educator-schools-shouldnt-merely-allow-students-to-protest-they-should-support-them/.

214: **Pollyanna Inc.—Every Voice Matters—Build Community—Host** https://pollyannainc.org/.

216: **Public High School History Teacher STOMPS ON AMERICAN** 20 Sep. 2016, https://dailycaller.com/2016/09/20/public-high-school-history-teacher-stomps-on-american-flag-in-front-of-class-photo/.

216: **Elementary School Can't Say 'God Bless America' Following** 6 Jan. 2016, https://dailycaller.com/2016/01/06/elementary-school-cant-say-god-bless-america-following-aclu-complaint/.

217: **Elementary School Can't Say 'God Bless America' Following** 6 Jan. 2016, https://dailycaller.com/2016/01/06/elementary-school-cant-say-god-bless-america-following-aclu-complaint/.

218: **National Embarrassment: Only 43% of Americans Know the** 22 May 2020, https://www.studyfinds.org/national-embarrassment-only-43-of-americans-know-the-meaning-of-memorial-day/.

219: **Woke History Is Making Big Inroads in America's High Schools** Real Clear Investigations, https://www.realclearinvestigations.com/articles/2019/09/17/woke_history_is_making_big_inroads_in_americas_high_schools.

220: **Two Arizona School Districts Promoting Racial Divisions and...** https://townhall.com/columnists/rachelalexander/2020/01/13/two-arizona-school-districts-promoting-racial-divisions-and-social-justice-n2559391.

220: **We need patriotism, not severed heads, to make America** https://www.usatoday.com/story/opinion/2017/06/14/patriotism-not-severed-heads-make-america-great-column-eric-metaxas/102777768/.

222: **Parents 'horrified' after man performs surprise drag show at** https://www.nydailynews.com/new-york/education/parents-horrified-man-performs-drag-show-nyc-school-article-1.3213718.

224: **Several Hundred Parents Rally Against Planned Parenthood** https://www.lifenews.com/2019/10/01/several-hundred-parents-rally-against-planned-parenthood-pushing-its-sex-ed-agenda-on-their-kids/.

CHAPTER 9: INSTITUTIONS OF HIGHER INDOCTRINATION

227: **The Zogby Poll®: Trump's job approval tops . . .—Zogby Analytics.** 14 May 2019, https://zogbyanalytics.com/news/888-trump-s-job-approval-tops-50-a-majority-of-millennials-approve-of-trump-nearly-half-of-generation-z-voters-approve-of-trump-trump-is-winning-back-hispanic-independent-college-educated-and-urban-voters.

229: **Sean Spicer speaks on campus, looks back on time as press** 19 April 2019, https://www.dailycal.org/2019/04/18/sean-spicer-speaks-on-campus-looks-back-on-time-as-press-secretary/.

230: **Partisan Registration and Contributions of Faculty in Flagship** 17 Jan. 2020, https://www.nas.org/blogs/article/partisan-registration-and-contributions-of-faculty-in-flagship-colleges.

231: **Commencement Season in the Age of #MeToo: Conservative** 15 May 2018, https://www.yaf.org/news/commencement-season-in-the-age-of-metoo-conservative-women-still-left-out/.

232: **Notre Dame graduates walk out over VP Mike Pence speech** 22 May 2017, https://www.cnn.com/2017/05/22/politics/mike-pence-notre-dame-speech/index.html.

232: **Dan Crenshaw,** *Fortitude: American Resilience in the Era of Outrage* (Grand Central, 2020), https://www.amazon.com/Fortitude-American-Resilience-Era-Outrage/dp/1538733307.

235: **Results from a new survey—Brookings Institution.** 18 Sep. 2017, https://www.brookings.edu/blog/fixgov/2017/09/18/views-among-college-students-regarding-the-first-amendment-results-from-a-new-survey/.

235: **Gen Z at Work—8 Reasons to Be Afraid—Forbes.** 15 Oct. 2019, https://www.forbes.com/sites/remyblumenfeld/2019/10/15/gen-z-at-work-8-reasons-to-be-afraid/.

236: **Schools offer counseling to help students process Trump win.** 9 Nov. 2016, https://www.campusreform.org/?ID=8369.

236: **Barnard students mourn Hillary loss with 'feminist coloring'** 14 Nov. 2016, https://www.campusreform.org/?ID=8398.

236: **Evergreen State Asks Profs to Take Protesters' Feelings into** 7 July 2017, https://www.nationalreview.com/2017/07/evergreen-state-professors-grading-student-protesters-feelings/.

236: **College spending $60k to turn computer lab into 'safe space.'** 29 Nov. 2017, https://www.campusreform.org/?ID=10204.

237: **Prof. who called Trump's election 'act of terrorism' honored.** 20 March 2017, https://www.campusreform.org/?ID=8952.

237: **Campus group proposing broad countermovement against** 17 Aug. 2017, https://www.insidehighered.com/news/2017/08/17/campus-group-proposing-broad-countermovement-against-white-nationalism-and-racism.

237: **Before former ICE director speaks, Penn shuts the event down** 23 Oct. 2019, http://www.thedp.com/article/2019/10/ice-protest-perry-world-house-immigration-customs.

237: **Petition: Yale must disarm police and donate to BLM.** 22 April 2019, https://www.campusreform.org/?ID=12137.

237: **The College Formerly Known as Yale—WSJ.** 8 Aug. 2016, https://www.wsj.com/articles/the-college-formerly-known-as-yale-1470698364.

238: **College asks NYPD to use bathrooms out of sight from students.** 20 Nov. 2017, https://www.campusreform.org/?ID=10174.

239: **College student kicked out of class for telling professor there** 12 March 2018, https://www.foxnews.com/us/college-student-kicked-out-of-class-for-telling-professor-there-are-only-two-genders.

241: **Study: Top colleges don't require US history courses for history** 30 June 2016, https://www.goacta.org/news-item/study_top_colleges_dont_require_us_history_courses_for_history_majors/.

241: **Karl Marx is the most assigned economist in US college classes.** 31 Jan. 2016, https://www.marketwatch.com/story/communist-manifesto-among-top-three-books-assigned-in-college-2016-01-27.

241: **Resistance Studies Initiative | UMass Amherst.** https://www.umass.edu/resistancestudies/.

242: **Poli-Sci exam blames capitalism for 'sweatshop conditions.'** 15 March 2018, https://www.campusreform.org/?ID=10642.

242: **'America' and 'American' Listed Among Words to . . .—Townhall.** https://townhall.com/tipsheet/leahbarkoukis/2019/07/19/csu-words-america-n2550271.

242: **Brown students vandalize U.S. flags on eve of Veterans Day.** 12 Nov. 2016, https://www.campusreform.org/?ID=8382.

242: **Prof uses American flag as doormat in college 'art display.'** 29 Jan. 2018, https://www.campusreform.org/?ID=10443.

243: **Boston University hosted just 3 conservative speakers in 2016** 8 June 2018, https://www.campusreform.org/?ID=11002.

243: **Americans Have Shifted Dramatically on What Values Matter** 25 Aug. 2019, https://www.wsj.com/articles/americans-have-shifted-dramatically-on-what-values-matter-most-11566738001.

243: **Nearly 50% of Republican students say they've had a prof go** 5 Dec. 2019, https://www.thecollegefix.com/poll-nearly-50-percent-of-professors-have-gone-on-tangents-criticizing-trump/.

243: **Calif. prof: Trump supporters are 'white nationalist terror'** 5 Aug. 2019, https://www.campusreform.org/?ID=13533.

244: **EXCLUSIVE: Prof's office door has Trump-Hitler photo, KKK** 19 Sep. 2019, https://www.campusreform.org/?ID=13732.

244: **MBA Students Have Billions in Federal Loans, Data Show—WSJ.** 3 Aug. 2019, https://www.wsj.com/articles/m-b-a-students-have-billions-in-federal-loans-data-show-11564830000.2020.

244: **Duke recruits men for program to fight 'toxic' masculinity.** 12 Sep. 2017, https://www.campusreform.org/index.cfm?id=9749.

245: **Education Department Investigating Harvard, Yale Over** 13 Feb. 2020,

https://www.wsj.com/articles/education-department-investigating-harvard-yale-over-foreign-funding-11581539042.

247: **Trump's executive order on college campus free speech lacks** 23 March 2019, https://www.businessinsider.com/trump-executive-order-college-campus-free-speech-lacks-details-2019-3.

249: **Trump Signs Executive Order Protecting Free Speech on** 21 March 2019, https://www.nytimes.com/2019/03/21/us/politics/trump-free-speech-executive-order.html.

251: **University of Florida to Pay Conservative Student Group** 2 Aug. 2019, https://www.newsweek.com/university-florida-conservative-student-free-speech-settlement-1452348.

251: **UC Berkeley reaches settlement with College Republicans.** 3 Dec. 2018, https://www.mercurynews.com/2018/12/03/uc-berkeley-reaches-settlement-with-college-republicans/.

CHAPTER 10: JOURNALISM SCHOOL TO SOCIAL JUSTICE WARRIOR

254: **BA Journalism—University of Arizona School of Journalism.** https://journalism.arizona.edu/ba-journalism.

255: **Chomsky claims GOP, Christianity trying to 'destroy the world.'** 8 May 2018, https://www.campusreform.org/?ID=10875.

255: **Noam Chomsky's Support for Hezbollah—CAMERA.org.** 20 July 2006, https://www.camera.org/article/noam-chomsky-s-support-for-hezbollah/.

255: **Department of Journalism and Mass Communication.** https://www.ncat.edu/cahss/departments/journalism-and-mass-communication/index.php.

256: **Tucker Carlson DESTROYS Lauren Duca (Teen . . .—YouTube).** 24 Dec. 2016, https://www.youtube.com/watch?v=oVfqbHqGmyI.

256: **NYU Journalism School Hires Ex-New Yorker Fact Checker** 20 March 2019, https://www.thewrap.com/nyu-journalism-talia-lavin-new-yorker-fact-checker-false-ice-agent-nazi-tattoo/.

257: **Special Report: Columbia University** | Media Research Center. https://www.mrc.org/special-reports/special-report-columbia-university.

259: **Lee Bollinger: Journalism Needs Government Help—WSJ.** 14 July 2010, https://www.wsj.com/articles/SB10001424052748704629804575324782605510168.

259: **Addressing The Daily's coverage of Sessions protests.** 11 Nov. 2019, https://dailynorthwestern.com/2019/11/10/lateststories/addressing-the-dailys-coverage-of-sessions-protests/.